Char-Broil®

CANADA

GRILLS!

CREATIVE
HOMEOWNER®

Char-Broil®
CANADA
GRILLS!

222 FLAVOURFUL RECIPES THAT WILL FIRE UP YOUR APPETITE

CREATIVE HOMEOWNER®, Upper Saddle River, New Jersey

Char-Broil CANADA GRILLS!

EDITORS	Lisa Kahn, Fran Donegan, Kathie Robitz
CONTRIBUTING EDITOR	Barry "CB" Martin
PROOFREADER	Sara M. Markowitz
PRINCIPAL PHOTOGRAPHER	Glen E. Teitell, Freeze Frame Studio
FOOD STYLIST	Dyne Benner
PHOTO COORDINATOR	Mary Dolan
DIGITAL IMAGING SPECIALISTS	Frank Dyer, Mary Dolan
INDEXER	Erica Cardidio, The Last Word
DESIGN AND LAYOUT	David Geer

CREATIVE HOMEOWNER

VICE PRESIDENT AND PUBLISHER	Timothy O. Bakke
MANAGING EDITOR	Fran J. Donegan
ART DIRECTOR	David Geer
PRODUCTION COORDINATOR	Sara M. Markowitz

Current Printing (last digit)
10 9 8 7 6 5 4

Manufactured in the United States of America

Canada Grills! First Edition
Library of Congress Control Number: 2010942808
ISBN-10: 1-58011-525-X
ISBN-13: 978-1-58011-525-4

CREATIVE HOMEOWNER®
A Division of Federal Marketing Corp.
24 Park Way
Upper Saddle River, NJ 07458
www.creativehomeowner.com

All photography by
Freeze Frame Studio
except as noted.

page 8: Scott Heimendinger
page 14: courtesy of Char-Broil

Acknowledgements

This book is dedicated to backyard cooks everywhere who believe the best way to celebrate—or even just spend time—with family and friends is to fire up the grill and start cooking. We would also like to recognize the many home and professional cooks who share their secrets on the internet. Some of their favourite recipes appear in Char-Broil's *Canada Grills!*

Contents

8 Introduction

CHAPTER 1
10 ALL FIRED UP

CHAPTER 2
28 APPETIZERS

CHAPTER 3
68 BEEF

CHAPTER 4
100 PORK

CHAPTER 5
134 LAMB & GAME

CHAPTER 6
150 POULTRY

CHAPTER 7
186 SEAFOOD

CHAPTER 8
228 SIDES

CHAPTER 9
260 DESSERTS

CHAPTER 10
278 MARINADES,
SAUCES & RUBS

294 Resources

297 Index

Introduction

CANADIANS LOVE TO GRILL—and to eat, especially when there's something deliciously different on the menu. Char-Broil's *Canada Grills!* presents scrumptious new recipes and tips for grillin' and chillin' with family and friends. It's all about the flavour—without the fuss—of meals that will keep everyone coming back for more.

Whether you're a grilling novice or an experienced home chef, it's important to know that great grilled, barbecued, and smoked foods are about timing and temperature. So first get "All Fired Up," beginning on page 10, starting with some basic information. (You'll also find specific prep and cook times, along with serving sizes, listed with each recipe in the book. We've included recommended marinate and chill times where appropriate, too.)

Next, if you're hungry for great grilled taste, check out what we've got cookin'—over two dozen tempting appetizers, such as "CB's Feta-Stuffed Portobellos," page 61, or "The Big Easy Yardbird Wings," page 65. Serve these tasty morsels as starters or as bite-size snacks. Move on to the main course with dishes such as our hearty, beefy "Smoky Grilled Meat Loaf," page 83; "CB's Chili-Rubbed Ribs," page 109; a "Butterflied Leg of Lamb with Chinese Seasonings," page 140; "Bourbon-BBQ Cornish Hens," page 166; or "Grilled Shrimp & Blue Cheese Grits," page 218. You'll find plenty of sides to accompany them—"Aunt Sylvia's Buttermilk Cole Slaw," page 230; "Savoury Corn Pudding," page 233; and "Grilled Potato Planks," page 250, to name a few. For a grand finale to your meal, get the dish on dessert. Our recipes include "CB's Pie-Iron Peach Pie," page 264; "Nectarine Pizza with Goat Cheese & Thyme," page 272; "Peanut Butter & Marshmallow Finger Sandwiches," page 275; and many more delectable treats. And PS: you don't want to miss the collection of marinades, sauces, and rubs that make many of Char-Broil's *Canada Grills!* recipes extra special.

Barry "CB" Martin

1 All Fired Up

13 Sear It, Grill It, Smoke It
- Infrared Cooking—It's Hotter Than...
- That Great Grilled Taste
- Adding Smoky Flavours to Grilled Food
- Adding Flavour before Cooking
- Frying without Oil?
- Hot Off the Spit

20 Play It Safe, and Handle with Care
- Keep It Clean
- That Goes for Your Grill, Too
- Keep Cold Foods Cold and Hot Foods Hot

22 The Big Thaw
- Refrigerator Thawing
- Cold-Water Thawing
- Microwave Thawing

23 Grill Safety

24 Cooking Temperature Guidelines
- Beef and Lamb Cooking-Temperature Table
- Poultry Cooking-Temperature Table
- Pork Cooking-Temperature Table
- Standard Terminology and Temperature Guidelines
- Fish and Seafood Cooking Temperatures and Times
- Grilling Temperature Guidelines
- Rotisserie Temperature Guidelines
- Roasting Temperture Guidelines
- Smoking Temperature Guidelines

WHO'S COOKING OUTDOORS TODAY? Who *isn't?* According to the Hearth, Patio & Barbecue Association, "over 82 percent of all North American households own a grill or smoker," and the majority of those people enjoy outdoor cooking so much that they are doing it year-round. That's one thing about which most Canadians can agree—we love to fire up that heat. After all, outdoor cooking methods, such as grilling and barbecuing, are easy ways to prepare a meal—and the food tastes great, too. Besides, that Canadian pastime, the barbecue, is a summertime tradition and a fun way to spend time outdoors—at home, at the game, at the beach, or camping. But why stop when the weather turns cool? As year-round grillers will attest, you can enjoy the deliciousness of food cooked on the grill anytime. When the temperature dips, an outdoor heater or fire pit can keep you toasty while you're waiting for the cheese to melt on your burgers.

Grilled Oysters with Bacon, Tomato & Tarragon, page 34

SEAR IT, GRILL IT, SMOKE IT

Because steaks, chicken parts, fish fillets, burgers, chops, and other foods eaten in individual portions can become dry quickly, it's important to lock in the juices by searing the meat first. Besides, searing is what produces that delicious crust that makes many people want to grill in the first place.

For the most satisfying grilled or barbecued meals, know your heat. You may have heard the terms *direct heat* and *indirect heat.* Understanding these two terms and employing their methods is the key to preparing mouth-wateringly moist and delicious outdoor-cooked dishes.

Grilling, or **direct-heat** cooking refers to preparing food directly over the heat source (propane- or natural-gas-powered burners, hot coals, burning wood), usually at a high temperature. It's a popular technique for cooking burgers, steaks, chops, and fish. Rotisserie cooking is done by direct heat, too, as is frying a turkey.

Large, less-tender cuts of meat are best cooked by **indirect heat.** This process of slow roasting at a low temperature, or **barbecuing,** takes longer, but adds flavour and tenderness to meat. Using a smoker? Then you're cooking with indirect heat. Sometimes, you might start cooking over direct heat, to brown or sear a piece of meat, for example, and then finish with indirect heat. You'll find references to direct and indirect heat in almost every outdoor cooking recipe.

Finally, don't forget to practise safe food-handling habits, and always start with a clean grill.

Cocoa & Coffee Grilled Chicken Thighs, page 168

SEARING locks in the meat's juices and adds a delicious smoky taste.

Infrared Cooking—It's Hotter Than...

With an affordable line of *infrared* gas grills, Char-Broil has made the technology used by professional chefs for decades available to backyard grillers. You'll find it in Char-Broil's Quantam and RED grills, as well as The Big Easy, an infrared turkey fryer that cooks without using oil.

Infrared heat is a great way to cook because it can generate higher temperatures than conventional grills for faster cooking and searing. Infrared waves start to cook the food the instant they reach its surface, quickly creating a sear on the meat that locks in moisture and creates exceptional browning. Char-Broil's infrared cooking systems offer a wide temperature range, from high-heat searing to "low and slow" barbecuing and rotisserie grilling. Because most flare-ups are eliminated, you can simply drop unsoaked wood chips between the grill grates to create a slow-cooked smokehouse flavour in a fraction of the time, using one-third less fuel than standard convection gas grills.

Experience with your new infrared grill will help you determine what temperatures and cooking times deliver the best results. At first, you may want to adjust your regular cooking times. If you have cooked on a charcoal fire, this should be fairly easy to do. If you are more familiar with cooking on a regular convection gas grill, reduce the heat settings you normally use by at least 30 percent, and the cooking time by about 50 percent. Here are some other ideas that will help you master infrared cooking:

■ Coat each piece of meat, fish, or poultry with a light spritz of high-heat oil, such as canola.

■ Plan your cooking according to technique, required times, and the best use of the grill surface. For example, steaks can be seared over high heat, then finished over medium or low heat. Begin with steaks you intend to cook to medium doneness, and end with those you want rare.

TIP: To Sear ... Or Maybe Not to Sear

Not every cut of meat is right for searing. Cuts with a lot of connective tissue, such as beef brisket, pork shoulder, or ribs, are best slowly roasted, or barbecued, at a low temperature. This "low and slow" method of cooking literally melts the cartilage in the meat, making it juicy and tender.

CHAR-BROIL'S RED uses infrared technology that lets you sear meat at a high-heat setting.

CB's Slow-Grilled Rib Eyes, page 82

THIS RECIPE starts on low heat, and then finishes on high heat for a crispy crust.

That Great Grilled Taste

Many people make the mistake of over-grilling their food. To get tasty grill marks on your food, particularly meat, and still keep it moist and done-to-perfection, use the "sear and hold" technique that's practised by professional chefs. Over direct heat, sear both sides. Then finish the food in a 350°F oven or place it on a tray loosely covered with foil, and set it on the grill away from direct heat until it reaches the desired internal temperature. That's it.

However, getting a yummy caramelized crust using a conventional gas grill can be challenging because you need very high heat (550°F to 650°F); gas flames simply don't get as hot as the hottest charcoal fire that can be banked up in a heap. So to get the grates as hot as possible, cover them with aluminum foil; turn up the heat to high; and close the lid.

Wet meat won't sear; it will steam, which isn't the way to grill a piece of meat. So while the grates are heating, blot off any moisture on the meat using a paper towel. Then spray one side of the food with a high-smoke-point oil, such as canola; open the grill lid; remove the foil; and place the meat directly on the hot grates, sprayed-side down. Check for sear marks by lifting one edge of the meat, using tongs. As soon as you see sear marks, spray the top side of the meat, and then flip it over onto a clean section of the hot grates.

When searing is done, use tongs to remove the meat to a holding tray that you can cover. Lower the heat, and allow the meat to finish at about 200°F to 300°F. Use an instant-read thermometer to check for doneness. If you want to apply a glaze, do so when the meat is fully cooked, and then place it once more directly on the hot grates *for just a few seconds* prior to service.

1. Season meat with spices.

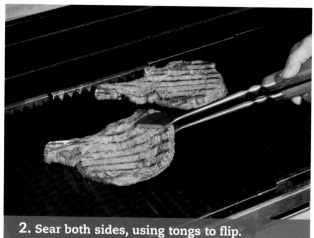
2. Sear both sides, using tongs to flip.

3. Remove to a holding tray, and cover.

4. Check internal temperature for doneness.

Adding Smoky Flavours to Grilled Food

Smoking is a low-and-slow cooking method that infuses food with flavour imparted by smouldering wood, charcoal, or aromatics. (Be sure to follow individual recipes for specific directions.) You can smoke food in several easy ways. The first uses a smoker box that sits under the grates, but on top of the grill burners, holding wood, such as mesquite, hickory, apple, cherry, or alder. The chips will not burn; instead, they'll produce smoke, which penetrates the food and flavours it. Just remember: the more smoke you create, the stronger the flavour.

You can also wrap wood chips in a couple of layers of aluminum foil shaped into something that looks like a large snowball. Puncture the foil in several places to create small holes. Then place your "smoke bomb" on the grill above the heat. The holes you've made in the foil will release the smoke of the smouldering wood, which will flavour your food.

If you prefer, you can use chunks of your favourite wood or aromatic branches or herbs directly on the grill and let them smoke. Another method, called "wet smoking," is done with a pan of water—or fruit juice or wine for extra flavour—placed inside the grill or smoker away from the direct heat. As the liquid evaporates in the dry air of the cooker, it adds flavour to the meat.

Adding Flavour before Cooking

Many recipes call for marinating before cooking. But be careful: the container you use to marinate should not react with the food. For example, acids in a marinade can react with copper or aluminum, giving the food a metallic taste. To prevent this, marinate only in nonreactive cookware, such as stainless steel, glass, and ceramic.

TIP: Capture the Flavour

Whatever method you choose for smoking, keep that aromatic hot air trapped inside the grill. Resist the urge to keep "checking." Keep the grill closed until food is cooked.

Smoker Box (shown on top of grates for clarity)

"Smoke Bomb"

Wood Chips

Frying without Oil?

The Big Easy is a safe and oil-less way to "fry" a turkey or cook rotisserie-style chicken, BBQ pork, roast beef, or even vegetables using infrared technology. And you can use dry rubs and seasonings on the outside of the bird, unlike with traditional fryers. See how to use The Big Easy, below; the complete recipe for The Big Easy Cider-Brined Turkey is on page 185.

1. Brine the bird up to 24 hours for extra flavour.

2. Spray cooking basket with vegetable oil.

3. Place bird—breast facing up—in the basket.

4. Allow the bird to rest for 20 to 30 minutes.

Hot Off the Spit

Rotisserie cooking is yet another way to roast large pieces of meat or poultry. A rotating spit driven by an electric or battery-powered motor is set directly over the heat source and turns at a constant, consistent speed to allow for even cooking. Use an instant-read thermometer inserted into the deepest part of the food to check for doneness—just be sure to stop the rotisserie motor first. It's also a good idea to wear heat-resistant gloves when you're removing the spit rod from the grill.

CB's Low & Slow Lamb Roast, page 142

A ROTISSERIE cooks large roasts and whole poultry over direct heat.

PLAY IT SAFE, AND HANDLE WITH CARE

I can't overemphasize the importance of good grilling hygiene. The food you serve to your family and friends must be wholesome as well as tasty. By adopting safe food-handling practises in your kitchen—and outside at your grill—you can significantly decrease your risk of food-borne illness.

Keep It Clean

Wash your hands thoroughly with hot water and antibacterial soap, especially after handling raw meat. Better yet, consider using food-safe disposable gloves—they're great for handling hot chili peppers, too. Be sure to toss them away before moving on to other tasks.

If you're using a paper towel to wipe up excess moisture from uncooked meat, seafood, or poultry, dispose of it immediately when you're done. Sterilize a damp sponge in the microwave, set on high, for about 60 seconds or more until it becomes hot. Then let it cool before you grab it, or use tongs to remove it. Launder dish towels and rags in hot water.

Plastic cutting boards can be thrown in the dishwasher. Use several colour-coded boards—one for raw poultry, one for vegetables, one for cooked food, and so forth—to prevent cross-contamination. And don't forget to sanitize the sink. Pour diluted bleach down the drain or waste-disposal unit to kill any lingering bacteria, especially after preparing raw meat.

Herb-Marinated Grilled Turkey & Panzanella Salad, page 174

CLEAN CUTTING BOARDS AND COUNTERTOPS before and after preparing food.

That Goes for Your Grill, Too

Burned gunk on the grates is not "seasoning." It's just old, dirty food and will add bad flavours to your next grilled meal. Take care of your grill's grates as you would a favourite cast-iron pan by preseasoning them *before the first use.* (Refer to your product manual for complete instructions.)

If you don't own one of Char-Broil's infrared gas grills with a built-in self-cleaning feature, here's a secret: fold a large piece of heavy-duty aluminum foil into three layers, forming a sheet that measures about 11 x 24 inches. (A disposable foil tray works well.) Place the sheet on the grates immediately after grilling. Keep the heat turned on high on a gas grill, or lower the grates on a charcoal grill until they are just about touching the coals. The foil concentrates the heat on the grates, which helps to burn off any cooking residue. The stuff usually turns to a white ash that is easy to brush off once the grates are cool again. Follow this by spritzing the grates with a little canola oil spray to season.

CB'S Pie Iron Peach Pie, page 264

MAKE THIS DELICIOUS DESSERT on the grill using an old-fashioned pie iron.

Keep Cold Foods Cold and Hot Foods Hot

Uh, oh! Did you forget to defrost that package of chicken thighs you were going to grill for dinner? Should you run hot water over it to thaw it quickly? What if you remembered to take the chicken out of the freezer but left the package on the counter all day while you were at work?

Both of these scenarios are bad news. As soon as food begins to defrost and become warmer than 40°F, any bacteria that may have been present before freezing can begin to multiply. So, even though the centre of those chicken thighs may still be frozen as they thaw on the counter, the outer layer of the food is in the danger zone. Maintain the temperature of frozen foods at under 0°F, and raw, unfrozen foods at under 40°F.

For hot foods, the minimum safe-holding temperature is above 140°F. Food can certainly pass through this temperature zone during cooking, but if it does not rise above 140°F, you are flirting with bacteria growth that will make you sick. Use an accurate meat thermometer.

As a rule of thumb, veal, beef, pork, and most seafood should be cooked to at least 145°F; ground beef, pork, lamb, and veal should be cooked to at least 160°F; chicken and turkey breasts, as well as ground poultry, should be cooked to at least 165°F.

See the cooking temperature charts and guidelines on pages 24–27 for more specific information.

Harvest Slaw with Sweet Potatoes, page 249

CHILL this salad up to 8 hours before serving.

THE BIG THAW

There are three safe ways to defrost food: in the refrigerator, in cold water, and in the microwave.

Refrigerator Thawing

Planning ahead is the key. A large frozen turkey requires at least a day (24 hours) for every 5 pounds of weight. Even a pound of ground meat or boneless chicken breasts needs a full day to thaw. Remember, there may be different temperature zones in your refrigerator, and food left in the coldest one will take longer to defrost.

After thawing in the refrigerator, ground meat and poultry can be chilled for an additional day or two before cooking; you can store defrosted red meat in the refrigerator for 3 to 5 days. You can also refreeze uncooked foods that have been defrosted in the refrigerator, but there may be some loss of flavour and texture.

Cold-Water Thawing

This method is faster than refrigerator thawing but requires more attention. Place the food in a leak-proof plastic bag, and submerge it in cold tap water. Change the water every 30 minutes until the food is defrosted. Small packages of meat or poultry—about 1 pound—may defrost in an hour or less. A 3- to 4-pound roast may take 2 to 3 hours. For whole turkeys, estimate about 30 minutes per pound. Cook the food immediately after it defrosts. You can refreeze the cooked food.

Microwave Thawing

This is the speediest method, but it can be uneven, leaving some areas of the food still frozen and others partially cooked. The latter can reach unsafe temperatures if you do not completely cook the food immediately. Foods thawed in the microwave should be cooked before refreezing.

GRILL SAFETY

As I cruise around my neighbourhood, I often notice grills on apartment terraces and backyard decks, and I get the chills. Why? Because many of these devices are way too close to wooden railings, siding, and fences. Regardless of the type of cooker you own, keep it at least 3 feet from any wall or surface, and 10 feet from other flammable objects. Here are some other tips for safe outdoor cooking from the Hearth, Patio & Barbecue Association.

■ **Read the owner's manual.** Follow its specific recommendations for assembly, usage, and safety procedures. Contact the manufacturer if you have questions. For quick reference, write down the model number and customer service phone number on the cover of your manual.

■ **Keep outdoor grills outdoors.** Never use them to cook in your trailer, tent, house, garage, or any enclosed area because toxic carbon monoxide may accumulate.

■ **Grill in a well-ventilated area.** Set up your grill in a well-ventilated, open area that is away from buildings, overhead combustible surfaces, dry leaves, or brush. Avoid high-traffic areas, and be aware of wind-blown sparks.

■ **Keep it stable.** Always check to be sure that all parts of the unit are firmly in place and that the grill can't tip.

■ **Follow electrical codes.** Electric accessories, such as some rotisseries, must be properly grounded in accordance with local codes. Keep electric cords away from walkways or anywhere people can trip over them.

■ **Use long-handled utensils.** Long-handled forks, tongs, spatulas, and such are designed to help you avoid burns and splatters when you're grilling food.

■ **Wear safe clothing.** That means no hanging shirt-tails, frills, or apron strings that can catch fire, and use heat-resistant mitts when adjusting hot vents.

■ **Keep fire under control.** To put out flare-ups, lower the burners to a cooler temperature (or either raise the grid that is supporting the food or spread coals out evenly, or both, for charcoal). If you must douse flames, do it with a light spritz of water after removing the food from the grill. Keep a fire extinguisher handy in case there is a grease fire. If you don't have one, keep a bucket of sand nearby.

■ **Install a grill pad or splatter mat under your grill.** These naturally heat-resistant pads are usually made of lightweight fibre cement or plastic and will protect your deck or patio from any grease that misses the drip pan.

■ **Never leave a lit grill unattended.** Furthermore, don't attempt to move a hot grill, and always keep kids and pets away when the grill is in use and for up to an hour afterward.

1

ALL FIRED UP

BEEF AND LAMB COOKING-TEMPERATURE TABLE

CUT OF MEAT	INTERNAL TEMPERATURE	VISUAL DESCRIPTION
Roasts		Depending upon how the meat is
Steaks and chops:		being prepared and which cut, different
beef, lamb, veal		temperatures may be used.
medium rare	145°F	Centre is very pink, slightly brown, or grey toward the exterior portion
medium	155°F	Centre is light pink, outer portion is brown or grey
medium well	Above 155°F	No pink
well done	Above 165°F	Steak is uniformly brown or grey throughout
Ground meat: beef, pork, lamb, veal	160°F to 165°F	No longer pink but uniformly brown or grey throughout

POULTRY COOKING-TEMPERATURE TABLE

MEAT	TEMPERATURE	VISUAL DESCRIPTION
	USDA guidelines	
General poultry	165°F	Cook until juices run clear.
Whole chicken, duck, turkey, goose	165°F	Cook until juices run clear and leg moves easily.
Parts of chicken, duck turkey, goose	165°F	Cook until juices run clear.

NOTE: Always cook meat, poultry, and fish to at least the recommended temperatures to prevent food-borne illness. However, some parts of poultry, such as legs and thighs, cooked to 165°F, while safe, would be considered undercooked by many people. Consult individual recipes for finish cooking temperatures. ALSO NOTE: A 12-pound turkey can easily require up to 60 minutes of resting. During that time, the internal temperature can rise 30 degrees if not exposed to drafts.

PORK COOKING-TEMPERATURE TABLE

CUT OF MEAT	INTERNAL TEMPERATURE	VISUAL DESCRIPTION
Roasts, steaks, chops	145°F	Medium-rare, pale pink centre
	160°F	Medium, no pink
	160°F and above	Well done, meat is uniform colour throughout
Pork ribs, pork shoulders, beef brisket	160°F and above	Depending upon how the meat is being prepared and which cut, different temperatures may be used. A pork shoulder may be prepared as a roast and would be done at 160°F, whereas the same cut when barbecued "low and slow" for pulled pork may be cooked to an internal temperature of 195°F to 200°F.
Sausage, raw	160°F	No longer pink
Ham, raw	160°F	Dark pink colour throughout
Ham, precooked	Follow printed instructions	Dark pink colour throughout

STANDARD TERMINOLOGY AND TEMPERATURE GUIDELINES

HEAT SETTING	GRATE TEMPERATURE RANGE	PULL YOUR HAND AWAY (5 in. above grate)
High	Approx. 450°F to 550°F	Approximately 2 to 4 seconds
Medium	Approx. 350°F to 450°F	Approximately 5 to 7 seconds
Low	Approx. 250°F to 350°F	Approximately 8 to 10 seconds

FISH AND SEAFOOD COOKING TEMPERATURES AND TIMES

FRESH OR THAWED FISH	INTERNAL TEMPERATURE	VISUAL DESCRIPTION
Salmon, halibut, cod, snapper (steaks, filleted, or whole)	145°F	Fish is opaque, flakes easily
Tuna, swordfish, marlin	145°F	Cook until medium-rare. (Do not overcook, or the meat will become dry and lose flavour.)
Shrimp	**TIME COOKED**	
medium-size, boiling	3 to 4 min.	Meat is opaque in centre.
large-size, boiling	5 to 7 min.	Meat is opaque in centre.
jumbo-size, boiling	7 to 8 min.	Meat is opaque in centre.
Lobster		
boiled, whole in shell, 1 pound	12 to 15 min.	Shell turns red, meat is opaque in centre.
grilled, whole in shell, 1½ pounds	3 to 4 min.	Shell turns red, meat is opaque in centre.
steamed, whole in shell, 1½ pounds	15 to 20 min.	Shell turns red, meat is opaque in centre.
baked, tails in shell	15 min.	Shell turns red, meat is opaque in centre.
grilled, tails in shell	9 to 10 min.	Shell turns red, meat is opaque in centre.
Scallops		
baked	12 to 15 min.	Milky white or opaque, and firm
seared	varies	Brown crust on surface, milky white or opaque, and firm
Clams, mussels, oysters	varies	Point at which the shell opens, throw out any that do not open

GRILLING TEMPERATURE GUIDELINES

METHOD OF HEAT	GRATE TEMPERATURE RANGE	DESCRIPTIVE LANGUAGE MOST OFTEN USED
Direct	Approx. 450°F to 650°F and higher	Sear, searing, or grilling on high
Direct	Approx. 350°F to 450°F	Grilling on medium
Direct	Approx. 250°F to 350°F	Grilling on low

ROTISSERIE TEMPERATURE GUIDELINES

METHOD OF HEAT	BURNER TEMPERATURE RANGE	DESCRIPTIVE LANGUAGE MOST OFTEN USED
Direct	Approx. 350°F to 450°F	Rotisserie or "spit" roasting

ROASTING TEMPERATURE GUIDELINES

METHOD OF HEAT	COOKING CHAMBER TEMPERATURE RANGE	DESCRIPTIVE LANGUAGE MOST OFTEN USED
Indirect	Approx. 350°F to 450°F	Indirect grilling or indirect cooking
Indirect	Approx. 250°F to 350°F	Indirect grilling or indirect cooking, "low and slow"

SMOKING TEMPERATURE GUIDELINES

METHOD OF HEAT	COOKING CHAMBER TEMPERATURE RANGE	DESCRIPTIVE LANGUAGE MOST OFTEN USED
Indirect, with wood smoke	Approx. 250°F to 350°F	Hot smoking "low and slow"
Indirect, with wood smoke	Approx. 150°F to 250°F	Smoking "low and slow"

2 Appetizers

30 Smoky Baby Blue
    Artichokes

31 Hot Sweet-Onion Dip

32 Grilled Portobello Mushrooms
    with Pepperoni & Cheese

33 Hot Corn Dip

34 Grilled Oysters with
    Bacon, Tomato & Tarragon

36 Grilled Oysters
    with Blood Orange & Ginger

37 Smokin' Soon's
    Hobo Potato Skins

38 CB's Avocado, Crab &
    Jalapeño Roll-Ups

40 Tall Paul's Scotch Eggs
    on the Grill

41 CB's Fire-Charred Green
    Beans with Vinaigrette

42 Spiced Cranberry Wings

44 Patio Daddio BBQ Pulled-
    Pork Pasties

45 Avocado Chimichurri
    Bruschetta

46 Frittata on the Grill

48 Reuben Dip

49 Moink Balls

50 Pirate Mike's Peg-Leg
    Chicken Drums

52 CB's Smoked Eggs

53 'Shroom Bombs

54 Grilled Romaine Salad

56 Smoked Chicken "Pâté"

57 CB's Prosciutto-Wrapped Dates

58 Thai Grilled
    Salt & Pepper Squid

60 CB's Caramelized
    Onion "Lollipops"

61 CB's Feta-Stuffed Portobellos

62 Dr. BBQ's Bacon-Brie Appetizer

64 CB's Grilled Scallops
    with Prosciutto

65 The Big Easy Yardbird Wings

66 CB's Grilled Melon Salad

*(Right) Grilled Oysters with
Bacon, Tomato & Tarragon, page 34*

SMOKY BABY BLUE ARTICHOKES

12 baby artichokes
Nonstick cooking
spray
Salt and pepper
½ cup blue cheese,
crumbled
Balsamic vinegar

To prepare the baby artichokes for cooking, snap off the lower petals until you reach the core. Trim each baby artichoke by cutting off the top ½-inch and the bottom stem. Place artichokes in a saucepan filled with water. Bring water to a boil, and parboil artichokes for approximately 3 to 4 minutes. Artichokes are done when a toothpick or knife tip will go into the base of the artichoke easily.

Preheat outdoor grill to medium. Directly spray either mesh grill basket or aluminum foil with nonstick cooking spray. Add artichokes to grill basket or foil, and cook over direct heat for 5 minutes or until artichokes are evenly browned.

Add salt and pepper to taste, and sprinkle blue cheese on top of artichokes. Keep the basket on the grill for one minute or until the blue cheese melts.

Remove the artichokes from the grill, and arrange them on a plate. Drizzle balsamic vinegar over the artichokes, and serve. ✤

HOT SWEET-ONION DIP

1 (4-ounce) package cream cheese, softened

½ cup mayonnaise

½ cup Parmigiano-Reggiano, grated

½ cup sweet onion (Vidalia or Maui), chopped

Black pepper to taste

Make this dip while you get your main course going; just mix everything in a baking dish, and cook on the top rack.

Stir all ingredients together in a baking dish or aluminum pan. Place on top rack of grill that has been preheated to medium. Cook about 30 to 50 minutes, or until top is browned. Serve with crackers, vegetables, or toasted bread. ✤

GRILLED PORTOBELLO MUSHROOMS WITH PEPPERONI & CHEESE

4 large Portobello mushrooms, stems removed, cleaned with paper towel

2 tablespoons butter

½ cup mozzarella, shredded

½ cup Parmesan cheese, shredded

Italian seasoning

16 slices pepperoni

These mushrooms taste like a pepperoni-and-cheese pizza—and you don't have to fling dough.

Preheat grill to medium. Lightly butter a baking sheet lined with foil. Place mushrooms on baking sheet; add a bit of butter to each; pile shredded cheeses (generously); sprinkle with herbs; and arrange pepperoni on top. Grill until mushrooms are slightly softened and cheese is golden brown, about 10 minutes. Cut in wedges or serve whole. ✚

⏰ Quick Snack • 6 Servings • Prep: 10 min. • Grill: 10–20 min.

33

HOT CORN DIP

2 tablespoons unsalted butter

2 cups corn kernels (from 2
  ears corn)

Salt and pepper to taste

½ cup yellow onion, chopped

¼ cup red bell pepper, chopped

¼ cup chopped green onions
  (green and white parts)

1 jalapeño, chopped

2 teaspoons garlic, chopped

¼ cup mayonnaise

½ cup Monterey Jack cheese, grated

¼ teaspoon cayenne

½ cup sharp cheddar, grated

*This warm, sweet dip is perfectly balanced by the heat of the
jalapeños and the cayenne pepper. It's great served with tortilla chips.*

Melt one tablespoon of the butter in a pan. Add the corn; season
with salt and pepper; and sauté until the corn starts to turn golden
brown, about 5 minutes. Remove from the pan, and set aside.

Melt the remaining tablespoon of butter in the same pan.
Add the onion and pepper, and sauté until softened, about 2
minutes.

Add the green onions, jalapeño, and garlic; sauté until softened, about 2 minutes. Mix the corn, onions, peppers, mayonnaise, Monterey Jack, and cayenne in a bowl. Pour the mixture
into an 8 x 8-inch baking dish or aluminum pan, and top with
the cheddar cheese.

Place on the top rack of a grill that has been preheated to
medium, and cook until bubbling and golden brown on top, about
10 to 20 minutes. ✦

2

APPETIZERS

GRILLED OYSTERS WITH BACON, TOMATO & TARRAGON

3 tablespoons unsalted butter
1 tablespoon shallot, minced
1 green onion, sliced thinly on the bias
2 tablespoons cider vinegar
2 tomatoes, peeled, seeded, and diced
2 teaspoons tarragon, minced
½ teaspoon ground black pepper
2 strips bacon, fried and crumbled
1 dozen oysters, shucked, shell reserved

TO SERVE THE OYSTERS
2 to 3 cups of coarse salt (kosher or rock)

Preheat one side of the grill to medium. (The oysters will be cooked over the indirect side.)

In a skillet over medium heat, melt the butter; add the shallot and green onion; and cook until they are softened, 4 minutes. Add the cider vinegar, and cook until bubbly and reduced, 3 minutes.

Add in the diced tomatoes, and stir gently to heat through, 2 minutes. Do not mash or break up the tomato chunks.

Remove from the heat, and stir in the tarragon and black pepper. Top each oyster with 1 to 3 teaspoons of the tomato mixture.

Grill over indirect heat, with lid closed, for 5 to 10 minutes. The oysters are done when the edges have curled and the topping is bubbly. Serve on a bed of coarse salt. ✤

GRILLED OYSTERS WITH BLOOD ORANGE & GINGER

**1 cup blood orange juice
(from about 3 oranges)**

**3 tablespoons unsalted
butter**

2 teaspoons minced ginger

2 teaspoons minced shallot

**1 teaspoon blood orange
zest**

**1 tablespoon unseasoned
rice wine vinegar**

1 dash hot sauce (optional)

**1 dozen oysters, shucked;
shells reserved**

TO SERVE THE OYSTERS

**2 to 3 cups coarse salt
(kosher or rock)**

Winter is blood orange season, but if you can't find them, try Valencia oranges.

Preheat one half of the grill to medium. (The oysters will be cooked over indirect heat.) In a small saucepan over medium heat, reduce the blood orange juice to ¼ cup, about 10 minutes; it should have a syrupy consistency.

Meanwhile, in a skillet over medium heat, melt the butter with the ginger, shallots, and orange zest; and cook for 4 to 5 minutes until everything is aromatic and the shallots are translucent. Add the rice wine vinegar, and stir frequently for 2 more minutes. Do not let the ginger burn. Remove from the heat, and stir in the reduced blood orange juice. Spoon 1 to 2 teaspoons of blood orange mixture over each oyster.

Grill oysters, hood closed, for 5 to 10 minutes. The oysters are done when the edges have curled and the topping is bubbly. Serve on a bed of coarse salt. ✤

SMOKIN' SOON'S HOBO POTATO SKINS

4 baked Russet potatoes, halved and scooped out, ¼ inch of flesh remaining

¼ cup olive oil or melted butter

Hot sauce to taste

Coarse salt and black pepper to taste

4 tablespoons finely grated Parmesan cheese (about 1½ teaspoons per potato skin)

You can use the scooped-out potato left over from this recipe for mashed potatoes.

After slicing and scooping the baked potatoes, mix the oil or butter with hot sauce in a plastic bag. Add the potato skins to the bag, and massage to coat them, about 1 minute.

Preheat grill to medium high. Remove skins from bag; place flesh side down on grill to brown; turn with tongs; remove; and season with salt, pepper, and Parmesan. Serve immediately. ✤

2

APPETIZERS

Smokin' Soon is a frequent contributor to Char-Broil's "Sizzle on the Grill" users' forums.

CB'S AVOCADO, CRAB & JALAPEÑO ROLL-UPS

2 large, ripe avocados
3 large garlic cloves,
   roasted and smashed
¼ teaspoon cumin
2 roasted jalapeño peppers
   (stems and seeds removed),
   finely chopped
½ pound crabmeat, picked
   clean of shell fragments
¼ cup shallots, finely chopped
1 can (18 ounces) diced
   tomatoes
½ cup fresh cilantro, chopped
Juice from ½ fresh lime
½ teaspoon coarse salt
24 leaves of romaine lettuce,
   hearts removed
Extra-virgin olive oil to taste

To enjoy these, wrap a lettuce leaf around a spoonful of the crab mixture and then eat it like a spring roll.

Halve avocados, remove pits and skins, and coarsely chop in a large, nonreactive bowl. Add roasted garlic and cumin; gently combine.

Add jalapeños, crabmeat, shallots, tomatoes, and all but two tablespoons each of the cilantro and lime juice. Stir until just combined.

Arrange romaine leaves on a serving plate, and place a dollop of crabmeat mixture on top of each.

Combine remaining two tablespoons of cilantro and olive oil in a small bowl; season with salt; and stir until thoroughly mixed. Drizzle the oil mixture over the lettuce before serving. ✤

2

APPETIZERS

4 Servings
Prep: 25 min.
Grill: 30–40 min.
or until sausage is
cooked to 160°F

TALL PAUL'S SCOTCH EGGS ON THE GRILL

1 pound bulk pork sausage
½ cup shredded cheese (cheddar or
    Monterey Jack)
½ cup crisp bacon, crumbled
4 eggs, parboiled for 4 to 5 minutes

ADDITIONS
Chopped bell peppers, red pepper flakes,
    chipotle paste, seasoned bread crumbs,
    or any other condiment you prefer

Often you'll find this classic bar-food item deep fried, but in this recipe, cook them on your grill or in your smoker.

Divide the sausage into four thin patties. Lightly sprinkle cheese, bacon bits, and any other fillings over the centre of each patty. Peel the eggs, and place one on top of each patty. Wrap the sausage around the egg to cover evenly.

Preheat a grill or smoker set for indirect cooking to medium high. Place the sausage balls in a pan or directly on the grates over a drip pan on the side with indirect heat. Cook about 30 to 40 minutes or until the sausage is crispy on the outside. ✤

CB'S FIRE-CHARRED GREEN BEANS WITH VINAIGRETTE

1 to 2 pounds fresh green beans,
    washed, trimmed, and dried
Canola oil

This recipe also works well with sliced zucchini, asparagus, broccoli spears, or steamed artichoke quarters.

Place beans in a bowl, and coat lightly and evenly with canola oil.
In a nonreactive bowl, mix anchovy paste, garlic cloves, Dijon mustard, Tabasco sauce, Worcestershire sauce, red wine vinegar, and lemon juice, using a whisk or fork.

Gently add olive oil as you continue to stir until all of the ingredients emulsify. Add the salt and pepper as desired. Keep covered and cold until just before serving.

Preheat grill to high. Place the beans at a 90-degree angle to the grates. (Use a grill basket to keep the beans from falling through the grates.) The beans will brown quickly, and the oil can cause flare-ups, so use tongs to move beans often as they cook. When beans are lightly charred, remove to platter, and drizzle with vinaigrette immediately before serving. You can top this dish with shavings of Parmesan cheese after drizzling the dressing on the veggies. ✤

VINAIGRETTE

1 egg
1 teaspoon anchovy paste
1 to 2 mashed garlic cloves
1 tablespoon Dijon mustard
½ teaspoon Tabasco sauce
1 teaspoon Worcestershire
    sauce
2 to 3 tablespoons red wine
    vinegar
2 tablespoons freshly
    squeezed lemon juice
Extra-virgin olive oil, as
    needed
Freshly ground coarse
    salt and black pepper
    to taste
Shavings of Parmesan
    cheese, if desired

2

APPETIZERS

SPICED CRANBERRY WINGS

3 to 4 pounds chicken wings
1 cup balsamic vinaigrette dressing
1 (14-ounce) can jellied
    cranberry sauce

2 tablespoons Tabasco
    sauce
½ teaspoon salt
¼ teaspoon pepper

2

APPETIZERS

This is a great appetizer for a holiday cocktail party.

Remove and discard tips from chicken wings. Combine remaining ingredients in a bowl, and whisk with a fork until smooth. Refrigerate half of the sauce to serve with the cooked wings.

Put the chicken and the remaining sauce in a resealable plastic bag; shake to coat well; and refrigerate from 3 hours to overnight.

Preheat grill to medium. Remove chicken from the marinade, and place on the grill skin side down. Discard marinade. Cook wings for about 10 to 12 minutes per side, basting often with the reserved sauce. Serve hot with remaining dipping sauce. ✚

PATIO DADDIO BBQ'S PULLED-PORK PASTIES

1 cup pulled pork or other grilled meat, shredded

1 package refrigerated roll-up or extra-large biscuits

Use leftover grilled pork, chicken, fish, or beef to make these tasty appetizers.

If filling is too dry, mix in a few drops of water, chicken stock, or barbecue sauce.

Roll out the biscuit dough, and separate into precut triangles, squares, or rounds. Place about 1 teaspoon of the meat mixture in the centre of each. Roll up dough to cover the meat; then pinch the sides. You can also use a fork to poke a few small holes in the crust to allow steam to escape.

Preheat one side of the grill to medium. Place pasties on a baking sheet on the grill over indirect heat, cooking until the dough is browned. Serve with a dipping sauce, such as mustard or your favourite barbecue sauce. ✦

John Dawson, a.k.a. Patio Daddio BBQ, is a regular contributor to "Sizzle on the Grill."

AVOCADO CHIMICHURRI BRUSCHETTA

2 ripe avocados

¼ cup parsley, chopped

¼ cup cilantro, chopped

½ shallot, finely diced

2 tablespoons red wine vinegar

1 tablespoon honey

Olive oil, enough to bring everything together

Salt and pepper to taste

6 slices thick Italian bread

1 garlic clove, peeled and cut in half

Cut the avocados in half; remove pits; and cut into cubes.

Combine avocados, parsley, cilantro, shallots, vinegar, honey, and olive oil. Season mixture with salt and pepper.

Brush olive oil on slices of bread, and grill on each side for a couple of minutes until toasted.

Rub the cut side of the garlic clove on grilled bread slices. Spread avocado mixture on bread, and serve immediately. ✤

FRITTATA ON THE GRILL

[*This recipe is presented courtesy of Gary House,*
"The Outdoor Cook" at Cooking-Outdoors.]

2

APPETIZERS

4 eggs

2 green onions, sliced

4 large crimini mushrooms,
  stemmed and sliced

½ red bell pepper, diced

1 teaspoon capers (no juice)

½ cup sharp cheese

2 tablespoons grated Parmesan cheese

½ cup frozen shredded hash browns

1 teaspoon dried parsley flakes

2 cloves garlic, minced

Salt and pepper to taste

½ cup milk or more as needed

This recipe provides savoury sustenance as a light lunch or while you await the dinner bell—all with some very simple preparation.

Preheat the grill to medium high. Grease the inside of a cast-iron pan or heavy skillet.

Scramble eggs and milk together in a bowl; add all the other ingredients; and mix. Pour mixture into the pan, and place on grill over indirect heat. Close hood, and cook for about 15 minutes. You may want to move the skillet around on the grates to ensure even cooking. Frittata is done when eggs are set and an instant-read thermometer inserted in centre registers 160°F. Slice into wedges, and serve hot or warm. ✤

REUBEN DIP

2 pounds deli corned beef

1 pound Swiss cheese

1 jar Thousand Island
dressing and dip

15-ounce can sauerkraut

4 tablespoons coarse
Dijon mustard

2 packages cocktail-size
rye bread

Finely chop corned beef and Swiss cheese in a food processor. Add dressing, sauerkraut, and mustard to the processor, and pulse a few times to mix. Lightly butter one side of each bread slice, and wrap slices in aluminum foil to toast. Pour dip into a small aluminum pan, and place on the warming rack of a preheated grill. Close hood, and allow bread to toast and cheese to melt, about 10 to 15 minutes. Serve the dip with the toasted bread. ♣

MOINK BALLS

6 slices bacon
12 precooked beef meatballs
Favourite dry rub
Favourite BBQ sauce

Cut each bacon slice in half lengthwise to make 12 thin strips. Place one meatball in the centre of each strip. Wrap bacon around meatball, and secure with a toothpick. Dust with your favourite rub, if desired.

Preheat one side of grill to low, and add smoker chips if desired. Place the moink balls in an aluminum pan. Set the pan over indirect heat, and cook about 30 minutes, checking and turning moink balls as necessary. Brush with BBQ sauce, and continue cooking for additional 20 minutes or until bacon is crisp and sauce has set. Serve hot. ❧

2

APPETIZERS

"MOO (beef) + OINK (pork) = MOINK"
is the way barbecue chef Larry Gaian
explains how he came up with the name
for these bacon-wrapped meatballs.

PIRATE MIKE'S PEG-LEG CHICKEN DRUMS

12 chicken legs
12 strips thin-sliced bacon cut in half lengthwise
¼ cup brown sugar
Ground salt and pepper to taste
Favourite dry rub or poultry seasoning
Toothpicks as needed
Favourite barbecue sauce
This recipe is courtesy of competitive barbecue champion Mike "Pit Pirate" Hedrick.

Rinse drumsticks thoroughly under cold, running water; pat dry with paper towels. Using poultry scissors, remove skin by trimming all the way around the bottom of the drumstick. Peel off the lower skin and knuckle. (Sometimes you may need to cut around the knuckle, too.)

Place bacon strips on a clean, dry surface, and liberally sprinkle them on one side with brown sugar and freshly cracked salt and pepper. Coat the chicken with the dry rub.

Set a drumstick at the end of a bacon strip, seasoned side up. Wrap the bacon around the chicken several times, making sure the bacon strip does not overlap too much. Secure with heavy-duty plain toothpicks. Repeat until all the drumsticks are wrapped.

Place bacon-wrapped chicken legs on a standing grill rack so that they can cook using indirect heat. (They can also be smoked or fry-roasted in The Big Easy.)

When the bacon is almost crisp, insert an instant-read thermometer into one of the drumsticks to test for doneness (180°F). Lightly brush the drumsticks with barbecue sauce to glaze. ✤

CB'S SMOKED EGGS

1 dozen large eggs in a cardboard carton, lid removed

Coarse salt

You can eat these straight out of the smoker or over a green salad dressed with crispy bacon and vinaigrette dressing.

Place eggs in a saucepan in an even layer. Cover with cool water, and add salt. Bring to a boil over high heat on the side burner of the grill or on a stove. When the water begins to boil, cover the pan and remove from the heat. Let eggs sit for 10 minutes.

Remove the lid, and run hot tap water over the eggs. After a minute, pour out the hot water, and add lukewarm water. After another minute, pour this out, and add cold water. Repeat until eggs are cool, about 4 to 5 minutes. Roll eggs on a counter or cutting board to crack the shells, but don't remove them.

Preheat one side of the grill to low, and add your choice of wood chips. (For a more delicate smoke flavour, try apple or almond wood.) Poke a hole in the bottom of each section of the egg carton to allow smoke to penetrate, and then return the eggs to the carton. Place the carton over the unheated side of the grill; close the hood; and smoke for approximately 1 hour. Serve eggs immediately, or refrigerate in a sealed container for up to a week. ✤

'SHROOM BOMBS

12 medium-sized cremini or white
  mushrooms

Olive oil

12 garlic cloves, peeled and crushed
  (1 per mushroom cap)

Sliced jalapeño peppers, sausage,
  shredded cheese, or other
  ingredients for stuffing

12 slices thin, centre-cut bacon

Salt and pepper to taste

Hot sauce, if desired

Wipe the mushrooms with a paper towel to clean them; pull the stems to remove them. Set the stems aside for future use.

Brush each mushroom with olive oil to prevent sticking to the grill. Insert a crushed garlic clove into each mushroom cap; then add a jalapeño slice and any other stuffing you desire.

Wrap each mushroom with a strip of bacon. (Take one turn around the top, and twist to go around the sides, ending inside the cap.) Preheat the grill to medium. Place bacon-wrapped stuffed mushrooms, filling side up, on a rack or pan over the heat. Roast, hood closed, for 25 to 30 minutes or until the bacon is crisp. Remove and let mushrooms cool for a bit before serving. ♣

This recipe is from Ka Honu, an active contributor to the "Sizzle on the Grill" users' forums.

GRILLED ROMAINE SALAD

1 teaspoon honey
½ cup balsamic-vinaigrette dressing
2 heads romaine lettuce, washed and dried
Olive oil
Coarse salt and pepper
½ cup feta cheese, crumbled

In the time it takes to fire up the grill, you can make an easy side dish with enough "wow factor" to impress your family or guests.

Preheat grill to medium. Add honey to prepared salad dressing; set aside. Split each head of lettuce lengthwise. Drizzle the cut side of each half evenly with a tablespoon or two of oil. Season the cut side of each half with salt and pepper. Sear each half, cut side down, over direct heat for about 90 seconds. Remove to a sheet pan; sprinkle evenly with the cheese; and let cool.

   Drizzle each half with an equal amount of dressing. Cut each section in half width-wise, and serve immediately. ✦

[*Recipe courtesy of John Dawson, who writes a food blog called "Patio Daddio BBQ."*]

SMOKED CHICKEN "PÂTÉ"

1½ cups smoked chicken thigh meat, bones and skin removed

8 ounces mild goat cheese, softened Camembert (rind removed), or French Neufchâtel*

3 tablespoons finely chopped onion

2 tablespoons favourite dry rub

2 tablespoons mayonnaise

2 teaspoons lemon juice

Hot sauce to taste

Favourite BBQ sauce

Neufchâtel is a soft, slightly crumbly French cheese that resembles Camembert but with a saltier, sharper taste. American Neufchâtel, very different from the French version, is a lower-fat cream-cheese product.

Grind smoked chicken in a food processor until pieces resemble coarse cornmeal. Using clean hands in food-safe gloves, combine chicken with remaining ingredients in a large bowl.

Transfer mixture to a 2-cup mould that has been coated with cooking spray.

Lightly press mixture into the mould, and cover with wax paper before storing in the refrigerator to set.

At serving time, turn pâté out onto a plate, and sprinkle with additional rub. Drizzle with your favourite BBQ sauce. ♣

"Sizzle on the Grill" contributor Larry Gaian says this appetizer is a great way to use left-over smoked chicken thighs.

CB'S PROSCIUTTO-WRAPPED DATES

24 large pitted dates (Medjool is a good variety)
1 cup cheese (Manchego, feta, goat, or blue),
   crumbled and chilled
1 (6 ounce) package prosciutto
24 plain wooden toothpicks

2

APPETIZERS

Seems like everyone's crazy about bacon-wrapped this or that. But a big problem with many of these recipes is that the bacon takes forever to crisp up, while the filling gets overcooked. Using thin slices of prosciutto from the deli case solves this problem deliciously.

Slit the dates lengthwise, and stuff each one with about ½ teaspoon of cheese. Wrap a prosciutto slice completely around each cheese-filled date; secure with a toothpick. You can prepare these in advance and keep up to one day in the refrigerator.

Preheat one side of the grill to medium high. Arrange the dates about 1 inch apart in a disposable aluminum tray, and place on the unheated section of the grill. (You may want to use a wire rack to help prevent sticking and overcooking, or place a drip tray under the grates.)

Roast dates for about 10 minutes with the hood down. Use tongs to turn; then roast another 10 minutes or until the prosciutto is crispy and the cheese is slightly melted. ✤

THAI GRILLED SALT & PEPPER SQUID

½ to ¾ pound cleaned calamari tubes (fresh or frozen)
1 tablespoon vegetable oil
¾ teaspoon ground white pepper
1 teaspoon salt
½ teaspoon cayenne pepper
½ teaspoon dried crushed chili
¼ teaspoon ground black pepper
1 teaspoon garlic powder
½ lime cut in wedges
¼ cup fresh coriander, lightly chopped
Thai sweet chili sauce (available in most supermarkets)
½ package prewashed baby greens
1 tablespoon Asian fish sauce, optional
Canola oil spray

Using a knife, cut open the calamari tubes so that they lie flat. Rinse and place the calamari on a clean kitchen towel. Dry them as thoroughly as possible to ensure that the spice mixture sticks.

Cut the calamari lengthwise into strips approximately 1 inch wide, and place in a mixing bowl. Drizzle the oil over the strips to coat them.

Mix the dry spices together in a cup or small bowl, and then sprinkle the mixture over the oiled calamari. Mix well until all of the strips are coated. Set aside to marinate while you heat the grill.

Preheat grill to medium. Place a piece of foil over the grill surface, and lightly spray with oil. Place calamari on top of the foil, and cook until edges curl. (Some strips may curl completely into a circle.) Cooking only takes 30 seconds to 2 minutes for each side, depending on the heat of your grill. Try not to overcook the calamari, because it will turn rubbery instead of tender.

Place the calamari on a serving platter over a bed of baby greens. Squeeze lime juice over calamari, and add salt and fish sauce if desired. Finish with a sprinkling of fresh coriander, and serve with Thai sweet chili sauce for dipping. ✤

2

APPETIZERS

CB'S CARAMELIZED ONION "LOLLIPOPS"

1 large or medium yellow onion

8 wooden skewers, soaked in water for 30 minutes

Coarse salt

Canola oil spray

The skewers anchor the onion rings so that you can create attractive sear marks.

Peel away the outer layer of the onion, but do not cut or trim ends. Insert two wooden skewers about ½ inch apart into the onion. Repeat this three more times at evenly spaced intervals around the perimeter of onion.

Hold onto the skewers as you carefully trim off the ends of the onion and cut it into four slices, each slice containing two skewers.

Once sliced, make sure to push the skewers about ½ inch deeper into the slice. This keeps the slices stable as you oil, season, and grill them.

Preheat grill to medium. Season the onion slices on all sides with a pinch of coarse salt; allow them to rest for a few minutes. Spray all sides with oil, and place on the grill.

Let onions cook until the edges begin to brown; then turn them over using tongs.

Once the onions show good sear marks and caramelization, place them in a holding pan or on the warming rack of the grill, and allow them to continue to roast until tender. Remove skewers before serving. ✤

CB'S FETA-STUFFED PORTOBELLOS

6 large Portobello mushroom caps (about 3 to 4 inches across)
¼ cup olive oil
¼ cup white balsamic vinegar
Salt and ground black pepper
½ cup feta cheese, crumbled
¼ cup sun-dried tomatoes, chopped
½ cup baby spinach leaves washed, dried,
    stems removed
1 teaspoon thyme
1 teaspoon curry powder

You can vary the size of the mushrooms to make bite-size hors d'oeuvres, or serve larger ones as a first course.

Place mushrooms in a large bowl. Add half of the oil and all of the vinegar, coating mushrooms on both sides. Season with salt and pepper, and set aside.

In the same bowl, add the feta cheese, tomatoes, and spinach. Add dry seasonings and remaining oil, and toss to coat.

Preheat one side of grill to medium high. Place the mushrooms on the heated side of the grill, and cook for 2 to 3 minutes on both sides. Remove the mushrooms to a pan on the unheated part of grill.

Carefully spoon enough stuffing mixture into each mushroom to fill each cap. Close the hood, and continue to cook the mushrooms over indirect heat. When the cheese begins to melt, remove mushrooms using tongs, and place on a serving plate. ❖

🕐 **Quick Snack** • **8 Servings** • **Prep: 15 min.** • **Grill: 15–20 min.**

DR. BBQ'S BACON-BRIE APPETIZER

1 pound bacon
1 16-ounce Brie wheel
½ cup BBQ sauce

Cook the bacon in a large skillet over medium heat until just crispy. Meanwhile, prepare the grill for indirect cooking, heated to medium.

Unwrap the Brie, and place it in a disposable pie pan. Top with the BBQ sauce. When the bacon is cooked, drain on a paper towel, and then chop the bacon medium fine. Top the cheese with the bacon.

Place the pan with the Brie on the unheated side of the grill, and cook until the cheese is soft, about 15 to 20 minutes.

Add crackers around the Brie, and serve warm. ♣

[
Recipe courtesy of Ray Lampe, who writes the food blog "drbbq.com."
]

⊕ **Quick Snack • 4 Servings • Prep: 25 min. • Grill: 6–8 min. (until internal temp. is 145°F)**

CB'S GRILLED SCALLOPS WITH PROSCIUTTO

12 jumbo sea scallops, about 2 ounces each

6 slices prosciutto, cut into thin strips

12 plain wooden toothpicks or 6 wooden skewers,
   soaked in water

Canola oil

OPTIONAL GLAZE

Melted butter, lemon juice, and touch of anchovy paste

When I try to grill bacon-wrapped seafood, either the bacon is undercooked or the seafood is overcooked. I've switched to prosciutto, and I'm so glad I did.—CB

If the scallops are still in their shells, have your fishmonger remove the shells and the tough side muscle. If desired, you can freeze these muscle pieces for making fish stock.

Wrap one slice of prosciutto around each scallop, and secure with a toothpick; or thread two scallops on each wooden skewer.

Preheat one-half of the grill to medium high. Spray the wrapped scallops with canola oil, and use tongs to place them on the heated grates. Sear for about 3 to 4 minutes per side or until grill marks appear, using tongs to turn.

When the scallops appear to be opaque in the centre (about 145°F), set them in a holding tray placed on the unheated section of the grill.

Whisk together butter, lemon juice, and anchovy paste. You may glaze the scallops with this butter sauce before serving. ❧

THE BIG EASY YARDBIRD WINGS

Around 24 chicken wings
½ cup canola or vegetable oil
½ cup or more lemon juice
½ cup favourite seasoning
** or rub for chicken wings**
Salt and pepper to taste

[*BBQ competitor Mike "Pit Pirate" Hedrick uses The Big Easy to prepare these crispy wings.*]

Mix seasoning ingredients together in a nonreactive container. Wash and cut off the wing tips, and then the drum, from each 2-bone wing. Add prepped chicken parts to container, and allow them to marinate at least two hours or overnight.

Place all of the wings in The Big Easy cooking basket. (Use either the EZ-Out Cooking Rack or the Half Racks to fit all the wings in the basket.)

Place the loaded cooking basket into The Big Easy; cover with the lid; and set heat to high. Let wings cook for at least 5 to 10 minutes. Pay close attention to the wings, turning the basket and using tongs to move the wings around for even cooking. Serve wings with your favourite dipping sauce. ✦

CB'S GRILLED MELON SALAD

1 cup balsamic vinegar
4 green onions
Extra-virgin olive oil
1 small melon (such as cantaloupe or honeydew),
  sliced into about 1-inch-thick crescents
1 head Boston or Bibb lettuce, washed and dried
¾ cup goat or feta cheese, crumbled
Sliced onions

On the grill's side burner or a stovetop, pour balsamic vinegar into a shallow sauce pan, and over low heat, cook until liquid is reduced to about half. Reserve.

Preheat grill to high. Lightly oil the green onions, and place on grill, using tongs to turn as each is browned with sear marks. Remove onions, and cut into short diagonal pieces.

Use paper towel to blot surface moisture on each melon slice, and immediately place them on clean hot grates until sear marks appear. Keep an eye on each piece, and use tongs to turn them.

Remove sear-marked melon slices from the grill, and place two or three on each lettuce leaf. Top the warm melon slices with some crumbled goat cheese and sliced onions. Drizzle a thin line of the reduced balsamic vinegar over each in a single curving line. Drizzle in the opposite direction with a thin stream of extra-virgin olive oil. ♣

3 Beef

70 CB's Burgers with Caramelized Onion Spread

71 Tomato-Mozzarella-Polenta Burgers

72 CB's Sliders

74 Jamaican Jerk Burgers

75 Cajun Meat-Loaf Muffins

76 Thai-Style Burgers

77 Grilled Beef Tacos with Avocado Salsa

78 CB's Rib Eyes with Balsamic-Mushroom Sauce

80 CB's Grilled Flat-Iron Steaks with Mustard-Bourbon Sauce

81 Ginger-Maple Steak with Napa Cabbage & Grilled Onions

82 CB's Slow-Grilled Rib Eyes

83 Smoky Grilled Meat Loaf

84 Beef "California Roll" Salad

86 Pomsey's Tailgate Tips

87 CB's Polynesian-Style Tri-Tip

88 CB's Salted Margarita Flank Steak

89 Flank-Steak Tournedos with Goat Cheese

90 Livefire's Grilled Beef Wellington

92 CB's Grilled Hanger Steak "Moutarde"

93 Szechuan Steak Wraps with Spicy Peanut Mayonnaise

94 Grilled Flank Steak with Lemon & Rosemary Marinade

95 CB's Beef Skewers "On Fire"

96 Turkish-Style Sirloin with Roasted Garlic-Fig Sauce

98 The Big Easy Coffee-Brined Beef Roast

99 CB's Cowboy-Style Beef Ribs

(Right) Turkish-Style Sirloin with Roasted Garlic-Fig Sauce, page 96

2 Servings • Prep: 60 min. • Grill: 10–20 min. (until meat temp. is 160°F)

CB'S BURGERS WITH CARAMELIZED ONION SPREAD

1 pound 80-percent lean ground chuck

1 tablespoon garlic powder

1 teaspoon cumin powder

1 teaspoon coarse salt or less to taste

1 teaspoon freshly ground black pepper or to taste

Chopped or shredded spinach leaves

1 medium tomato

2 sesame-seed burger buns

CARAMELIZED ONION SPREAD

1 large yellow onion

Canola oil spray

¼ cup ketchup

1 tablespoon mustard

2 tablespoons sour cream

1 teaspoon balsamic vinegar

1 teaspoon brown sugar or honey

Combine ground beef, garlic, cumin, salt, and pepper in a large mixing bowl. Gently form into two patties about ½–1 inch thick. Place in refrigerator for at least 1 hour prior to grilling.

While patties are chilling, heat grill to medium high. Slice onion into ½-inch disks; separate into rings; and spray with canola oil. Use tongs to place on the grill. When the onions are caramelized and soft, place them into a food processor or blender. Add ketchup, mustard, sour cream, balsamic vinegar, and brown sugar. Pulse until mixture is thick and chunky. Cover with foil, and place on warming rack while burgers cook.

Remove patties from refrigerator, and lightly spray with canola oil before placing them on the grill over medium-high heat. Cook for about 4 to 5 minutes per side, turning once with a spatula that has been sprayed with canola oil. Place patties in a foil pan on cooler section of the grill to continue cooking over indirect heat. Cook until meat reaches an internal temperature of 160°F.

While the patties are finishing, butter the buns, and toast on the grill. Add each burger to a bottom bun, and spread with spoonfuls of the caramelized onion mixture. Top with sliced tomatoes and spinach leave and then with the top bun. ✲

TOMATO-MOZZARELLA-POLENTA BURGERS

1½ pounds ground beef

⅔ cup balsamic vinegar

Salt and pepper

1 package (16 to 18 ounces) refrigerated polenta, cut into 8 disks

2 tablespoons olive oil

1 package (8 ounces) fresh mozzarella cheese, cut into 8 slices

2 medium tomatoes cut into 4 slices each

Fresh basil, thinly sliced

Bring vinegar to a boil in a 2-quart saucepan. Reduce heat; simmer uncovered for 9 to 10 minutes or until reduced to ⅓ cup. Set aside.

Preheat grill to medium high. Lightly shape ground beef into eight ½-inch-thick patties. Season burgers with salt and pepper. Brush polenta slices with oil.

Place patties in centre of grill; arrange polenta disks around patties. Grill patties for 4 to 5 minutes per side, turning once and basting with 2 tablespoons reduced vinegar after turning. About 2 minutes before burgers are done, top each with a slice of mozzarella to warm and soften, taking care not to let cheese melt onto grill. Cook until centres of burgers reach 160°F. Cook polenta, turning once, until heated through and light grill marks appear on each side, about 9 to 10 minutes. For each serving, place burger on top of polenta and tomato slice. Drizzle with remaining vinegar, and sprinkle with basil to garnish. ❀

3

BEEF

CB'S SLIDERS

1 pound ground chuck
20 dinner rolls
American-style cheese (or other favourite),
   sliced into 20 1-inch squares
Canola oil spray
1 medium onion, diced

Combine dry seasoning ingredients in a small bowl. In a large bowl, add the meat; sprinkle with the dry seasoning mixture; and incorporate gently, making sure not to overwork the meat.

Place the meat mixture in the centre of a sheet pan that has been lined with parchment paper or foil. Loosely cover meat with plastic wrap. Using a rolling pin or bottle, evenly roll out the meat until it covers the surface of the pan and is about ¼ inch thick.

Using the parchment paper, lift the meat, and fold it in half lengthwise. Gently press the halves together, and re-cover with the plastic wrap. Refrigerate meat for at least 20 minutes to chill.

Slice each dinner roll in half, and arrange rolls on a large square of foil; loosely wrap and seal.

Preheat the grill to medium. Remove the meat from the refrigerator, and discard the plastic wrap. Using a pizza cutter or sharp knife, cut meat into 20 2 x 2-inch squares.

Use a pan or the griddle portion of your grill to cook the onions until lightly browned. Remove onions from the heat, and set aside.

Place foil packet containing rolls over indirect heat to warm. Add meat patties to grill, and cook approximately 3 minutes per side, turning once.

After turning the patties, top each with one square of cheese. Close the grill lid to melt. Place bottom halves of warmed buns on a serving plate. Using a spatula and tongs, remove cooked patties from the grill, and place one on each of the buns. Top with a teaspoon of grilled onions and the other half of the bun. Serve with condiments. ❀

DRY SEASONING

½ teaspoon garlic powder

½ teaspoon freshly

ground black pepper

½ teaspoon coarse salt

¼ teaspoon cumin

TOPPINGS

Butter pickles

Sliced cherry tomatoes

Mayonnaise

Ketchup

Mustard

Relish

3

BEEF

JAMAICAN JERK BURGERS

1 pound ground beef, pork, or turkey	2 tablespoons soy sauce
	2 teaspoons ground ginger
2 tablespoons lime juice	4 tablespoons Jamaican jerk seasoning

Whisk together all the ingredients except the beef. Then mix in the beef until combined, taking care not to overmix. Form into patties, and grill. Serve with Chipotle-Lime Mayonnaise. (See below.) ✺

CHIPOTLE-LIME MAYONNAISE

2 egg yolks

3 teaspoons lime juice

1 teaspoon chipotle purée

3 tablespoons cilantro, finely chopped

Salt and white pepper to taste

1 cup olive oil

Bring the egg yolks to room temperature. In a food processor, purée the yolks, lime juice, chipotle purée, cilantro, salt, and white pepper. Once fully incorporated, slowly drizzle in the olive oil while the food processor is still running.

Note: to avoid consuming raw eggs for health reasons, use pasteurized eggs, or substitute about 1½ cups store-bought mayonnaise for eggs and oil.

CAJUN MEAT-LOAF MUFFINS

1¾ pounds 80-percent lean ground chuck

⅓ cup yellow onion, diced

⅓ cup celery, diced

⅔ cup green bell pepper, diced

1 large egg, beaten with dash of milk or cream

1 cup plain cornbread crumbs

2 tablespoons Tabasco sauce

1 tablespoon Worcestershire sauce

½ teaspoon ground cumin

½ teaspoon ground mustard

¼ cup ketchup

¼ cup cooked brown or white rice (optional)

Salt and pepper to taste

Canola oil spray

[
Make a few extra portions of these individual meat loaves to pop into a lunch box the next day.—CB
]

3

BEEF

Prepare the grill for indirect cooking by preheating one side to high. Temperature inside the grill should reach between 425°F and 450°F.

In a large bowl, combine ground beef and rest of ingredients. Insert foil-covered muffin liners into a 12-cup muffin pan. Using a spoon or ice cream scoop, completely fill each cup with the meat mixture. Place pan in the centre of the grill.

Close hood, and cook for about 20 minutes or until internal temperature of meat reaches 155°F.

Remove muffin pan from grill, and loosely cover with foil. Meat will continue to cook until it reaches 160°F degrees.

You can either serve meat-loaf muffins immediately or wrap and store them in the refrigerator or freezer for later meals. ✺

THAI-STYLE BURGERS

1 pound coarse-ground 80-percent lean beef

1 large shallot, finely chopped

2 green onions, coarsely chopped, including greens

4 to 7 garlic cloves, finely chopped

1 roasted poblano pepper, finely chopped (or use paste)

1 roasted habanero pepper, finely chopped (or use paste)

2 to 3 tablespoons ginger, freshly grated

2 to 3 tablespoons Thai green curry paste, plus additional for topping

Cayenne pepper to taste (optional)

Coarse salt

Black pepper

Bread crumbs (optional)

½ lime

Canola oil spray

½ bunch fresh cilantro or watercress sprigs

3 to 4 buns, toasted

Bean sprouts

Basil

In large nonreactive bowl, thoroughly mix the 10 ingredients that follow the ground beef. Gently fold mixture into the meat, being careful not to overwork. If the meat is too loose, add bread crumbs until you can form 3 or 4 patties about 1 inch thick. Chill for at least 1 hour.

Preheat grill to medium high. Remove burgers from refrigerator, and lightly spray with canola oil before placing them on the grill. When you see some browning at the edges (about 2 to 3 minutes), spray a spatula with canola oil. Slip the spatula under the burger patty; away from the heat, spray the uncooked side; and then place it down on a clean section of grate. Grill over direct heat for another 2 to 3 minutes or until the meat is seared. Use the same method to lift patties and place them in a holding pan over indirect heat. Cook until internal temperature of patties reaches 160°F.

Before serving the burgers on toasted buns, squeeze a few drops of lime juice onto each one, along with some grated lime zest. Serve with cilantro or watercress and bean sprouts topped with a dollop of green curry paste if desired. ❀

6 Servings • Prep: 45 min. • Marinate: 15 min.–2 hr. • Grill: 10–14 min.

77

GRILLED BEEF TACOS WITH AVOCADO SALSA

4 beef top-blade (flat-iron) steaks, about 8 ounces each

18 small corn tortillas (6- to 7-inch diameter)

MARINADE

1 cup prepared tomatillo salsa

⅓ cup chopped fresh cilantro

2 tablespoons fresh lime juice

2 teaspoons minced garlic

½ teaspoon salt

¼ teaspoon pepper

AVOCADO SALSA

1½ cups prepared tomatillo salsa

1 large avocado, diced

⅔ cup fresh cilantro, chopped

½ cup white onion, minced

1 tablespoon fresh lime juice

1 teaspoon garlic, minced

½ teaspoon salt

TOPPINGS

Minced white onion

Chopped fresh cilantro

Lime wedges

3

BEEF

Combine marinade ingredients in a small bowl. Place steaks and marinade in a food-safe plastic bag; turn steaks to coat. Close bag securely, and marinate steaks in refrigerator for 15 minutes to 2 hours.

Remove steaks from marinade; discard marinade. Place steaks on grill over medium heat. Grill, covered, 10 to 14 minutes for medium-rare to medium doneness, turning once.

Meanwhile, combine avocado salsa ingredients in a medium bowl. Set aside.

Place tortillas on grill. Grill until warm and slightly charred. Remove; keep warm.

Slice steaks, and serve in grilled tortillas with avocado salsa. Top with onion, cilantro, and lime wedges as desired. ✸

CB'S RIB EYES WITH BALSAMIC-MUSHROOM SAUCE

2 rib-eye steaks,
  cut 1 to 2 inches thick
Coarse salt
Pepper
Canola oil spray

CB's Grilled Potatoes with Bacon, Cheese & Roasted Jalapeños, page 241

Pat the steaks dry with a paper towel. Lightly season both sides of the steaks with salt, and rub it in. This helps to draw out natural sugars and proteins that enhance searing.

Place salted steaks in a glass dish, and let rest in refrigerator for about 2 hours. Remove steaks about 30 minutes prior to grilling, and place on room-temperature plate.

Trim off ½ inch from the tip of each steak. Mince this up, season with a pinch of salt and pepper, and reserve.

Preheat grill to high; lightly spray both sides of each steak with canola oil. Place steaks on the grill, and don't move them until you see the bottom edge beginning to brown (about 3 minutes). Use tongs to turn steaks over, and move them to a fresh section of the grill. Cook for 3 minutes more or until that side of the meat begins to turn brown. Turn the steaks over again, and rotate them so that the grill grates are crossing the original sear marks. After 2 to 3 minutes, use the tongs to turn the meat over, and cross-hatch the other side. Place the steaks in an uncovered aluminum pan, and let them finish over indirect heat to desired doneness. Remove the steaks, and let them rest at room temperature for about 15 to 20 minutes.

To prepare mushroom sauce, spray a sauté pan with canola oil, and place over medium heat directly on the grill or on the side burner. Add all of the minced raw steak to brown.

When the meat has cooked, add the sliced mushrooms and a pinch of salt. Continue to sauté on medium until mushrooms are tender, about 3 to 5 minutes.

Remove mushroom mixture, and set aside. Add balsamic vinegar to skillet; increase heat to medium high. Cook 7 to 10 minutes, stirring up any browned bits remaining in the skillet with a spatula. When the sauce is reduced to ¼ cup, stir in butter, thyme, cooked mushrooms, and a pinch of salt. Cook and stir until heated through. Serve sauce with steaks. ✲

3

BEEF

MUSHROOM SAUCE

8 ounces thinly sliced cremini
  or white mushrooms
¼ teaspoon salt
¾ cup balsamic vinegar
2 tablespoons butter
1 teaspoon dried thyme leaves, crushed

CB'S GRILLED FLAT-IRON STEAKS WITH MUSTARD-BOURBON SAUCE

Flat-iron steaks are available at most grocery stores—ask your butcher.

2 beef shoulder top-blade steaks (flat-iron), about 8 ounces each

½ teaspoon each large-grain coarse salt and black peppercorns, crushed

SAUCE
½ cup whipping cream

¼ cup country Dijon-style mustard

2 tablespoons bourbon

1 tablespoon fresh chives or green onions, finely chopped

Press salt and pepper evenly onto both sides of steaks about 30 minutes before grilling. Spritz with canola or other high-heat vegetable cooking oil. (Do not use extra-virgin olive oil to grill at high temperatures.)

Heat grill to medium-high heat. Place prepped steaks on grates; grill for 13 to 15 minutes for medium-rare (145°F) to medium (160°F) doneness, turning twice. Remove steaks from grill, and wrap in foil to keep warm.

For the sauce: Combine cream, mustard, and bourbon in a small bowl. Add to skillet; cook and stir 1 to 2 minutes. Season with salt, as desired.

Serving suggestion: Carve steaks into slices; season with salt as desired. Spoon sauce over steaks; sprinkle with chopped chives. ❀

8 Servings • Prep: 15 min. • Marinate: 2 hr. • Grill: 15–20 min.

81

GINGER-MAPLE STEAK WITH NAPA CABBAGE & GRILLED ONIONS

2 boneless beef top loin (strip) steaks, about 10 ounces each

¼ teaspoon pepper

1 large red onion, cut into ½-inch thick slices

4 cups thinly sliced Napa cabbage

GINGER-MAPLE MARINADE AND DRESSING

½ cup soy sauce

⅓ cup pure maple syrup

¼ cup lemon juice

2 tablespoons fresh ginger, minced

1 tablespoon sesame oil

1½ teaspoons fresh garlic, minced

1½ teaspoons Asian chile-garlic paste

Whisk marinade ingredients in a medium bowl. Place steaks and ½ cup marinade in a plastic bag; turn steaks to coat. Seal bag, and refrigerate up to 2 hours. Cover and refrigerate remaining marinade for dressing.

Preheat grill to medium high. Remove steaks from marinade; discard marinade. Sprinkle steaks with pepper. Place steaks in centre of grill; arrange onion around steaks. Grill steaks, uncovered, 15 to 18 minutes for medium rare to medium, turning occasionally. Grill onions 15 to 20 minutes, turning occasionally.

Carve steaks into slices. Cut onion into quarters. Toss cabbage, onion, and 2 tablespoons reserved dressing in a large bowl. Arrange beef on cabbage mixture. Drizzle with the remaining dressing. ❀

2 Servings • Chill: 1 hr. • Rest: 1 hr. • Grill: 20–25 min.

CB'S SLOW-GRILLED RIB EYES

2 rib-eye steaks, 8 to 12 ounces each, at least 1½ inches thick
Coarse salt
Canola, safflower, or peanut oil spray
2 teaspoons maître d' butter (See recipe page 293.)

Here's a technique for grilling rib eyes that starts with low heat followed by an extremely hot finish for searing and crisping the meat.—CB

Trim away excess fat from around steaks. Blot excess moisture from meat using a paper towel. Generously sprinkle both sides of steaks with salt. Refrigerate for at least 1 hour.

Remove steaks from the refrigerator about 1 hour prior to grilling. Lightly brush off remaining salt.

Preheat one side of the grill to high, and leave the other side off. Spray steaks lightly with the oil, and place on the cool side of the grill, as far from the heat as you can.

When steaks reach an internal temperature of 90°F, use tongs to place them on the hot side of the grill. Sear steaks over direct heat until they reach a temperature of 140°F (rare) to 145°F (medium rare). Turn steaks once, when sear marks appear on each side. Remove from grill, and top each steak with a teaspoon of maître d' butter before serving. ✽

SMOKY GRILLED MEAT LOAF

1 pound ground pork

1 pound ground beef

1 pound ground turkey

1 pound centre-cut bacon

¼ cup carrots, chopped

¼ cup celery, chopped

¼ cup white onion, chopped

3 large eggs, lightly beaten

¼ cup fine bread crumbs

5 large cloves garlic, roughly chopped

½ teaspoon ground cumin

½ teaspoon mustard powder

½ teaspoon Worcestershire sauce

½ teaspoon balsamic vinegar

¼ cup ketchup

Salt and pepper to taste

In a skillet, cook bacon until it starts to brown. Remove bacon, but reserve fat in the skillet.

Add carrots, celery, and onion and a pinch of salt to the bacon fat. Cover, and cook until the vegetables are softened and slightly browned, about 3 to 5 minutes. Remove from heat, and let vegetables cool.

In a large bowl, thoroughly mix the meat with the eggs, cooked vegetables, and all remaining ingredients except for the bacon. Place the meat mixture into a metal loaf pan, and weave bacon strips on top.

Preheat grill to high for about 10 minutes with hood closed. Turn centre burner off, and reduce heat on outer burners. Temperature of cooking chamber with hood closed should remain steady at 350°F.

Put soaked wood chips in a smoker box or foil on the grill. Place meat loaf in centre, and close the hood.

After about 30 minutes, check temperature inside grill. Add more wood chips if desired.

You can remove meat loaf from grill when a thermometer inserted in the centre registers 160°F. Cover with foil, and let rest at room temperature for 15 to 20 minutes before serving. ❋

3

BEEF

BEEF "CALIFORNIA ROLL" SALAD

3 boneless beef top loin strip steaks, cut ¾ inch thick (about 8 ounces each)

MARINADE

⅓ cup hoisin sauce

¼ cup pomegranate juice

2 tablespoons garlic, minced

2 tablespoons fresh ginger, minced

1 tablespoon sesame oil

½ teaspoon pepper

WASABI CUCUMBERS

2 teaspoons wasabi paste

1 teaspoon pomegranate juice

1 English cucumber, thinly sliced

GINGERED CARROTS

1 tablespoon mayonnaise

1½ teaspoons fresh ginger, minced

2 cups packaged matchstick carrots

GARNISH

1 tablespoon sesame seeds, toasted

1 medium avocado, diced

½ cup fresh pomegranate seeds

Combine marinade ingredients in small bowl. Place steaks and marinade in food-safe plastic bag; turn steaks to coat. Close bag securely, and marinate in refrigerator 15 minutes to 2 hours.

Prepare wasabi cucumbers. Combine wasabi paste and pomegranate juice in medium bowl; add cucumbers; toss to coat. Set aside; refrigerate until ready to serve.

Prepare gingered carrots. Combine mayonnaise and ginger in another medium bowl. Add carrots; toss to coat. Set aside in refrigerator until ready to serve.

Preheat grill to medium. Remove steaks from marinade; discard marinade. Place steaks on grill, and cook, covered, 7 to 10 minutes for medium-rare (145°F) to medium (160°F) doneness, turning occasionally.

Carve steaks into thin slices. Place cucumbers and carrots side by side on plate; top with beef. Top with avocado and pomegranate seeds; sprinkle with sesame seeds. ❀

POMSEY'S TAILGATE TIPS

9 pounds sirloin tips or rib-eye cubes
French rolls
American-style cheese
Vidalia onion

SAUCE

1 cup ketchup
⅛ tablespoon molasses
⅓ teaspoon spicy brown or Dijon mustard
⅙ teaspoon soy sauce
⅓ teaspoon garlic powder
⅓ teaspoon hot pepper sauce
1 teaspoon black pepper

Trim any excess fat (keeping in mind the meat needs some fat to remain juicy throughout the grilling process), and cut meat into 2-inch cubes. Place tips in a large plastic container or bag.

In a large mixing bowl, combine sauce ingredients. Set aside some sauce for basting if you desire, and pour the rest of the sauce over tips. Mix well so that meat is completely coated. Refrigerate for 24 to 30 hours.

Preheat grill to medium-high heat. Place tips on the medium-high grill, and grill to your desired doneness. **Note:** to avoid a messy grill, coat your tips well the day before so that there's no need to slather on extra sauce. ✽

"Sizzle on the Grill" contributor Greg from Quincy, Massachusetts, writes that his gang enjoys these tips on fresh French rolls with American-style cheese and grilled Vidalia onions. This recipe feeds 10 if other main courses are served.

6–8 Servings • Prep: 15 min. • Rest: 1 hr. • Grill: 15–20 min. • Rest after cooking: 15–20 min.

87

CB'S POLYNESIAN-STYLE TRI-TIP

2½ **pounds tri-tip roast**
   (triangular tip of the sirloin)
Pineapple slices
Vegetable oil spray

DRY RUB

2 **tablespoons coarse salt**
½ **tablespoon cracked black**
   pepper
1 **tablespoon garlic, minced**

GLAZE

1 **tablespoon brown sugar**
2 **tablespoons melted butter**
1 **tablespoon light soy sauce**
1 **tablespoon fresh ginger,**
   finely grated

Combine dry-rub ingredients; apply to all surfaces of the meat; wrap meat in plastic; and allow meat to rest at room temperature for 1 hour.

Preheat one side of grill to high. Remove meat from plastic, and lightly spray with vegetable oil on all sides. Place on hot side of grill to sear for about 2 to 3 minutes on each side, using tongs to turn.

Thoroughly combine glaze ingredients in a small bowl. Place seared roast in pan on cool half of grill; apply glaze with silicon brush; and close hood. Cook until internal temperature of meat reaches 145°F for medium rare, 160°F for medium. (Tri-tip is best enjoyed medium rare.) Transfer roast to carving board; tent with foil; and let stand for 15 to 20 minutes. Grill pineapple slices 2 to 3 minutes on each side. ❄

3

BEEF

The glaze for this steak reminds me of the flavours of Hawaii, where one of my favourite meals is the "Plate Lunch." It usually features either chicken, fish, beef, or pork prepared with fresh ginger, garlic, and soy sauce.—CB

CB'S SALTED MARGARITA FLANK STEAK

2 pounds skirt steak

Coarse salt

3 shots tequila

1 tablespoon Cointreau

2 tablespoons lime zest

2 tablespoons fresh cilantro, chopped

2 large garlic cloves, minced

2 tablespoons hot sauce

This dish benefits from an overnight "salt cure" to tenderize and flavour the meat.

Dry the meat with a paper towel. Liberally salt both sides of the steak; seal in plastic wrap; and place in refrigerator for at least 4 hours or overnight.

Mix together all remaining ingredients in a sealable plastic bag. Remove steak from plastic wrap; do not rinse off salt. Add steak to bag, and seal. Allow steak to marinate for up to 2 hours.

Preheat grill to high. Remove the steak from the marinade, and pat it dry. Spray the meat with canola oil. Cook until grill marks form, about 5 minutes. Use tongs to turn and sear the other side, about 5 minutes. Use an instant-read thermometer to check the temperature of the meat: 140°F rare, 145°F medium rare, 160°F medium.

Transfer steak to a cutting board, and let rest for 5 minutes. Cut the steak across the grain at an angle to expose more of the pink meat—about ⅛- to ¼-inch-thick slices. Serve with your favourite salsa on the side. ✺

FLANK-STEAK TOURNEDOS WITH GOAT CHEESE

4 2-to-3-ounce flank-steak slices, approximately 6 inches long and ½ inch or less thick

2 teaspoons coarse salt

2 teaspoons fresh ground black pepper

4 tablespoons extra-virgin olive oil

2 medium-size garlic cloves, minced

2 ounces goat cheese or other soft, creamy cheese

Butchers twine

Flank steak is a flavourful cut that lends itself quite well to this recipe.

Place steak on cutting board or other hard surface, and cover with wax or parchment paper. Use mallet to flatten slightly.

Season meat with salt and pepper, and place in a shallow bowl. Cover with olive oil and minced garlic. Marinate for at least 45 minutes at room temperature. Lay the pieces of meat flat on a sheet of wax paper; spread softened goat cheese on each slice; roll up each one; and individually tie with the twine.

Preheat grill to high. Use tongs to place tournedos on grill, and allow them to sear for approximately 3 to 4 minutes. Turn meat; place on fresh section of grill; and sear for another 3 to 4 minutes.

Remove meat to a warming rack in a foil pan. Sprinkle additional crumbled goat cheese on tournedos, and allow to rest for a few minutes. Serve with sliced tomatoes, cucumbers, or other raw vegetables. ✺

3

BEEF

Livefire's Holiday Potato Torte, page 243

LIVEFIRE'S GRILLED BEEF WELLINGTON

[*This recipe is courtesy of Curt McAdams, a creative cook, photographer, and writer of Livefire, a popular grilling blog.*]

Add the mushrooms and shallots to a dry skillet, and place over medium heat to evaporate moisture, about 5 minutes or until mushrooms are springy but no longer wet. Set mushroom mixture aside.

Wipe out the skillet; return to medium-high heat; and sear the beef on all sides, about 1 minute per side. Remove string from roast. Set aside the skillet for sauce to be prepared later.

Arrange prosciutto slices on a large sheet of plastic wrap, overlapping each slice by about half. Spread with Dijon mustard, followed by mushroom mixture, and sprinkle evenly with the thyme. Place the tenderloin along one edge of the prosciutto/mushroom layer, and carefully roll up in the plastic wrap. Once rolled up tightly, refrigerate for 30 minutes.

Line up 2 sheets of puff pastry so that edges overlap. Gently press together edges to seal and make a single sheet. Using a rolling pin, gently roll out the sheet until it is approximately ¼ inch thick. Place the tenderloin in the centre of the sheet. Fold pastry over the meat, and seal the seam using the egg wash as glue. Place the roast on a pizza stone or cookie sheet with the pastry seam facing down. Lightly brush egg wash over the top of the pasty, making sure that the ends are well closed. Cut off any excess pastry, and use it to form leaves or other decorations along the top of the pastry if desired.

Preheat one side of the grill to high, and prepare for indirect cooking. Put the tenderloin on the indirect side. Cook for about 40 minutes or until roast reaches an internal temperature of 145°F. Remove the tenderloin from the grill, and let it rest, covered with foil.

About 10 minutes before carving, add 2 cups of beef stock to the skillet. Bring stock to a low boil, whisking up any browned bits remaining in the pan, until liquid is reduced by about half. Then stir in cream and coarsely ground pepper. Reduce heat, and simmer sauce for another 2 to 3 minutes. Ladle over slices of roast, and serve. ✳

Whole beef tenderloin (about 4 pounds), trimmed of excess fat, rolled, and tied
Ask the butcher to fold and tie the roast so that it is of even thickness.
1½ pounds button mushrooms, finely chopped
1 shallot, finely chopped
12 slices prosciutto, medium thickness
2 tablespoons grainy Dijon mustard
Fresh thyme
1 package frozen puff pastry sheets
1 egg, beaten
2 cups beef stock
1 cup heavy cream

CB'S GRILLED HANGER STEAK "MOUTARDE"

12-to-18-ounce hanger or flank steak
½ cup grainy Dijon mustard
2 tablespoons maple syrup
1 tablespoon cider vinegar
¼ teaspoon dried tarragon
¼ teaspoon hot sauce
Salt and pepper to taste
Canola oil spray

Combine all ingredients in a plastic bag, including the meat; massage gently to coat. Marinate in refrigerator for up to 8 hours.

Preheat grill to high. Remove steak from bag; spray with canola oil; and grill on each side for about 4 minutes. Remove; place in an aluminum pan; and cover with foil. Place on warming shelf over indirect heat, and continue cooking for about 10 minutes.

Remove from grill, and let steak rest, covered, for about 5 minutes. Slice into thin strips across the grain. ✺

Several years ago, I had the opportunity to visit the Burgundy region of France, where I was delighted to see a grilled steak with "frites"(fries) on the menu at just about every restaurant! Here's my interpretation of those steaks.—CB

SZECHUAN STEAK WRAPS WITH SPICY PEANUT MAYONNAISE

1 beef top-round steak, ¾ inch thick (about 1 pound)
2 baby bok choy, cut lengthwise in half
4 spinach wraps or tortillas (8- to 10-inch diameter)

MARINADE

2 tablespoons rice vinegar
2 tablespoons dark sesame oil
2 tablespoons reduced-sodium or regular soy sauce
1 tablespoon fresh ginger, minced

SPICY PEANUT MAYONNAISE

2 tablespoons reduced-fat or regular mayonnaise
2 tablespoons dry-roasted peanuts, finely chopped
1½ teaspoons fresh ginger, minced
1 to 1½ teaspoons chili-garlic paste
¾ teaspoon reduced-sodium or regular soy sauce
¾ teaspoon rice vinegar
½ teaspoon dark sesame oil

3

BEEF

Combine marinade ingredients in small bowl. Cover and refrigerate 1 tablespoon for bok choy. Place steak and remaining marinade in food-safe plastic bag; turn steak to coat. Close bag securely, and marinate in refrigerator 6 hours or overnight.

Remove steak from bag; discard marinade. Preheat grill to medium. Grill steak, covered, 10 to 11 minutes for medium-rare doneness, turning occasionally. (Do not overcook.)

Brush bok choy with reserved 1 tablespoon marinade. Grill bok choy, uncovered, 4 to 5 minutes or until tender and lightly browned, turning once.

Meanwhile combine Spicy Peanut Mayonnaise ingredients in a medium bowl; mix well.

Carve steak into thin slices. Cut each bok choy section in half lengthwise again, forming quarters. Cut core from each quarter. Spread mayonnaise mixture evenly on spinach wraps. Divide steak slices and bok choy among wraps. Roll up tightly. ✸

GRILLED FLANK STEAK WITH LEMON & ROSEMARY MARINADE

1 flank steak, about 3 pounds

¼ cup olive oil

2 lemons, zested and juiced

2 tablespoons fresh rosemary, chopped

2 cloves garlic, minced

1 teaspoon fresh ground black pepper

½ teaspoon coarse salt

Grilled Potato Planks, page 250

Combine the marinade ingredients. Put the steak in a large plastic bag with the marinade, and seal. Turn several times to coat the steak. Refrigerate for 30 minutes to 4 hours.

Preheat one side of grill to high. Spray grates lightly with canola oil. Remove the steak from the marinade, and place directly on the high-heat side of the grill. Leave it alone until it develops a rich brown crust—3 to 5 minutes. Turn the steak, and repeat. Remove steak when it reaches 145°F for medium-rare. Cover loosely with foil, and let rest for 5 minutes. Carve into long slices at an angle, against the grain. ❁

This recipe is courtesy of Brys Stephens at cookthink.com.

4 Servings • Prep: 10 min. • Marinate: up to 4 hr. • Grill: 10–12 min.

95

CB'S BEEF SKEWERS "ON FIRE"

1½ pounds beef tri-tip or sirloin,
   trimmed of fat and cut into
   1-inch cubes

4 12-inch metal skewers

4 small yellow onions cut in quarters

1 each red, green, and yellow bell
   peppers, seeds removed
   and cut into chunks

MARINADE

½ cup Chinese-style or other hot
   mustard

½ cup soy sauce

¼ cup brown sugar

Dash Tabasco or other favourite hot sauce

Juice from ½ fresh lime

5 tablespoons garlic, crushed

1 tablespoon powdered ginger

1 teaspoon cumin

Dried red pepper flakes to taste

Serve these kabobs with Pan Pacific Rice. (See page 256.)

In large nonreactive bowl, whisk together the marinade ingredients. Remove and reserve ½ cup for basting while skewers grill.

Add beef cubes and marinande to large sealable plastic bag. Seal bag, and refrigerate for up to 4 hours.

Remove the beef cubes from the bag, and discard the marinade. (It's a good idea to use food-safe gloves whenever you handle raw meat and poultry.)

Thread beef, onions, and peppers onto each of four 12-inch metal skewers. Grill on medium-hot grates, uncovered, for 10 to 12 minutes for medium-rare to medium doneness, basting frequently with reserved ½-cup marinade and turning occasionally. When finished grilling, squeeze remaining half of lime over skewers, and serve immediately. ✺

3

BEEF

6 Servings • Prep: 15 min. • Marinate: 15 min.–2 hr. • Grill: 15–20 min.

97

TURKISH-STYLE SIRLOIN WITH ROASTED GARLIC-FIG SAUCE

1 boneless sirloin steak (1½ pounds) cut 1 inch thick
2 cloves garlic, minced
1 teaspoon pumpkin pie spice
½ teaspoon pepper
⅓ cup dry red wine
1 tablespoon olive oil
Salt and pepper
Chopped almonds and fresh mint (optional)

BULGUR

1 cup uncooked bulgur wheat
1½ cups water
½ teaspoon salt
½ teaspoon pumpkin pie spice
¼ cup roasted unblanched almonds, chopped
¼ cup fresh mint, chopped

ROASTED GARLIC-FIG SAUCE

½ cup dry red wine
⅓ cup roasted garlic-onion jam
⅓ cup thinly sliced dried figs, stems removed
½ teaspoon pumpkin pie spice

Combine garlic, pumpkin pie spice, and pepper; press evenly onto steak. Place steak and ⅓ cup wine in food-safe plastic bag; turn steak to coat. Close bag securely, and marinate in refrigerator 15 minutes to 2 hours, turning once.

Combine bulgur, water, salt, and pumpkin pie spice in small saucepan; bring to a boil. Reduce heat to low; cover; and simmer about 15 minutes or until tender and water is absorbed. Fluff with a fork. Stir in mint and almonds; keep warm.

Meanwhile, combine sauce ingredients in small bowl. Set aside.

Remove steak from bag; discard marinade. Preheat grill to medium. Place steak on grill; cook 15 to 20 minutes for medium-rare (145°F) to medium (160°F) doneness, turning occasionally. Remove to cutting board; keep warm.

Add sauce mixture to a medium saucepan. Cook and stir 1 to 2 minutes or sauce thickens and coats the back of a spoon. Remove from heat.

Carve steaks into slices; season with salt and pepper. Serve steak over bulgur; drizzle with sauce. Garnish with additional almonds and mint if desired. ✺

THE BIG EASY COFFEE-BRINED BEEF ROAST

Sirloin tip beef roast
  (5 to 7 pounds)
1 tablespoon flour
½ tablespoon butter

COFFEE BRINE

4 cups warm water,
  or enough to
  cover roast
2 cups brewed coffee
½ cup salt
¼ cup white sugar
¼ cup brown sugar
3 tablespoons oil
2 teaspoons white
  pepper
2 teaspoons black
  pepper
¼ cup Worcestershire
  sauce
2 tablespoons
  onion flakes

Mix brine ingredients, and let mixture cool to room temperature. Place roast in a large pan or container; pour brine over meat. Cover meat, and refrigerate for a minimum of 8 hours.

Remove meat from brine about 1 hour before cooking; set in shallow pan or bowl to allow brine to drip off. Do not rinse.

Line the drip tray of The Big Easy with aluminum foil. Place meat vertically in the cooking basket (using skewers to hold it in place); lower basket into the cooking chamber; and cover with mesh lid. Set control knob to high; ignite.

After approximately 30 minutes, remove lid, and turn the control knob to about halfway between high and off. Continue cooking for approximately 1 hour or until meat reaches an internal temperature of 145°F degrees for medium rare.

Lift cooking basket from cooker; carefully remove meat from basket; and wrap with foil. Place in shallow bowl or tray to rest for 30 minutes.

Pour drippings from the drip tray into a measuring cup. Skim off fat and solids, and add remaining juices to saucepan. Add one teaspoon of flour and ½ tablespoon of butter. Cook, stirring occasionally, until sauce is reduced by about half, approximately 5 minutes. Slice roast; arrange on platter; and serve. ✺

Recipe courtesy of Tommy Bommarito, Guest Chef for The Big Easy Users' Forum.

CB'S COWBOY-STYLE BEEF RIBS

2 racks of beef back ribs (7 ribs per rack)
2 tablespoons black pepper
1 tablespoon smoked paprika
1 tablespoon ground mustard powder
½ teaspoon ground cayenne pepper

Peg's Magic Beans, page 231

Combine all spices. Rub over surface of ribs to coat well. Wrap with plastic, and chill for up to 4 hours.

Set grill for indirect cooking, and preheat to medium-high with hood closed. Place ribs on rack in roasting pan. Add ½-inch of water to bottom of pan. Tent pan with foil, but leave sides open to allow smoke to enter. Place wood chips in smoker box or on grate. Cook ribs for about 2 hours. Remove ribs from pan, and place on grill over medium heat for 15 minutes. Cut between ribs to serve. ✹

When I lived in Texas, I learned that a Texan's concept of barbecue is an appreciation of the meat—the flavours that evolve after careful preparation and attention to spices, heat, and smoke. So serve these ribs with sauce if you dare!—CB

4 Pork

102 Brined Pork Chops
with Mustard & Herbs

103 CB's Five-Spice Pork Chops

104 CB's Grilled Pork Chops
with Garlic, Citrus & Cilantro

106 CB's Grilled
Pork Chops Marsala

107 CB's Caribbean-Spice
Pork Roast

108 CB's Fennel & Vermouth
Pork Tenderloin

109 CB's Chili-Rubbed Ribs

110 CB's Bacon-Wrapped
Pork Loin

112 CB's Grilled Pork Paillards
with Two-Mustard Sauce

113 CB's Pork Neck Roast
with Cumin-Spice Rub

114 CB's "Cincinnati-Chili"
Pork Chops

115 Grilled Stuffed Pork Chops

116 CB's Tailgate
Grilled Baby Back Ribs

118 CB's Pork Loin with Chili,
Curry & Coffee Rub

119 CB's "Get Creative"
Pork Chop Casserole

120 CB's Grilled Pork Burgers
with Chorizo

121 CB's Char Siu
Pork Tenderloin

122 CB's Herb & Honey
Glazed Ham

124 Grilled Breaded Pork Chops

125 Grilled Pork &
Pineapple Tacos

126 CB's Mojito-Mopped
Pulled Pork

128 Cola Ribs

129 Uncle Dane's Grilled
Pork Patties

130 Indian Tandoori Ribs

131 Pork Spareribs
with Coconut-Peanut Sauce

132 CB's Nut-Crusted Ribs
with Bourbon Mop Sauce

(Right) CB's Chili-Rubbed Ribs, page 109

2–4 Servings • Prep: 10 min. • Chill: 45 min. • Grill: 18–24 min.

BRINED PORK CHOPS WITH MUSTARD & HERBS

2 thick pork loin
  chops
1½ cup coarse salt
2½ quarts (10 cups)
  water
1 tablespoon
  fresh marjoram,
  chopped
1 tablespoon fresh
  rosemary, chopped
1 tablespoon fresh
  thyme, chopped
4 tablespoons
  Dijon mustard
Salt and pepper to
  taste
Olive oil

In a large mixing bowl, stir the salt into the cold water until dissolved. Place chops in the brine. Refrigerate for 45 minutes.

When you're ready to grill, rinse the chops, and pat dry. Preheat one side of the grill to high and one side to low. In a small bowl, whisk together the herbs, mustard, salt, and pepper. Lightly coat the chops with olive oil, and place on the high-heat side of the grill. Let them brown well on the first side, 4 to 6 minutes. Turn the chops over, and generously coat the browned side with the mustard-herb mixture. Brown the second side for another 4 to 6 minutes. Turn the chops over, and move them to the low-heat part of the grill. Coat the second side with the mustard-herb mixture.

Turning once more, cook the chops until they're 150°F in the thickest part, another 10 to 12 minutes. Remove them to a clean plate to rest, loosely covered with foil, 5 minutes before serving. ✺

Soaking pork chops in brine before grilling ensures that they will be exceptionally tender.
Recipe courtesy of cookthink.com

CB'S FIVE-SPICE PORK CHOPS

4 thick-cut bone-in pork chops
2 tablespoons Chinese five-spice
powder
Coarse salt and freshly ground
black pepper, to taste
1 teaspoons garlic powder
Vegetable oil spray

FRESH CITRUS SALSA

2 large navel oranges, peeled and
cut into cubes
2 kiwi fruits, peeled and cut into
cubes

Most large supermarkets carry Chinese five-spice powder, which is usually composed of cinnamon, clove, fennel seed, star anise, and peppercorns.

Combine five-spice powder, salt, and pepper with garlic powder. Dry the pork chops with a paper towel, and rub with the spice mixture.

Spray the chops with oil, and place on the clean grates of preheated medium-high grill. Cook about 5 minutes or until meat browns and sear mark appear. Use tongs to turn. When the chops have sear marks on both sides, remove to a holding pan to finish over indirect heat. Serve with rice and fresh citrus salsa. ⊛

4

PORK

CB'S GRILLED PORK CHOPS WITH GARLIC, CITRUS & CILANTRO

4 pork chops (Use centre-cut pork chops or the cut you prefer.)
Canola oil spray
Coarse salt to taste

Preheat one side of your grill to medium high for direct grilling, and reserve the other side of the grill for indirect cooking in a tray or pan.

Season chops on both sides with pinches of salt, and spritz with canola oil. Grill chops over direct heat for 3 to 4 minutes per side until grill marks appear. To finish cooking, remove chops from direct heat, and finish in the pan.

Serve on platter with sauce. Garnish with grated or sliced citrus rinds. ✺

Cookout Potatoes, page 247

SAUCE

6 to 8 large garlic cloves, finely minced

⅓ cup fresh orange juice with pulp, rind reserved for grating or slicing at presentation

⅛ cup fresh lime juice with pulp, rind reserved for grating or slicing at presentation

⅛ cup olive oil

4 tablespoons chopped fresh cilantro, several sprigs reserved for garnish

½ teaspoon coarse salt

⅓ teaspoon red pepper flakes

⅓ teaspoon anchovy paste

1 teaspoon butter to finish sauce prior to serving

Mix together all of the ingredients except the butter and citrus rinds in a large glass or non-reactive bowl, and let rest for 3 hours so that flavours will meld. Prior to use, heat on low until vapours appear; then lower to a simmer. Just before serving, add the butter. Ladle over chops, and serve with grated or sliced citrus to taste.

4

PORK

2–3 Servings • Prep: 15 min. • Grill: 20 min. (until meat temp. is 150°F)

CB'S GRILLED PORK CHOPS MARSALA

1 pound pork chops (about 2 or 3 double-thick cut)

Coarse salt to taste

¼ cup Parmesan cheese

⅛ cup Italian flat leaf parsley, chopped

Dry pork chops on both sides with paper towels, and lightly season with salt. Allow to rest while you preheat grill to medium high. Spray the chops on both sides with canola oil, and place on clean, hot grates. Sear for about 3 to 4 minutes per side. If the chops are very thick, you may wish to cross-hatch sear marks.

When the chops are seared, place in a foil pan or tray with the Marsala sauce to finish over indirect heat. The pork is done when it reaches at least 150°F internal temperature. Arrange the chops on a platter; drizzle Marsala sauce over them; and top with Parmesan cheese and chopped parsley. ❀

SAUCE

1 tablespoon butter

1 tablespoon virgin olive oil

1 shallot, finely chopped

Lemon-pepper seasoning

¼ cup Marsala wine

Melt butter and olive oil in small skillet over medium heat on the side burner. Add shallots, and allow to cook until translucent. Add lemon-pepper seasoning. Reduce heat, and warm for a few minutes. Add Marsala wine; remove mixture from heat; and pour into a holding pan placed on the warming rack of the grill over indirect heat.

CB'S CARIBBEAN-SPICE PORK ROAST

2½-pound pork sirloin roast

Brine the roast, and remove it from the brine at least 1 hour prior to cooking; then rinse and pat dry.

Set up grill or outdoor cooker for indirect heat and low temperature.

Place roast over direct heat to brown; then cook over drip pan on the indirect side of the cooking chamber. Close lid, and cook to approximately 150°F internal temperature.

Remove; place on cutting board; and cover loosely with foil to rest for up to 30 minutes. Serve with the sauce. ✵

BRINE

1½ cup dark brown sugar
2 cups apple cider
¼ cup coarse salt
1 jigger gin
1 tablespoon fresh rosemary leaves, roughly chopped
2 tablespoons freshly ground black pepper
2 garlic cloves, smashed

Simmer all ingredients in a small saucepan until salt is dissolved. Cool to room temperature. Cover meat with brine and cool water; refrigerate for at least 12 hours.

CARIBBEAN-SPICE SAUCE

1 tablespoon olive oil
1 pear, peeled, cored, and cut into ½-inch cubes
1 tablespoon jerk spice
8 ounces warm chicken stock as needed
Salt and pepper to taste
½ cup dark rum
1 tablespoon butter

Add first five ingredients to a saucepan, and heat over medium-high heat. Bring to a boil; lower to simmer to reduce the sauce. As the pears soften, mash with a fork to blend into the mixture. Add the rum and butter to finish the sauce.

4

PORK

CB'S FENNEL & VERMOUTH PORK TENDERLOIN

1 pound pork tenderloin

1 teaspoon crushed fennel seeds

Coarse salt and fresh ground pepper

2 tablespoons extra-virgin olive oil

2 tablespoons unsalted butter, cut into pieces

3 garlic cloves, smashed

½ cup chicken broth

¼ cup dry white vermouth

1 tablespoon fresh lemon zest

1 tablespoon parsley or fennel fronds, chopped, to garnish

CB's Grilled Fennel, page 240

Preheat one side of the grill to medium high. Dry pork tenderloin with a paper towel; apply crushed fennel seeds and about 1 teaspoon each of salt and pepper. Spray pork tenderloin with canola oil; use tongs to place it on the grill grates; and sear each side, turning as necessary.

When the pork is seared on all sides, remove to a pan to finish over indirect heat. Cover lightly with foil, and allow meat to finish with the hood closed until the pork's internal temperature is 150°F or more. Remove pork to cutting board to rest, reserving the pan juices.

For the sauce: Add pan juices to heavy saucepan over medium heat. Add butter and crushed garlic to pan, and cook until garlic begins to release its aroma. Add warmed chicken stock and vermouth; simmer until reduced and thickened a bit.

Slice the tenderloin across the grain into ½-inch slices. Arrange on platter; spoon pan sauce over the slices; and then drizzle with olive oil. Garnish with chopped parsley and lemon zest. ✼

CB'S CHILI-RUBBED RIBS

4 pounds of pork ribs,
   trimmed of excess fat

CHILI RUB

2 tablespoons chili powder
2 tablespoons garlic powder
1 tablespoon ground ginger
1 tablespoon smoked paprika
1 tablespoon ground cumin
1 teaspoon salt
1 teaspoon ground black
   pepper

Whisk chili-rub ingredients together in small bowl to blend. After drying ribs with a paper towel, rub spice mixture all over ribs. (Use food-safe gloves.) Wrap ribs in plastic wrap, and refrigerate for at least 6 hours or overnight.

4

PORK

SAUCE

6 ounces dark beer
18 ounces barbecue
   sauce
1 cup water
2 tablespoons honey
1 tablespoon instant
   espresso powder

Combine in saucepan, and simmer until sauce thickens. Cool slightly; then cover and refrigerate until needed.

Preheat grill, and set up for indirect heat to 200°F to 225°F (low). Add wood chips, if desired. Remove ribs from refrigerator, and unwrap. Place them on indirect heat side of the grill, bone-side down. Pour some of the sauce into a pan, and place over indirect heat. Close hood, and slow cook, monitoring temperature regularly. After 1 hour, brush ribs with sauce. Close

hood, and allow ribs to cook 1 hour more, checking at 20-minute intervals and applying more sauce.

Ribs should be fully cooked after 2 hours. To keep warm on the grill for up to 1 hour, wrap ribs in 2 layers of heavy-duty aluminum foil (shiny side out) that has been sprayed on the dull side with canola oil. Add the remainder of the sauce before sealing. ❀

*Greek Potato Salad with Sun-Dried
Tomatoes, page 232*

CB'S BACON-WRAPPED PORK LOIN

1 pork loin roast, about 3 to 5 pounds
Coarse salt and freshly ground pepper to taste
⅛ cup dark brown sugar
⅛ cup mild horseradish sauce
3 cloves garlic, crushed
1 pound hickory-smoked bacon, thin-sliced

Dry pork roast using paper towels. Season all surfaces with salt and pepper. Mix together brown sugar, horseradish sauce, and garlic, and coat the roast with it.

Create a bacon weave on a sheet of wax paper. Place the pork roast in the centre of the weave so that the presentation side is down. Use the wax paper to help wrap the bacon weave around the roast; then secure with plain wooden toothpicks, if necessary.

Place the pork loin above a drip pan in a preheated grill or outdoor cooker set up for indirect cooking and registering 400°F (medium high). Cook until the roast reaches an internal temperature of 150°F and the bacon is crispy. Remove the roast, and let it rest, covered lightly with foil.

Using a sharp knife, slice into servings about the thickness of one slice of bacon. Serve with rustic applesauce or chutney. ❈

CB'S GRILLED PORK PAILLARDS WITH TWO-MUSTARD SAUCE

4 boneless pork loin chops, about 1 inch thick

¼ cup olive oil

2 tablespoons apple cider vinegar

1 clove garlic, minced

1 tablespoon coarse-grain mustard

1 tablespoon Dijon-style mustard

1 teaspoon brown sugar

Coarse salt and freshly ground black pepper to taste

Toasted baguettes

Place the pork chops between two pieces of plastic wrap. Using the flat end of a meat cleaver, pound and tenderize them. When all the chops are pounded, season with salt and pepper to taste. Refrigerate chops in a plastic bag until ready to grill.

After the seasoned pork has rested for at least 30 minutes, remove from bag while you preheat grill to medium high. Spray meat surfaces with canola oil, and using tongs, place on grill just long enough to sear on both sides. Be careful not to overcook the meat, or it will be too dry.

For the sauce: Mix olive oil, vinegar, garlic, mustard, and brown sugar in a non-reactive bowl, and set aside.

Remove pork from grates when seared on both sides. Fold into toasted baguettes, and serve along with the sauce. ⊛

CB'S PORK NECK ROAST WITH CUMIN-SPICE RUB

1 pork neck fillet (bones removed), rolled and tied

1 teaspoon coarse salt

1 teaspoon black pepper, freshly ground

1 teaspoon cumin, ground

1 teaspoon ginger, ground

1 teaspoon garlic, minced

⅓ cup olive oil

1 medium onion, roughly chopped

¾ cup dried apricots, roughly chopped

8 ounces warm chicken stock

Dash Worcestershire sauce

Pork neck—also known as hog jowl—is best when cooked "low and slow."

Dry the meat with paper towels. Untie roast, and lay it flat. Combine salt, pepper, cumin, ginger, and garlic with olive oil, and brush onto the surface of the meat. Spoon the onion and apricot into the centre of the roast. Roll up, and tie with butcher's twine.

Preheat grill to medium, and set up for indirect cooking. Brown the meat on all sides. Remove roast to a pan on the unheated side of the grill, and finish until internal temperature reaches 180°F. Remove and let roast rest for 20 minutes covered with foil. The temperature should rise another 10 degrees. Serve with sauce.

For the sauce: Add the pan juices to a sauce pan with warm chicken stock, and simmer over medium heat until sauce reduces. Season with Worcestershire sauce and salt and pepper to taste. If desired, strain sauce before serving. ✳

4

PORK

CB'S "CINCINNATI-CHILI" PORK CHOPS

6 pork loin chops, 1 inch thick
½ cup apple cider vinegar
3 large russet potatoes
Salt and pepper, freshly ground

CINCINNATI RUB

1 tablespoon smoked paprika
1 tablespoon chipotle chili powder
1 tablespoon garlic powder
2 teaspoons unsweetened cocoa powder
1 teaspoon mustard powder
1 teaspoon cumin, ground
1 teaspoon cinnamon
1 teaspoon black pepper, ground
½ teaspoon coarse salt

Whisk together rub ingredients in a large bowl until well blended.

This recipe uses a rub inspired by Cincinnati-style chili.

Brush each chop with the vinegar, and then press a generous amount of the Cincinnati rub on all surfaces. (Use food-safe gloves.) Place the chops on a plate; cover with plastic wrap; and refrigerate for up to 2 hours. Remove from the refrigerator 1 hour prior to grilling.

Preheat grill to medium high, and spritz chops with canola oil. Sear over direct heat for about 1 to 2 minutes per side. When both sides are seared, move chops to a foil pan on the warming rack with no direct heat. Close the hood lid. Chops are done when they reach an internal temperature of 160°F.

While chops are cooking, spray potatoes with canola oil; season with salt and pepper; and grill 8 to 10 minutes per side. ✸

GRILLED STUFFED PORK CHOPS

8 centre-cut boneless pork chops, each
  1¼ to 1½ inches thick

BRINE

3 tablespoons mustard seeds

1 cup coarse salt, plus more for
  seasoning

1 cup maple syrup

1 cup bourbon whiskey

3 (4-inch) sprigs rosemary, lightly
  crushed

STUFFING

1 large head garlic

1 teaspoon olive oil

Black pepper, freshly ground

6 ounces bacon (about 5 slices),
  cut into ¼-inch pieces

10 ounces baby spinach,
  washed and trimmed

12 ounces feta cheese

1 teaspoon thyme,
  chopped

½ teaspoon rosemary,
  chopped

4

PORK

Toast the mustard seeds in a stock pot. Remove from heat. Add 16 cups water and other brine ingredients to the pot. Bring to a boil; then allow the mixture to cool to room temperature. Brine the pork chops in the refrigerator overnight.

Heat oven to 325°F. Cut off the end of the garlic head. Season with oil and salt and pepper. Roast it, wrapped in foil, for 1 hour. Cool; then squeeze the garlic from the bulb.

Render the fat from the bacon. Set cooked bacon aside. Pour off all but 1 tablespoon of fat.

Reheat the bacon fat over medium heat. Stir in the spinach in bunches. When just wilted, drain the spinach. Allow it to cool slightly; then chop.

Combine all of the stuffing ingredients together, adding some black pepper. Refrigerate until needed.

Remove the pork chops from the brine. Slice a pocket into the side of each chop. Stuff each chop. Close the pockets with a toothpick or two.

Heat a grill to medium. Grill chops 6 to 7 minutes per side, 150°F for medium; about 8 minutes per side for well. Remove toothpicks before serving. ❀

CB'S TAILGATE GRILLED BABY BACK RIBS

1-pound rack of baby back ribs per person
¼ cup brown sugar per rack of ribs
¼ cup apple cider vinegar per rack
¼ cup your favourite barbecue sauce per rack
Coarse salt and freshly ground pepper to taste

This is an easy recipe to prepare at home and finish at a tailgate party.

Have the butcher remove the thin membrane from the back of the ribs. Rinse the ribs, and pat dry. Rub each rack with salt and pepper and then the ½ cup of brown sugar—make sure it's all rubbed in. **Note:** It's a good idea to use food-safe gloves during this process.

Place the ribs meat-side down in a nonreactive bowl or pan, and pour cider vinegar over them. Cover ribs with plastic wrap and refrigerate. Marinate for a minimum of 2 hours.

Remove the ribs from the refrigerator, and discard the marinade.

Preheat one side of the grill to medium high; reserve the other side for indirect cooking. You can add wood chips for smoke flavour for the first hour.

Place the ribs on the hot side, and sear for about 5 minutes. Then use tongs to transfer to the side without direct heat. Close hood; reduce heat to low; and roast for about 2 hours. You want to maintain an even temperature of about 225°F to 250°F.

Note: You can also finish the ribs in the oven. Just place them on a baking sheet in an oven set to about 225°F to 250°F for about 1½ hours to 2 hours. Use tongs to grab each rack. If the rib rack bends and starts to separate, ribs are ready!

To transport: Up to 1 hour in advance, baste ribs with barbecue sauce, and seal in aluminum foil. Place in insulated carrier. Once on site, you can place one or two of the foil packages on the grill, heated to low, and close the lid to warm the ribs. When the ribs have warmed, remove them from foil, and turn grill to medium high. Sear ribs on direct heat, brushing on remaining sauce, if needed. To serve, slice individual ribs, and pile on platter with more sauce if desired. ✺

4

PORK

CB'S PORK LOIN WITH CHILI, CURRY & COFFEE RUB

2-pound boneless pork loin roast

Dash apple cider vinegar

2 tablespoons espresso coffee, finely ground

2 tablespoons chili powder

2 tablespoons curry spice powder

1 teaspoon dry mustard

1 teaspoon garlic powder

1 teaspoon kosher salt

1 teaspoon black pepper, freshly ground

Brine pork roast overnight in a standard brine of water, salt, and a dash of apple cider vinegar. Remove pork roast from brine; rinse with cold water; pat dry; and refrigerate for about an hour.

Mix all dry ingredients. Remove pork roast from refrigerator, and apply dry rub to all sides of the roast. Wrap in plastic wrap, and refrigerate until ready to grill.

Preheat one side of the grill to medium high. Unwrap roast and spray with canola oil. Sear meat on all sides, about 3 to 5 minutes per side.

Set seared roast in disposable aluminum pan on section of grates without direct heat. Close hood, and roast until internal temperature is at least 160°F.

Let the cooked meat rest for 15 minutes before carving into thin slices. Serve on toasted, buttered buns or slices of crusty bread with your favourite cole slaw. ❀

Marinated Portobello Mushrooms, page 237

CB'S "GET CREATIVE" PORK CHOP CASSEROLE

4 boneless thin-cut pork
   loin chops
Favourite casserole recipe
   (See below.)
Salt and pepper to taste
Canola oil spray

A casserole, or "hot dish," is pure comfort food. This is an easy, make-ahead recipe that can be prepared in advance and finished at the picnic or before dinner at the table. It works using leftover chops, too.

Use your favourite casserole recipe, or try mixing together par-boiled egg noodles, a touch of garlic, grated Parmesan cheese, frozen peas, 1 tablespoon of butter, and ¼ cup of milk. Bake in a greased baking dish for 25 to 30 minutes.

Preheat grill to high. Pound chops as thin as you can without tearing meat. Season with salt and pepper, and spray both sides with canola oil.

Sear the meat quickly on both sides; then place the chops on top of casserole that is hot from the oven. Cover chops tightly with aluminum foil to allow heat from casserole to warm and finish cooking chops. ✺

6–8 Servings • Prep: 15 min. • Chill: 1 hr. • Grill: 15–20 min. (until meat temp. is 160ºF)

CB'S GRILLED PORK BURGERS WITH CHORIZO

1 pound ground pork or ground pork sausage

2 chorizo or other spicy sausages, finely chopped

3 garlic cloves, finely chopped

1 teaspoon cumin, ground

2 tablespoons olive oil

1 red pepper, grilled and cut into 6 to 8 strips

Salt and pepper to taste

Canola oil

6 to 8 burger buns, warmed

For juicy burgers, roast seared patties in a holding tray over indirect heat with the grill lid closed.

In a large bowl, mix together the ground pork, chorizo, garlic, cumin, and olive oil. Form into 6 to 8 meatballs; cut each in half; place a red pepper strip on the cut surface. Reform the meatballs; and then work into 6 patties. Chill for at least 1 hour.

Preheat the grill to medium high. Season the burgers with salt and pepper, and spritz with canola oil. Sear burgers for about 2 minutes per side. When both sides are seared, place patties in a disposable aluminum tray on the warming rack away from direct heat. Allow to finish with the grill hood closed and the internal temperature of the cooking chamber about 350ºF until the meat reaches 160ºF. ❄

CB'S CHAR SIU PORK TENDERLOIN

2 pork tenderloins, unprocessed or brined

4 tablespoons Chinese five-spice powder

1 teaspoon coarse salt

BARBECUE MOP

½ cup rice wine

¾ cup Tamarind sauce

3 garlic cloves, finely minced

1 teaspoon dark sesame oil

1 teaspoon ginger, finely minced

1 teaspoon dry Chinese-style mustard

1 teaspoon cumin, ground

Harvest Slaw with Sweet
Potatoes, page 249

Char Siu is the Cantonese version of barbecue, a low-and-slow technique for crispy, caramelized pork and duck.

Mix the mop ingredients in a bowl, and warm on side burner. Make a rub of the salt and five-spice powder, and rub into meat. Cover with plastic wrap, and chill in the refrigerator for 2 to 3 hours. Remove meat from refrigerator 1 hour prior to cooking.

Set up your grill for indirect heat and to maintain a constant temperature of 225°F to 250°F (low). Grill tenderloins using indirect heat for about 20 minutes. When the internal temperature of the meat reaches 100°F, apply mop sauce. You can move the meat to a pan, but continue to use indirect heat. Repeat mopping every 10 minutes until the internal temperature reaches 150°F. Allow the pork to rest at least 15 to 20 minutes before cutting it across the grain into very thin slices. ⊕

4

PORK

CB'S HERB & HONEY GLAZED HAM

1 (12-to-14-pound) boneless fully cooked ham, at room temperature for at least 1 hour prior to cooking

4 tablespoons unsalted butter

2 tablespoons fresh thyme, chopped

2 tablespoons fresh rosemary, chopped

2 tablespoons fresh lemon sage, chopped

1 teaspoon cinnamon, ground

2 bay leaves, crushed

¼ cup unfiltered apple cider

½ cup pure honey

1 teaspoon Worcestershire sauce

½ teaspoon Tabasco sauce

1 tablespoon white vinegar

This recipe calls for a precooked ham. (Do not buy a preglazed or spiral sliced ham.) Use your grill or outdoor cooker to heat it for the holiday meal, and add a tasty glaze that will please your family and friends!

Peel off and discard any rind or skin from ham, leaving ¼ inch of fat. Score fat on top of ham in a crosshatch pattern without cutting into meat. Preheat your grill or outdoor cooker set up for indirect cooking to medium with a drip pan under the unheated section of the grates. Place ham in the cooker over the drip pan, and loosely cover with a large sheet of aluminum foil—shiny side up. Do not wrap the ham; just create a tent. Cook for approximately 90 minutes.

Melt butter; add herbs and cinnamon in a saucepan over low heat; and gently warm to release the natural oils of the herbs. Cover and keep warm away from direct heat. In another saucepan, warm apple cider until it reduces by about one-half; slowly stir in honey, vinegar, Worcestershire, and Tabasco, and cover to keep warm away from direct heat.

When ham is fully heated, remove the foil tent, and place a fresh drip pan under the ham. Combine any pan drippings with the butter sauce and honeyed cider in one saucepan, and brush on the ham. Cook an additional 30 minutes, uncovered, until the glaze is a deep golden brown and the ham is completely heated. Remove the ham, and allow it to rest for 15 minutes prior to slicing. ✽

4

PORK

Black-Eyed Pea Salad, page 234

GRILLED BREADED PORK CHOPS

8 ¾-to-1-inch-thick bone-in centre-cut pork chops (4½ pounds)

4 cups fresh bread crumbs, finely grated

⅔ cup Parmigiano-Reggiano, finely grated

Rounded ½ teaspoon salt

¼ teaspoon black pepper

1 cup olive oil (not extra-virgin)

Toast bread crumbs in a 350°F oven for 7 to 10 minutes until dry. Cool bread crumbs completely.

Mix bread crumbs with cheese, salt, and pepper in a shallow bowl or a 9-inch pie plate. Lightly season pork chops with salt and pepper.

Line a baking sheet with wax paper. Pour oil in another shallow bowl. Dip each chop in oil, letting excess drip off; then dredge both sides of chops in bread-crumb mixture, pressing gently to help crumbs adhere, and transfer to baking sheet.

Preheat grill to medium high. Grill chops, turning over once or twice, until pork is cooked through and crumbs are golden brown, about 10 minutes or until a thermometer reads 160°F. ⊛

GRILLED PORK & PINEAPPLE TACOS

1 pork tenderloin (about 1 pound), trimmed

¼ cup onion, chopped

¼ cup fresh pineapple, chopped

3 garlic cloves, minced

3 chipotles in adobo sauce, sliced, with 1 tablespoon sauce reserved

1 tablespoon red wine vinegar

⅓ cup olive oil

¼ teaspoon cayenne pepper

1 tablespoon cumin

1 teaspoon smoked paprika

½ teaspoon ancho chili powder

1 teaspoon coriander

1 teaspoon dried oregano

SERVE WITH

Pineapple salsa

Guacamole

Tortillas

Fresh cilantro

In the bowl of a food processor, combine all ingredients except for the pork tenderloin. Pulse until a thick paste forms. Place the pork tenderloin in a large plastic bag and add the marinade. Place in the refrigerator for 1 hour before grilling.

Grill the tenderloin over medium heat for 35 to 40 minutes, until the centre of the tenderloin registers 150°F. Let the meat rest for 5 minutes before slicing into thin medallions. Serve in soft tortillas with pineapple salsa, guacamole, and a little fresh cilantro. ✸

4

PORK

CB'S MOJITO-MOPPED PULLED PORK

1 bone-in pork shoulder, 8 to 10 pounds

STEP 1: BRINE

½ cup kosher salt
½ cup dark brown sugar
⅛ cup apple cider vinegar
Water to cover

Add first three ingredients to a large sealable plastic bag placed in a bowl or tray to prevent leaks. Add the pork shoulder. Fill with water to cover; then seal and chill for at least 6 hours.

STEP 2: CUBAN-SPICE RUB

4 tablespoons garlic powder
1 tablespoon smoked paprika
1 tablespoon ginger, ground
1 tablespoon cumin, ground
1 tablespoon dried
   oregano
1 tablespoon
   kosher salt
1 tablespoon
   black
   pepper

Whisk together all ingredients in a bowl. Remove meat from brine; rinse in cold water; pat dry with paper towels; and massage spice rub into the meat (using food-safe gloves). Tightly wrap the meat in plastic wrap, and refrigerate for at least 12 hours.

STEP 3: COOKING

Prepare your grill for indirect cooking, and pre-heat to 200°F (low). If you're using a smoker box, have several ready and keep them rotating to ensure consistent smoke. (Use a fruitwood or pecan wood.)

Remove the pork from the refrigerator, and unwrap at least 2 hours before cooking. Insert a meat thermometer into the deepest part of the roast. Place the roast, fat side up, on the grates over indirect heat and a drip pan; leave undisturbed for at least 3 hours. Monitor regularly to ensure consistent smoke and temperature.

STEP 4: MOJITO MOP

¼ cup crushed mint leaves

¼ cup sugar

¾ cup lime juice

1 cup ginger ale

1 cup dark rum

Whisk mop ingredients together in a bowl. At 3 hours, mop the pork every 20 minutes while continuing to monitor cooking temperature. When the pork shoulder reaches an internal temperature of 190°F, remove from the cooker; wrap in foil covered with clean kitchen towels; and place in an insulated holder, such as a picnic cooler or an unheated oven. Let rest for at least 2 hours. Reserve the pan drippings.

STEP 5: SERVE

Shred the meat using food-safe gloves. Combine any unrendered gristle and fat in a saucepan along with pan drippings and additional water, and simmer. When mixture has rendered, pour through a sieve onto the meat. Serve on toasted Cuban or French-style bread with grilled onions and peppers.

6 Servings • Prep: 10 min. • Marinate: 4 hr. • Smoke: 3 hr. • Rest: 10 min.

COLA RIBS

2 racks baby back ribs,
   approx. 3 pounds each
3 sweet potatoes
3 ears corn
Canola oil

MARINADE

2 cups cola
½ cup bourbon
½ cup brown sugar
2 tablespoons mustard powder
2 tablespoons chili flakes
1 tablespoon garlic, minced
3 sprigs fresh rosemary
½ bag char wood (⅔ soaked
   in cool water for 2
   hours or until
   saturated)

Place ribs in nonreactive glass dish. Mix marinade ingredients in medium-size bowl. Pour marinade over ribs, and cover with plastic wrap. Allow ribs to marinate for 4 hours.

Preheat grill to medium heat for indirect cooking. Add two-thirds of drained soaked wood and remaining dry char wood to smoking tray. Mix, and allow wood to smoke. Once smoke is achieved, reduce heat to low, and add more wet chips.

Place ribs over the side of the grill that does not have direct heat. Close lid, and smoke for 3 hours or until ribs are falling off the bone. While cooking, continue to add wet chips to the tray. Remove ribs from grill, and loosely tent them with foil. Let ribs rest for 10 minutes before serving.

Spray potatoes with canola oil. Sear potatoes 3 minutes on each side. Move to tray over indirect heat, and cook for 20 minutes or until tender; grill corn over direct heat, turning often, for about 5 minutes.

UNCLE DANE'S GRILLED PORK PATTIES

1 pound ground pork,
  unseasoned
1 red onion, finely diced
¾ cup saltine cracker crumbs
½ cup buttermilk
2 eggs, lightly beaten
Coarse salt and freshly
  ground pepper to taste
Canola oil

SERVE WITH
Toasted rye bread
Mustard
Grilled onions

CB's Cucumber Salad, page 236

4

PORK

Uncle Dane is Danish, and he loves to serve these pork patties on lightly toasted rye bread with mustard and grilled onions.

Mix all of the ingredients in a large bowl, using your hands and food-safe gloves. Form 3 or 4 large meat patties with a slight indentation in the middle of each one. Place on a wax paper-covered plate, and set in freezer for up to 30 minutes to chill—but not freeze.

Preheat your grill to high. Remove the pork patties from the freezer, and spritz both sides with canola oil. Place the patties on clean grates. "Where they hit, they sit" until the side sears. Flip the patties to a clean section of the grates, and sear that side.

When both sides of the pork patties are seared, remove to a holding pan on the warming rack (not over direct heat) and finish to an internal temperature of 160°F. ❀

INDIAN TANDOORI RIBS

2 slabs pork spareribs

MARINADE
2 8-ounce cartons plain yogurt
2 garlic cloves, crushed
3 tablespoons ginger root, grated
2 jalapeño chilies, seeded
½ cup fresh cilantro leaves
1 tablespoon cumin, ground
Red food colouring

Tandoori refers to the Indian traditional red-orange tint of tandoor-oven cooking. Serve with flatbread or naan, seasoned rice mixed with peas, and cucumber salad.

In a blender, combine yogurt, garlic, ginger, chilies, cilantro, and cumin, and purée. Reserve a small amount for dipping sauce if desired. Add a few drops of red food colouring. Place ribs in large plastic bag; coat with marinade; seal bag; and refrigerate overnight.

Preheat grill to medium. Drain ribs, and discard marinade. Place ribs over drip pan; close grill hood; and cook for 1½ hours over indirect heat, until ribs are tender. ❈

PORK SPARERIBS
WITH COCONUT-PEANUT SAUCE

3 to 4 pounds pork spareribs

COCONUT-PEANUT SAUCE

⅓ **cup light coconut milk**

¼ **cup creamy peanut butter**

2 tablespoons soy sauce

1 tablespoon sesame oil

1 tablespoon ginger, minced

1 tablespoon cilantro, snipped

¼ **to** ½ **teaspoon red pepper, crushed, to taste**

1 garlic clove, minced

Why make the same old barbecued ribs? Try this sauce for your next barbecue. Serve with tropical fruit salad and rice.

Grill ribs over indirect medium heat for 1 hour. Stir together sauce ingredients until well combined; reserve half of sauce to serve with finished ribs. Brush remaining sauce on ribs; grill for 30 minutes longer until ribs are tender and meat pulls from the bone. Warm reserved sauce, and serve with ribs. ✳

4

PORK

CB'S NUT-CRUSTED RIBS WITH BOURBON MOP SAUCE

2 whole racks (about 4 to 5 pounds) pork spareribs

½ cup apple cider vinegar

½ cup dark porter beer, or stout

3 to 4 cups pecans, walnuts, or almonds, finely chopped

DRY RUB

1 tablespoon garlic powder

1 tablespoon chili powder

1 tablespoon onion powder

1 tablespoon mustard powder

1 tablespoon cumin

1 teaspoon kosher salt

1 teaspoon black pepper, freshly ground

1 cup dark brown sugar

BOURBON MOP SAUCE

¼ pound butter

1 cup dark brown sugar

4 cups ketchup

½ cup apple cider vinegar

6 garlic cloves, crushed and finely minced

2 teaspoon curry powder

Contents of 1 Earl Grey tea bag

1 tablespoon stone-ground mustard

4 ounces Worcestershire sauce

1 ounce Tabasco sauce

2 cups Kentucky bourbon

Mix together dry-rub ingredients, and set aside. In a large nonreactive pot, add the butter and brown sugar, stirring over low heat. Add ketchup, cider vinegar, and garlic, and then heat. Stir in the other ingredients, except the bourbon, and simmer briefly. Add the bourbon; then remove from heat. Place in a covered nonreactive container. Refrigerate for at least 2 days, stirring occasionally. If the mop seems too thick, add equal parts water and bourbon to thin.

The night before cooking the ribs, allow them to air dry in the refrigerator for 1 hour. Then place one rack at a time on a sheet pan. "Paint" the ribs with a mixture of vinegar and beer. Massage the dry rub into the meat. Wrap the ribs tightly in plastic wrap, and chill in the refrigerator overnight.

Preheat grill set up for indirect heat to maintain consistent 225°F (low). Add smoker box with dry chips of your choice. When the chips begin smoking, remove the plastic wrap from the ribs; place them on the grates away from direct heat; and allow them to cook.

Warm the mop sauce, but do not boil.

After about 2½ hours of smoking at a low indirect heat, place racks on sheets of heavy-duty aluminum foil. Mop all sides of the ribs with the warmed mop sauce, and use your hands to press nuts onto the top of the ribs.

Wrap the ribs tightly, and return to the cooker. Cook for at least 1 hour with the lid closed.

After 1 hour, check to see whether the meat is pulling away from the bone. Mop if desired, but be mindful to not scrape away the nuts. When the meat pulls back easily to expose the bones, you know it is nearly fully cooked.

Open the foil, and place the ribs back on the cooker to finish (adding more mop sauce and nuts). You may wish to raise the heat to develop a crust. Remove ribs after cooking, and keep warm until ready to serve. ✳

4

PORK

5 Lamb & Game

136   CB's Lamb Chops with
Toasted Cumin & Rosemary

137   CB's Grilled Lamb Sirloin
with Red-Wine Sauce

138   Five-Spice Lamb Chops with
Grapefruit-Fennel Salad

140   Butterflied Leg of Lamb
with Chinese Seasonings

141   Lamb Burgers
with Feta Spread

142   CB's Low & Slow
Lamb Roast

143   Grilled Lamb &
Mango Tostadas

144   Chef Erik's Lamb Kabobs
with Mint Pesto

146   CB's Grilled Wild Boar
Tenderloin

147   CB's Spit-Roasted Rabbit

148   CB's Grilled Loin of Venison

*(Right) CB's Low & Slow
Lamb Roast, page 142*

134

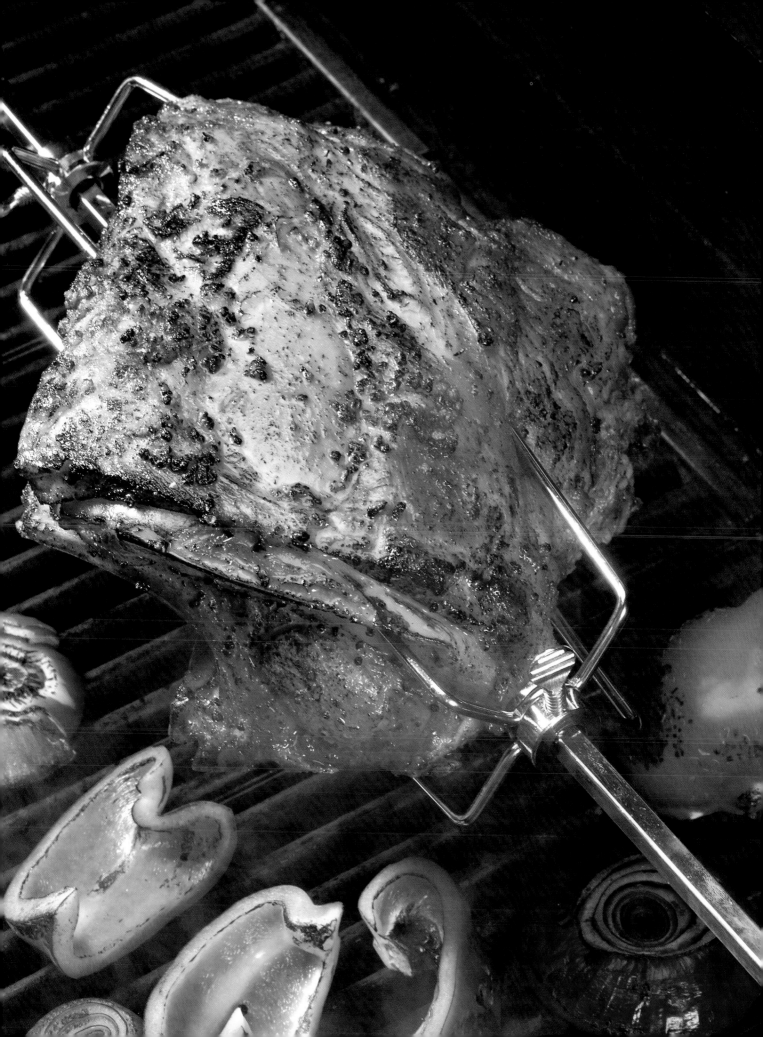

CB'S LAMB CHOPS WITH TOASTED CUMIN & ROSEMARY

4 lamb chops

1 tablespoon toasted cumin seeds

1 teaspoon whole toasted mixed peppercorns

1 teaspoon coarse salt, if desired

2 tablespoons fresh rosemary, finely minced

For the chops: Remove chops from package, and dry meat using paper towels. Trim off any excess fat or silver skin. Generously rub spice mixture into the meat using food-safe gloves. Let the meat rest at room temperature for at least 20 minutes. (If preparing a rack of lamb, cut it into two chops for even grilling.)

Preheat the grill to medium high. Spray the chops with canola oil. Place them on clean grates to sear, about 2 minutes per side. Use tongs to turn, and sear all sides.

When chops are seared, remove them to a holding pan away from direct heat to finish cooking (135°F internal temperature for rare). Remove from heat, and let rest for 10 to 15 minutes prior to serving. ⚙

For the rub: Toast the cumin seeds and peppercorns in a preheated, heavy skillet over medium-low heat, stirring to prevent burning. If desired, add the salt. It takes about a minute for the spices to toast, so remove them from the heat as soon as they release their aroma. Grind the toasted spices in a spice grinder, or smash them using a meat mallet. The spices should be coarsely ground, not fine. Add the minced rosemary, and set aside.

CB'S GRILLED LAMB SIRLOIN WITH RED-WINE SAUCE

6 lamb sirloin steaks, about 1 inch thick

Coarse salt and pepper to taste

2 tablespoons olive oil

¼ cup shallots, minced

¼ cup full-bodied dry red wine (such as Syrah or Zinfandel)

4 ounces chicken stock

2 tablespoons balsamic vinegar

1 tablespoon fresh thyme, finely chopped

½ tablespoon dark brown sugar

2 tablespoons unsalted butter

Trim off excess fat from the steaks, and reserve. Dry the lamb with paper towels, and season lightly with salt on both sides; then let meat rest for at least 30 minutes prior to grilling.

Preheat grill to high. Lightly spray both sides of the meat with canola oil, and sear on each side about 2 minutes or until sear marks appear. Remove seared lamb to a foil pan away from direct heat to finish cooking until rare (135°F internal temperature). Spoon sauce over lamb, and serve. ☺

RED-WINE SAUCE

Heat olive oil in a sauté pan over medium-high heat. Add the reserved fat and brown; discard solid bits. Add shallots, and cook until browned, stirring constantly 1 to 2 minutes. Add wine, broth, vinegar, thyme, and brown sugar, and cook, stirring, until liquid is reduced by half, about 3 to 5 minutes. Reduce heat to medium low, and add meat juices from the foil pan; swirl in butter. Season with salt and pepper, and serve.

MARINADE

1 teaspoon Chinese five-spice powder

1 tablespoon honey

1 tablespoon soy sauce

2 tablespoons red wine

SALAD

1 ruby red grapefruit, segmented, pith removed

1 small bulb fennel, white part only, finely sliced

½ bunch cilantro, chopped

1 bunch watercress

1 tablespoon olive oil

1 tablespoon lemon juice

Coarse salt and freshly ground pepper to taste

FIVE-SPICE LAMB CHOPS WITH GRAPEFRUIT-FENNEL SALAD

8 lamb shoulder chops, trimmed

Place the lamb chops in a flat dish. Combine the five-spice powder, honey, soy sauce, and wine. Mix well. Pour over the chops, turning them so that they are fully coated in the mixture. Cover, and marinate 20 minutes to overnight.

Preheat the grill to medium, and cook the chops, turning occasionally, for 8 to 10 minutes or until cooked as desired.

To make the salad, combine the grapefruit, fennel, cilantro, and watercress in a bowl. Whisk together the oil and juice; season with salt and pepper to taste; and toss with the salad. ✦

8–10 Servings • Prep: 10 min. • Grill: 20–30 min. (until meat temp. is 145°F) • Rest: 5 min.

BUTTERFLIED LEG OF LAMB WITH CHINESE SEASONINGS

3- to 4½-pound leg of lamb, boned, butterflied, and trimmed of most fat

2 teaspoons cinnamon

2 teaspoons ground ginger

2 teaspoons brown sugar

1 teaspoon anise

½ teaspoon cayenne

1 large fresh clove garlic, minced

¼ cup peanut oil

1 teaspoon sesame oil

Salt to taste

Ask the butcher to bone and butterfly the leg for you. Mix seasonings and oil together, and rub into both sides of lamb, making sure all the nooks and crannies are coated. With the grill covered, cook lamb over medium-high heat, skin-side down to start, turning often. At its thickest point, the meat should register 145°F for medium rare—thinner parts will be medium rare to medium. Set lamb aside, covered loosely with foil, for about 5 minutes before slicing diagonally and serving. ⊙

LAMB BURGERS WITH FETA SPREAD

2¼ pounds ground lamb

½ cup shallots, minced

3 tablespoons fresh
   mint leaves, minced

1 tablespoon garlic, minced

1½ teaspoons salt

½ teaspoon cumin, ground

¼ teaspoon allspice, ground

¼ teaspoon cayenne pepper

¼ teaspoon cinnamon, ground

6 hamburger buns

Lettuce leaves

Sliced tomatoes

Sliced roasted red peppers

FETA SPREAD

⅛ teaspoon cayenne
   pepper

4 ounces feta cheese,
   crumbled

4 ounces cream cheese,
   softened

¼ cup mayonnaise

2 tablespoons green
   onion tops, minced

1 tablespoon plus 1
   teaspoon olive oil

¼ teaspoon lemon zest,
   finely grated

To make the feta spread, stir together all of the ingredients in a mixing bowl. Cover with plastic wrap, and refrigerate for at least 1 hour.

In a mixing bowl, combine the lamb, shallots, mint, garlic, salt, cumin, allspice, cayenne, and the cinnamon. Mix gently but thoroughly to combine. Using your hands and food-safe gloves, shape the mixture into 6 patties. Cover with plastic wrap, and refrigerate for at least 2 hours.

Preheat grill to medium high. Brush both sides of burgers with 1 tablespoon of olive oil. Cook for about 4 minutes on each side for medium. Transfer the burgers to a platter, and cover loosely with foil. Serve on toasted buns with feta spread and desired garnishes. ✿

5

LAMB & GAME

CB'S LOW & SLOW LAMB ROAST

1 bone-in lamb shoulder
   roast, 3 to 4 pounds
5 garlic cloves, finely
   minced
3 tablespoons thyme
   leaves, finely chopped
3 tablespoons sage leaves,
   finely chopped
1 teaspoon hot mustard,
   ground
1 teaspoon cumin, ground
Coarse salt and freshly
   ground black pepper to
   taste
¼ cup vegetable oil

Trim excess fat and silver skin from the lamb shoulder. Combine the garlic, thyme, sage, mustard, cumin, salt, pepper, and vegetable oil. Spread the paste all over the meat. Wrap roast in plastic wrap, and refrigerate overnight.

About 1 hour before cooking, remove the lamb from the refrigerator. Insert an oven-safe meat thermometer into the centre of the roast. Preheat your grill to 225°F (low) for indirect cooking, or prepare a smoker. Place the lamb on the grill over a drip pan, and close the hood. Cook until the thermometer registers about 145°F. Turn up the heat to 325°F (medium). Wrap the roast in two layers of foil, and add some chicken stock or apple cider before sealing. Continue cooking until the internal temperature of the roast reaches 180°F. Remove, and let rest for at least 30 minutes before carving. ✪

GRILLED LAMB & MANGO TOSTADAS

1 pound lamb shoulder chops, cubed
 (about 1½ inches thick), bones discarded

3¼ teaspoons coriander, freshly ground

¾ teaspoon kosher salt

1⅛ teaspoon black pepper, freshly ground

1 large red bell pepper

1 mango, peeled, pitted, and diced

1 small avocado, seeded, peeled, and diced

⅓ cup red onion, diced

1 tablespoon fresh mint, chopped

4 corn tostadas (4 to 5 inches in diameter)

Preheat grill to medium. Combine 3 teaspoons of coriander, ½ teaspoon salt, and 1 teaspoon black pepper in a small dish. Transfer spice mixture to a plate. Coat lamb well in spice mixture.

Slice the bell pepper in half, and remove the seeds and stem. Cook pepper halves and lamb cubes on grill over moderate heat, turning once or twice, until pepper is softened and lamb is browned. Remove both from heat; let lamb rest about 5 minutes. Transfer pepper to a cutting board, and dice. Combine diced pepper, mango, avocado, onion, and mint in a mixing bowl. Add remaining ¼ teaspoon salt, ⅛ teaspoon of pepper, and ¼ teaspoon coriander.

To serve, place one layer of lamb on top of a tostada. Cover with a large spoonful of the mango mixture. Repeat with another layer of lamb and mango mixture. Garnish with sprigs of mint and a lime wedge. ✲

5

LAMB & GAME

Garlic-Roasted Potatoes with Arugula, page 245

Chef Erik Lind is a regular contributor to "Sizzle on the Grill" and was the Pit Master for the Char-Broil Grilling Tour in 2006.

2 pounds boneless lamb leg or shoulder, cut into 1½-inch cubes (32 pieces)

½ cup extra-virgin olive oil

½ cup lemon juice

¼ cup honey

4 cloves garlic, minced

½ small onion, minced

¼ cup mint leaves, minced

¼ cup parsley leaves, minced

1 teaspoon rosemary leaves, minced

1 teaspoon oregano leaves, minced

16 skewers (if using wood, presoak for at least 30 minutes)

32 cherry tomatoes

32 pearl onions, or 4 medium onions, cut into 32 chunks

4 green bell peppers, cored, seeded, and cut into 1-inch squares (32 pieces)

16 fresh mushrooms

Salt and freshly ground black pepper

CHEF ERIK'S LAMB KABOBS WITH MINT PESTO

In a nonreactive bowl, combine the olive oil, lemon juice, honey, garlic, onion, mint, parsley, rosemary, and oregano. Add the lamb, and toss to coat well. Marinate in the refrigerator for at least 4 hours. Preheat the grill on high. On each skewer, thread tomato, lamb, onion, pepper, lamb, onion, mushroom, pepper, and tomato. Repeat until you have 16 prepared skewers. Season the skewers with salt and pepper. Grill to desired doneness, about 3 to 5 minutes per side for medium to medium rare. Serve with the mint pesto. ✪

MINT PESTO

Yield: 1 cup

½ cup fresh mint leaves

1 tablespoon honey

Pinch kosher salt

2 tablespoons white wine vinegar

Freshly ground black pepper

¾ cup olive oil

Combine all of the ingredients, except for the oil, in a blender. Pulse until well puréed. With the blender running on low, slowly drizzle in the olive oil. Taste, and adjust seasonings.

CB'S GRILLED WILD BOAR TENDERLOIN

2 wild boar tenderloins,
   about 12 ounces each

3 tablespoons chili powder

1 tablespoon garlic powder

1 tablespoon cumin, ground

1 tablespoon coarse salt

Many specialty butchers offer wild boar that is ranch raised. The meat is rich in flavour and can stand up to robust spices and assertive smoking.

Combine dry ingredients with whisk, and rub into surfaces of the meat. Wrap the tenderloins in plastic wrap, and refrigerate for at least 3 hours.

Remove the meat from the refrigerator at least 1 hour prior to grilling. Preheat the grill to medium high. Spray the meat with canola oil. Sear on all sides; then remove the meat to a holding pan away from direct heat until the internal temperature reaches 150°F (rare). Serve with pan juices and a chilled citrus fruit salsa. ✿

CB'S SPIT-ROASTED RABBIT

1 whole rabbit,
prepped by the
butcher, 1½ to 2½
pounds
4 cups buttermilk

FOR FINISHING
Extra-virgin olive oil
Roasted garlic cloves
Salt and pepper to
taste

Rabbit is delicious and can be prepared in just about any way you might cook poultry.

Place meat in large plastic bag, and add buttermilk. Refrigerate overnight. At least one hour before cooking, remove meat; rinse with cold water; and dry.

Place the rabbit on the spit of the rotisserie; truss the legs to the spit.

Cooking the rabbit: Preheat the grill to medium high. Place the spit with the rabbit firmly attached and balanced on the rotisserie over the heat.

Cook for about 40 minutes or until the meat reaches an internal temperature of about 155°F. During cooking, brush regularly with the glaze.

Cut into serving pieces; drizzle with olive oil; add garlic and salt and pepper; cover and hold at 200°F either on the closed grill or inside oven until the leg quarters reach 165°F internal temperature. ⊙

5

LAMB & GAME

GLAZE
4 tablespoons clarified butter
1 teaspoon rosemary
 leaves, crushed
1 teaspoon sage leaves, crushed
1 teaspoon mustard powder
1 teaspoon garlic powder
1 teaspoon coarse salt
½ teaspoon anchovy paste

Whisk together just before using, and keep warm during use.

⊕ **Quick Meal** • **2 Servings** • **Prep: 10 min.** • **Grill: 5 min.**

CB'S GRILLED LOIN OF VENISON

1 venison loin, about 1 pound
Coarse salt and freshly
  ground pepper to taste
Canola oil

[*Venison is VERY lean, and most recipes call for using bacon to lard it. I prefer to cook it fast over high heat and enjoy the flavour of the meat, not the pork fat. (Not that there's anything wrong with pork fat!)*—CB]

Cut the loin into medallions about 1 inch thick. Place the medallions between two pieces of heavy-duty wax paper or food-safe plastic. Gently pound the steaks with a meat mallet, working from the centre out, until the medallions are about ¼ to ½ inch thick. Dry off the medallions, and season with salt and pepper to taste.

Preheat the grill to high. Spray venison with canola oil, and use tongs to place on the grill. Sear both sides of meat, about 1 to 2 minutes per side.

Return to a warm plate, and serve with a sauté of spinach, chopped tomatoes, garlic, and mushrooms. Venison is also great on grilled polenta. ⊙

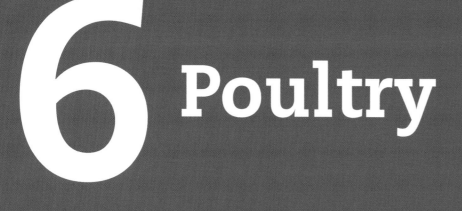

6 Poultry

152 CB's Grilled Chicken with Balsamic Garlic Sauce

153 CB's Korean-Style Chicken

154 CB's Chicken with Rosemary Butter & White BBQ Sauce

156 CB's Grilled Chicken Cacciatore

157 Grilled Yogurt-Mint Chicken

158 Grilled Stuffed Chicken Breasts with Artichokes & Italian Cheeses

159 Barbecued Chicken Thighs au Vin

160 Pacific Rim Chicken Burgers with Ginger Mayo

162 CB's V8 Chicken

163 Greek Salad Olive-Grilled Chicken

164 CB's Grilled Ginger Chicken Tenderloins with Spicy Peanut Sauce

165 Grilled Chicken Marsala

166 Bourbon-BBQ Cornish Hens

168 Coffee & Cocoa Grilled Chicken Thighs

169 Sesame-Crusted Chicken with Wasabi Cream Sauce

170 CB's Beer-Brined Chicken Quarters

171 Peach-Barbecued Chicken

172 Tequila Lime Chicken

173 CB's Grilled Chicken Meatballs

174 Herb-Marinated Grilled Turkey & Panzanella Salad

176 Jamaican Jerk Turkey Thighs

177 Lemonade Turkey Kebabs

178 Tangy Turkey Dogs

179 Lemon-Oregano Grilled Turkey

180 Thai Marinade Turkey Wings

181 Red-Hot Barbecued Turkey Tenderloins

182 Florentine Turkey Burgers

183 Jalapeño-Jelly-Glazed Turkey Thighs

184 The Big Easy Cider-Brined Turkey

(Right) Lemon-Oregano Grilled Turkey, page 179)

5 Servings • Prep: 15 min. • Grill: 20–25 min. (until thigh temp. is 180°F)

CB'S GRILLED CHICKEN WITH BALSAMIC GARLIC SAUCE

5 chicken quarters
**Sea salt and fresh
    cracked pepper**
Canola oil spray

Preheat one side of the grill to medium and the other side to low. Season the chicken with salt and pepper, and lightly spray all sides with canola oil.

Sear the chicken over medium heat, about 3 to 5 minutes per side; then remove it to a foil pan on the low-heat side of the grill. Keep the other side of the grill on medium, but shut off the burners under the pan. Close the lid. Cook until the temperature of the thick thigh meat is 180°F.

Sauce: Heat 1 tablespoon of olive oil and the butter in a saucepan over medium-high heat. Add the shallots, cooking until translucent, and then add the garlic. Combine with the vinegar and chicken broth, and bring to a boil.

In a small bowl, mix 1 tablespoon oil and flour. Drizzle it into the saucepan mixture, whisking to prevent lumps. Bring to a boil; then simmer on low for 1 to 2 minutes, whisking as necessary. Serve with the chicken. ❋

SAUCE

2 tablespoons olive oil	⅓ cup balsamic vinegar
1 tablespoon butter, softened	1 cup chicken broth
1 small shallot, chopped	2 tablespoons instant flour
3 cloves of garlic, minced	Chopped parsley for garnish

CB'S KOREAN-STYLE CHICKEN

3 pounds boneless, skinless chicken thighs
⅓ cup soy sauce
2 tablespoons sugar
1 tablespoon sweet rice wine
½ medium onion, grated
2 cloves garlic, mashed and minced
1 teaspoon ginger, grated
1 teaspoon Chinese-style dry mustard powder

¼ teaspoon black pepper
1 teaspoon sesame seeds, toasted for garnish
Green onions or chives, chopped for garnish

GLAZE
¼ cup soy sauce
1 tablespoon sesame oil
1 tablespoon melted butter

Mix glaze ingredients together in a small bowl and set aside.

Flatten chicken thighs. Mix the next six ingredients in a large plastic bag. Add chicken, and seal. Place the sealed bag in the refrigerator for 1 hour.

About 30 minutes before grilling, remove chicken from marinade. Pat chicken dry, and cover loosely with plastic wrap. Preheat grill to high; then lower one side to medium.

Spray the chicken with canola oil. Sear one side of it over high heat. Then move the chicken, seared side up, to the medium side of the grill. When the chicken reaches an internal temperature just below 160°F, remove it to a foil tray or pan, and put it back on the medium side of the grill. Brush on the glaze, and loosely cover the pan with foil. Chicken is ready when it reaches an internal temperature of 180°F.

Arrange the grilled chicken on a platter, and drizzle with glazing sauce. ❋

CB'S CHICKEN WITH ROSEMARY BUTTER & WHITE BBQ SAUCE

2 4- to-5-pound chickens, each cut in half along the back- and breast-bone

¼ cup kosher salt

¼ cup brown sugar

1 tablespoon apple cider vinegar (optional)

Freshly ground sea salt to taste

Freshly ground black pepper to taste

½ cup fresh rosemary, finely chopped, plus several sprigs for garnish

¼ pound unsalted butter, softened

If possible, brine overnight in a mixture of ¼ cup kosher salt, ¼ cup brown sugar, and water to cover. One hour before grilling, remove the chicken from the brine solution; rinse under cool water; and pat dry. Allow the chicken halves to air dry in the fridge for up to several hours if time permits.

Mix butter, salt, pepper, and all but about 2 tablespoons of the rosemary in a small bowl. Using your fingers and food-safe gloves, gently insert the compound butter under the skin. Any unused butter can be massaged into the skin of the chicken.

Set up your grill for indirect cooking with a drip

pan under the grates on the side without heat. Turn on the direct-heat burner. The hood temperature inside the closed grill should read about 400°F.

Place the seasoned chicken halves skin-side up on the indirect-heat side of the grill over the drip pan, and close the hood. After about 15 to 20 minutes, use tongs to move the chicken so that all of it is exposed equally to the "hot" side of the cooking area. Continue to cook with the hood closed about another 15 to 20 minutes until chicken browns.

Use tongs to place the chicken halves skin-side down on the hot side of the grill to sear. Check the internal temperature of the chicken at the breast and thigh, and remove chicken halves to a holding tray to finish cooking indirectly on the grill (to 180°F).

To serve, drizzle with CB's White BBQ Sauce, and garnish with pinches of chopped rosemary. ❊

6

POULTRY

CB'S WHITE BBQ SAUCE

1⅓ cups mayonnaise

2 garlic cloves, finely minced

½ cup fresh lemon juice

2 to 3 tablespoons lemon zest (or very finely chopped lemon peel)

¼ teaspoon smoked paprika

In a nonreactive bowl, whisk together the ingredients in the order listed. Spoon sauce over hot pieces of grilled chicken or pork.

4 Servings • Prep: 25 min. • Grill: 3–4 hr.

CB'S GRILLED CHICKEN CACCIATORE

2 to 3 pounds chicken thighs and drumsticks

3 tablespoons canola oil or spray

1 yellow onion, sliced

2 medium shallots, diced

2 cups red, yellow, and/or green peppers, diced

3 cloves garlic, minced

3 tablespoons flour

½ pound mushrooms, quartered

1 cup baby carrots

15-ounce can diced tomatoes

2 cups chicken broth

⅓ cup red wine

2 tablespoons fresh cilantro, chopped

2 tablespoons fresh parsley, chopped

1 tablespoon dried thyme

Kosher salt and freshly ground black pepper

¼ teaspoon red pepper flakes

Dash Tabasco sauce

Sliced black olives, if desired

Grilling the chicken adds a rich flavour that's even better if you use some wood chips to impart a bit of smoke. To get a head start, grill the chicken the day before.—CB

Preheat grill to high. Season chicken with salt and pepper. Brush or lightly spray chicken with oil. Place on hot grill skin-side down. Cook until browned on one side; then turn and brown the other side, but do not cook completely. Set aside.

Turn grill's side burner to high. In a large, non-reactive pan over the burner, heat the oil. Then reduce heat to medium, and add onion. Sauté for 2 to 3 minutes; add shallots. Continue to cook for 1 minute before adding bell peppers. When shallots and onions begin to caramelize and peppers soften, add garlic, making sure that mixture does not burn.

Add the flour to mixture 1 tablespoon at a time. Add mushrooms and the remaining ingredients.

Reduce heat to low, and add chicken. Cover and cook over indirect heat on grill for 3 to 4 hours. ✳

GRILLED YOGURT-MINT CHICKEN

1 whole chicken, cut
  into pieces

1 cup plain yogurt

6 tablespoons olive oil

4 cloves garlic, minced

1 cup fresh mint,
  chopped

Salt and pepper

Vegetable oil (for the
  grill)

*The refreshing combination of yogurt and mint creates a creamy marinade that is the
perfect complement to a warm-weather meal.*

In a large bowl, whisk together the yogurt, olive oil, garlic, mint, and a sprinkling of
salt and pepper. Submerge the chicken in the marinade; cover; and refrigerate for 2
to 6 hours.

If using a gas grill, preheat one side to high and one side to low. Oil the grates.

Remove the chicken from the marinade, and season generously with salt and
pepper. Put the chicken pieces on the high-heat side of the grill. Let them cook
until they get dark brown grill marks, 4 to 6 minutes. Turn the chicken, and brown
on the other side for 4 to 6 minutes.

Once seared, move the chicken pieces to low-heat side, and cook until internal
temperature reaches 180°F in thighs. Serve with the reserved sauce. ❁

6

POULTRY

4 Servings • Prep: 20 min. • Marinate: 2 hr.–overnight • Grill: 10 min.

GRILLED STUFFED CHICKEN BREASTS WITH ARTICHOKES & ITALIAN CHEESES

4 large, boneless, skinless
chicken breasts

1 bottle Italian salad
dressing

2 tablespoons olive oil

1 teaspoon thyme, dried or
fresh

¼ teaspoon red pepper
flakes

2 cloves garlic, minced

2 tablespoons fresh
basil, chopped

1 small jar (6 or 7 ounces)
artichoke hearts, rinsed
and drained

¼ teaspoon salt

A few grinds of pepper

1 cup shredded Italian cheese
such as Parmesan, Romano,
mozzarella, provolone, or
a blend.

Toothpicks

This recipe for grilled stuffed chicken breasts has just a few more steps than that for a standard chicken breast, but it's a real treat of flavours that keep the chicken juicy.

Using a sharp paring knife, create a 2- to 3-inch pocket in each breast. Marinate the chicken in the salad dressing in the refrigerator for 2 hours to overnight.

To prepare stuffing, combine olive oil, thyme, and pepper flakes in a saucepan over medium heat. Cook until the spices release their fragrance. Stir in the gar-lic, basil, artichoke hearts, salt, and pepper. Cook for about 3 minutes. Add the cheese, and blend well. Cook for another minute or two, until the cheese is partially melted. Remove from heat, and cool.

Spoon stuffing into each breast pocket, securing each one using 2 toothpicks.

Preheat the oven to medium high. Cook the chicken for 4 to 5 minutes on each side. Meat should be medium brown, with its juices running clear. Let the chicken rest before removing the toothpicks. ✽

BARBECUED CHICKEN THIGHS AU VIN

6 chicken thighs (about 1½ pounds)

1 tablespoon vegetable oil

1 tablespoon butter

2 tablespoons shallots, chopped fine

1 clove garlic, minced

¼ cup red currant jelly

½ cup red wine

¼ cup chicken stock or orange juice

1 teaspoon grated orange rind

½ teaspoon dry mustard

½ teaspoon ground ginger

Place chicken thighs in a plastic bag or large bowl. In saucepan, heat oil and butter; add shallots and garlic, and cook over medium heat for 5 minutes or until softened. Add jelly, wine, stock, orange rind, mustard, and ginger. Heat only until jelly has melted. Remove from heat; let cool to room temperature.

Pour marinade over chicken. Press air out of bag, and secure with twist tie. Marinate at least 3 hours to overnight in refrigerator. Pour marinade into saucepan; bring to a boil; simmer 5 minutes; reserve.

Place chicken thighs, skin side up, on greased grill heated to medium high. Cook for 20 minutes, with lid closed, brushing occasionally with marinade once most of the fat is rendered from the chicken pieces. Turn each thigh, and cook 10 to 15 minutes longer or until juices run clear when chicken is pierced with fork (180°F). ✳

6

POULTRY

8 Servings • Prep: 20 min. • Grill: 10–15 min.

PACIFIC RIM CHICKEN BURGERS WITH GINGER MAYO

¼ cup soy sauce

1 tablespoon hoisin sauce

1 tablespoon honey

1 tablespoon red chili paste

2 pounds ground chicken

2 green onions, thinly sliced

2 jalapeño peppers, minced

4 cloves garlic, minced

1 cup cilantro, finely chopped

1 cup tarragon leaves, finely chopped

1 egg, lightly beaten

⅔ to 1 cup panko or other

unseasoned bread crumbs

Vegetable oil

8 pineapple rings (fresh or canned)

1 cucumber, peeled and thinly sliced

8 hamburger buns

These burgers have a nice, tangy-but-sweet teriyaki flavour, with good caramelization on the outside. The surprisingly potent ginger mayonnaise, slices of cucumber—which add a contrast in texture and coolness—and grilled pineapple, provide the right combination of acidity and sweetness to keep things interesting.

In a pot over medium heat, warm the soy sauce, hoisin, and honey for 5 minutes, stirring periodically to dissolve the honey and hoisin. Mix in the chili paste, and let the sauce simmer for a few minutes. Remove from heat, and let cool. In a large bowl, combine ground chicken with vegetables and herbs.

After the marinade has cooled, add the egg. Work this mixture gently into the ground chicken.

Gently mix in the bread crumbs. Form the mixture into 8 patties by coating your hands (in food-safe gloves) liberally with vegetable oil. (The chicken mixture will be very sticky.)

Rub each patty with a bit of oil on all sides. Chill patties briefly in the refrigerator while you preheat the grill to medium high. Cook about 5 minutes per side, turning when underside has browned and releases easily from the grill. (Be careful that you don't scorch the patties; the sugar in the marinade can burn.)

Cook the pineapple on the grill for roughly 2 minutes per side, or until grill marks appear. To serve, place each burger on a toasted bun, and top with ginger mayo, pineapple, and cucumber slices. ✳

GINGER MAYONNAISE

½ cup mayonnaise
2 cloves garlic
1-to-2-inch knob of ginger
Juice of 1 lime
¼ teaspoon salt

Put all ingredients into a blender or food processor, and blend until smooth. Refrigerate.

6

POULTRY

CB'S V8 CHICKEN

1 fryer chicken, cut into 8 pieces
1 12-ounce can V8 vegetable
    juice cocktail
½ to 1 cup water
BBQ sauce for glaze

[*Sometimes the ingredients for great-tasting marinades are already made and ready for the using. By accident, I discovered this idea, and the flavours were very tasty!—*]

Trim chicken pieces of excess fat and place in a non-reactive bowl or plastic food bag. Add V8 juice and water until meat is covered. Cover bowl or seal bag and refrigerate overnight.

One hour before cooking, remove chicken from marinade.; rinse chicken; and pat dry with paper towels. Allow chicken to rest a bit at room temperature.

Preheat half of grill to high. Spray or lightly brush chicken parts with canola oil. Sear over high heat. Because wings and legs tend to cook faster, add them to the grill after starting the breasts and thighs. Use tongs to turn chicken when the skin is seared and releases from grill.

As pieces are seared and begin to brown, place them in a pan away from direct heat. Cover loosely with foil or another pan. Allow chicken to finish cooking in pan until individual pieces reach an internal temperature of at least 165°F.

During the final 5 to 10 minutes of indirect cooking, brush on a light coating of BBQ sauce. Serve. ❊

Roasted Asparagus with Cherry Tomatoes, Garlic & Olive Oil, page 254

GREEK SALAD OLIVE-GRILLED CHICKEN

6 split chicken breasts, bone-in
¼ cup olive oil
1 4½-ounce jar prepared black olive tapenade
¼ cup lemon juice
¼ cup fresh oregano, chopped

Place the first four ingredients in a resealable plastic bag; add chicken; seal bag; and shake gently to coat chicken with marinade. Refrigerate 4 to 24 hours.

GREEK SALAD

1 cup grape tomatoes, halved
12 pitted kalamata olives
6 ounces feta cheese, cubed
½ small red onion, diced
¼ cup extra-virgin olive oil
3 tablespoons lemon juice
1 tablespoon fresh oregano, chopped
8 cups mixed greens, preferably spinach, arugula, and romaine

Toss together the first seven ingredients in a bowl. Gently stir in greens. To serve, divide Greek Salad among plates, and top with chicken.

Preheat grill to medium high. Remove chicken from bag, and discard marinade. Arrange chicken on grill. Close lid, and open vents. Cook chicken, turning occasionally to cook all pieces evenly, for about 30 minutes or until a meat thermometer inserted in thickest part of breast registers 165°F. ❊

6

POULTRY

4 Servings • Prep: 1 hr. • Marinate: 1–4 hr. • Grill: 20 min. (until meat temp. is 165°F)

CB'S GRILLED GINGER CHICKEN TENDERLOINS WITH SPICY PEANUT SAUCE

1 pound chicken tenderloins or boneless, skinless chicken thighs, cut into large chunks

3 garlic cloves, minced

2 tablespoons fresh ginger, minced

2 teaspoons dark brown sugar

½ teaspoon cumin

½ teaspoon turmeric

½ teaspoon salt

Safflower or peanut oil, as needed

Juice of one lime and one lemon, as needed

PEANUT SAUCE

1 cup creamy peanut butter

½ cup ginger tea, hot

Hot sauce to taste

1 tablespoon garlic powder

1 tablespoon brown sugar

1 tablespoon soy sauce

1 tablespoon peanut oil

In a microwavable bowl, heat the peanut butter until it is runny, not bubbling, about 1 minute. Mix in the ginger tea and the remaining ingredients, reheating as necessary. Pour into container, and cover to keep warm until ready to serve.

In a large bowl, whisk together all of the ingredients except the chicken. Add to sealable plastic bag. Rinse and pat the chicken dry, and place in bag with marinade. Refrigerate for at least 1 hour and up to 4 hours before grilling.

Remove chicken pieces from marinade, and discard the contents of bag. Preheat grill to medium high. Turn individual pieces to form sear marks. When the chicken has seared on all sides and has an internal temperature of 165°F (180°F for thighs), it is done. Place on plate, and serve with peanut sauce for dipping. ❋

GRILLED CHICKEN MARSALA

4 4-ounce boneless, skinless chicken
    breasts
16 small carrots, peeled
2 teaspoons extra-virgin olive oil
8 ounces sliced fresh mushrooms
2 shallots, chopped
3 cloves garlic, minced
12 ounces Marsala wine or low-sodium
    chicken broth, or 6 ounces of each
1 teaspoon cornstarch (optional)
4 tablespoons nonfat yogurt
4 sprigs fresh rosemary
Chives, chopped for garnish

SPICE MIXTURE

1 teaspoon fresh rosemary, chopped
1 teaspoon sea salt
¼ teaspoon freshly ground black pepper
½ teaspoon red pepper flakes

Combine spices, and sprinkle over the chicken. Boil carrots for about 8 to 10 minutes; drain.

Add 2 teaspoons of oil to a large skillet, and heat over medium heat. Add mushrooms, shallots, and garlic. Season with salt and pepper. Cook until the mushrooms are slightly brown and soft. Add wine or broth. If thicker sauce is desired, stir in cornstarch, and simmer until liquid thickens and reduces to one-third, about 20 minutes.

Preheat grill to medium high. Grill chicken for 8 to 10 minutes on each side or until cooked through. Grill carrots for about 5 minutes, rotating until charred.

Once the mushroom sauce has reduced, remove from heat, and whisk in yogurt. Divide carrots among four plates, and top each with chicken, sauce, chives, and rosemary. ❋

Grilled Stuffed Tomatoes
Caprese, page 251

I love Marsala sauce, but the traditional version is packed with fat. This lighter recipe has so much creamy, wine-y, mushroom flavour.—CB
Recipe courtesy of danicasdaily.com

BOURBON-BBQ CORNISH HENS

4 Cornish game hens
1 tablespoon blackening
  spice
Your favourite spice blend
1 teaspoon salt
1 teaspoon ground black
  pepper

SERVE WITH

Red and yellow cherry
  tomatoes
Grilled asparagus
Garlic
Shallots
Basil
Citrus vinaigrette
Goat cheese

BBQ SAUCE

1 tablespoon olive oil
2 tablespoons jalapeño
  chiles, diced
1 tablespoon garlic,
  chopped
1 tablespoon shallots,
  chopped
2 ounces bourbon
2 cups ketchup
1 cup orange juice

¼ cup cola
½ cup molasses
½ cup brown sugar
1 teaspoon liquid smoke
1 teaspoon paprika
1 teaspoon garlic salt
1 teaspoon BBQ spice

Season Cornish hens with blackening spice, spice blend, salt, and pepper. Rub seasoning into meat to seal flavour.

Add olive oil, jalapeños, garlic, and shallots to a medium saucepan over medium-high heat. Stir until brown. Remove pan from heat, and pour in bourbon.

Add ketchup, orange juice, cola, and molasses, and mix well. Stir in brown sugar, liquid smoke, paprika, garlic salt, and BBQ spice. Remove from heat, and let cool.

Cook Cornish hens over indirect heat on grill for 30 minutes or until the thickest thigh section reads 180°F. Baste BBQ sauce over Cornish hens for last 10 minutes until well coated and caramelized.

Complement the Bourbon-BBQ Cornish Hens with a platter of red and yellow cherry tomatoes coupled with grilled asparagus, garlic, and shallots. Top with basil, citrus vinaigrette, and goat cheese. ✳

4 Servings • Prep: 10 min. • Rest: 1 hr. • Grill: 30–40 min. (until meat temp. is 180°F)

COFFEE & COCOA GRILLED CHICKEN THIGHS

8 pieces skinless chicken thighs, bone-in

1 tablespoon plus 2 teaspoons paprika

1 tablespoon chili powder

½ teaspoon sea salt

½ teaspoon sugar

½ teaspoon cumin, ground

½ teaspoon coriander, ground

½ teaspoon freshly ground black pepper

½ teaspoon garlic powder

1 tablespoon finely ground dark roast coffee

1 tablespoon cocoa or a dark hot chocolate mix

Combine spice ingredients in a sealable plastic bag. Add chicken pieces, and shake to coat. Massage spices into the chicken through bag. Allow the chicken to rest for at least 1 hour so that the spice flavours can set. Preheat grill to medium high. Grill, turing often, until a thermometer inserted into the chicken pieces reads 180°F.

Note: Use this easy barbecue rub to fully seal chicken pieces to yield the juiciest chicken. Use a strong, dark, powdered coffee, such as espresso, and a high-quality cocoa or hot chocolate. ❋

4 Servings • Prep: 20 min. • Marinate: 12 hr. • Grill: 15 min. (until meat temp. is 165°F)

169

SESAME-CRUSTED CHICKEN WITH WASABI CREAM SAUCE

4 boneless, skinless chicken breasts

1 cup bottled teriyaki sauce

½ to 1 teaspoon prepared wasabi*

½ cup light sour cream

2 teaspoons lemon juice

½ teaspoon grated lemon rind

¼ cup black sesame seeds**

¼ cup white sesame seeds

1 egg white, lightly
   beaten

* Wasabi is Japanese horseradish. It is green and spicy. Prepared wasabi is a ready-to-use paste that comes in a tube. Add more or less wasabi depending on your desire for heat.

** Black sesame seeds are available at Asian grocery stores. If you prefer, use ½ cup of white sesame seeds instead.

Pound chicken until slightly flattened. Marinate chicken in the teriyaki overnight in the refrigerator.

Stir wasabi, sour cream, lemon juice, and rind until smooth. Cover and refrigerate until serving time. Preheat the grill to medium. Mix black and white sesame seeds on a plate. Remove chicken from teriyaki sauce; pat it dry using paper towels.

Dip each piece in beaten egg; then coat with sesame seeds, pressing the seeds into the chicken. Transfer chicken to a wax paper-lined pan to stand for 10 minutes to allow the coating to set. Grill for 5 to 7 minutes per side with the lid down or until a meat thermometer reads 165°F. Serve immediately with wasabi cream sauce on the side. ❈

4 Servings • Prep: 15 min. • Brine: 8 hr. • Chill: 1 hr. • Grill: 45 min. (until meat temp. is 180°F)

CB'S BEER-BRINED CHICKEN QUARTERS

4 chicken quarters (legs and thighs)

4 cups water

¼ cup kosher salt

¼ cup packed brown sugar

12 ounces beer

RUB

1 tablespoon smoked paprika

1 tablespoon kosher salt

1 teaspoon garlic powder

1 teaspoon ground ginger

1 teaspoon powdered mustard

½ teaspoon pepper

Thoroughly mix together all rub ingredients, and set aside.

Brine the chicken in water, salt, sugar, and beer, adding the water last to ensure that chicken is covered. Store in refrigerator up to 8 hours.

Remove chicken from brine; rinse; and pat dry with paper towels. Refrigerate uncovered about 1 hour to air dry.

Remove chicken from the refrigerator, and apply the rub, massaging it into the skin using your hands in food-safe gloves.

Preheat half of grill to medium high. Spray chicken lightly on all sides with canola oil. Cook chicken pieces on hot section of the grill until they lift easily and sear marks appear. Turn and sear the other sides.

Move chicken to an aluminum pan on an unheated section of grates; lightly cover with foil; and close grill hood. Reduce the heat to low on the section furthest from the chicken. Cook, covered, until chicken reaches an internal temperature of 180°F. ❈

Brining is usually done with salted water, in which sugar and assorted flavours have been added. Brining helps the chicken stay moist when grilling.—CB

PEACH-BARBECUED CHICKEN

4 boneless, skinless chicken
  breasts

2 teaspoons onion salt

⅓ cup peach or apricot
  preserves

3 tablespoons barbecue
  sauce

SERVE WITH

Buttermilk biscuits

Carrot salad

[*Georgia is known as the "peach state" because the commercial peach industry originated there with the introduction of the delectable—and shippable—Elberta peach in 1875.*]

Sprinkle chicken with 1 teaspoon onion salt. Combine peach preserves, barbecue sauce, and remaining teaspoon of onion salt in a small bowl.

Grill chicken over medium-low heat, turning and brushing frequently with peach barbecue sauce, for 15 to 20 minutes or until the internal temperature is 165°F. ✳

6

POULTRY

TEQUILA LIME CHICKEN

4 split boneless, skinless
  chicken breasts
1 tablespoon fresh
  minced garlic
½ cup fresh squeezed
  lime juice
½ cup gold tequila
1 teaspoon kosher salt
½ teaspoon fresh
  ground black pepper
1½ teaspoon ancho
  chili powder
1 tablespoon
  olive oil

Combine the chicken with remaining ingredients, and marinate for 30 minutes at room temperature. (The acid in the lime juice cooks the chicken, so be careful not to over-marinate.) Heat the grill to medium high, and spray the grates with oil to prevent the chicken from sticking. Grill the chicken over direct heat for about 5 to 6 minutes per side. Cook until nicely browned—it should feel firm and the juices should run clear. The sugars in the tequila and lime juice will blacken the chicken—so move them to a lower heat if it gets out of control. Serve hot off the grill with lime wedges and rice. ❊

Recipe courtesy of Marcia Frankenberg, Minneapolis, MN

CB'S GRILLED CHICKEN MEATBALLS

2 pounds ground chicken

1 cup fresh bread crumbs

1 cup Parmesan cheese

2 onions, finely diced

1 medium carrot, finely chopped

1 tablespoon ketchup

1 tablespoon Worcestershire

Your favourite hot sauce to taste

Kosher salt and freshly ground
    pepper to taste

1 egg, beaten

¼ cup cilantro, roughly chopped

SERVE WITH

Marinara sauce

Toasted baguette or sub roll

Shredded mozzarella cheese

The night before, place ground chicken in a colander over a dish, cover, and refrigerate overnight to drain excess moisture.

The following day, combine chicken with remaining ingredients in a large nonreactive bowl using your hands. (Food-safe gloves are recommended.) Form ping-pong-ball-size meatballs, and spray them lightly with canola oil.

Preheat grill to medium high. Use tongs to place meatballs on grill, and turn as searing occurs. If meatballs are seared on all sides and internal temperature has not reached 165°F, use tongs to place meatballs in a disposable aluminum pan; loosely cover with foil; and finish cooking over indirect heat. Close hood.

To make a meatball sub sandwich, add your favourite marinara sauce to the aluminum tray while meatballs are finishing. When sauce is warm, serve meatballs on toasted baguette or sub bread, along with additional sauce. Top with shredded mozzarella cheese. ❁

6

POULTRY

HERB-MARINATED GRILLED TURKEY & PANZANELLA SALAD

6 turkey cutlets
¼ cup dry white wine
Juice of 1 lemon
Zest of ½ lemon
1 clove garlic, chopped

2 tablespoons olive oil
¼ cup fresh herbs, such as parsley, thyme, basil, rosemary, oregano, chopped

Combine wine, lemon juice, zest, oil, garlic, and fresh herbs in a sealable, food-safe plastic bag. Add turkey, and marinate at room temperature for 15 minutes.

Preheat grill to medium high. Place turkey 4 to 5 inches away from the direct heat, and grill for 5 to 6 minutes on each side until turkey is no longer pink in centre and the internal temperature reaches 165°F. Remove from heat; tent with foil; and set aside until you are ready to serve. ❋

PANZANELLA SALAD

8 cups 1-inch cubed ciabatta or other
  country bread

3 cloves garlic, minced

4 tablespoons olive oil, divided

3 tablespoons red wine vinegar

2 teaspoons Dijon mustard

4 cups tomatoes, coarsely chopped

1 cup cucumber, chopped

½ cup red onion, thinly sliced

3 slices bacon, cooked and crumbled

3 ounces fresh goat cheese, crumbled

½ cup fresh basil leaves, torn into large
  pieces

Preheat oven to 400°F. Toss bread cubes with garlic and 2 tablespoons of oil. Spread on baking sheet coated with cooking spray, and toast for about 12 minutes or until lightly browned. Toss once halfway through toasting.

In a large bowl, combine remaining 2 tablespoons of oil with vinegar and mustard; season with salt and pepper. Add tomatoes, cucumber, and onion, and gently toss. Allow to marinate for 10 minutes or up to 1 hour.

Just before serving, toss tomato mixture with toasted bread. Add bacon, crumbled cheese, and torn basil. Gently toss together, and serve with grilled turkey.

4 Servings • Prep: 15 min. • Marinate: 12 hr. • Grill: 50–60 min. (until meat temp. is 180°F)

JAMAICAN JERK TURKEY THIGHS

2 pounds turkey thighs, skinned and excess fat removed

Carrots & Raisins Revisited, page 235

MARINADE

½ cup medium onion, cut in large chunks
1 large clove of garlic
1 teaspoon fresh ginger, peeled and thinly sliced
2 jalapeño peppers, seeded and ribs removed
⅓ cup red wine vinegar
¼ cup orange juice
2 tablespoons reduced-sodium soy sauce
2 tablespoons olive oil
1 tablespoon maple syrup
1 teaspoon allspice
½ teaspoon cinnamon
½ teaspoon thyme
½ teaspoon salt
½ teaspoon pepper
¼ teaspoon cayenne pepper
¼ teaspoon nutmeg

In food processor fitted with metal blade or in blender, process marinade ingredients until smooth. Remove ⅓ cup; cover; and refrigerate.

In sealable plastic bag, combine turkey thighs and remaining marinade. Refrigerate overnight, turning occasionally to flavour evenly.

Preheat grill to medium. Cook thighs over indirect heat 25 to 30 minutes per side until meat thermometer, inserted in thickest portion of thigh, registers 180°F. During last 10 minutes, brush thighs with reserved marinade. Serve with favourite rice dish and grilled vegetables. ❁

4 Servings • Prep: 20 min. • Marinate: 2 hrs. • Grill: 10–12 min.

177

LEMONADE TURKEY KEBABS

1 pound turkey tenderloins, cut into
   1-inch cubes

Vegetable oil cooking spray

1 can (6 ounces) frozen lemonade, thawed

3 tablespoons soy sauce

3 tablespoons olive oil

1 ripe but firm mango (or 4 peaches),
   peeled and cut into 1½-inch chunks

¼ large honeydew melon, peeled and
   cut into 1½-inch chunks

8 10- or 12-inch skewers

In small bowl, combine lemonade, soy sauce, and olive oil. Reserve ¼ cup. Marinate turkey in remaining sauce for 2 hours in the refrigerator. Place mango and honeydew melon in reserved marinade.

Preheat grill to medium high.

Remove turkey from marinade, and discard marinade. Thread drained turkey cubes onto skewers. On separate skewers, thread fruit chunks, alternating fruits.

Grill turkey kebabs 10 to 12 minutes or until turkey is no longer pink in centre and the internal temperature is 165°F to 170°F. Add fruit kebabs to grill after turning turkey kebabs. ❋

4 Servings • Prep: 15 min. • Marinate: overnight • Grill: 12–16 min. (until meat temp. is 170°F)

TANGY TURKEY DOGS

2 8-to-10-ounce turkey
    tenderloins
4 hot dog buns
BBQ sauce

MARINADE

2 tablespoons fresh lemon juice
¼ cup dry sherry or red wine
2 tablespoons dehydrated onion
¼ cup soy sauce
¼ teaspoon ground ginger
¼ cup vegetable oil
Dash black pepper
Dash garlic powder

Using a sharp knife, slice each tenderloin in half lengthwise, yielding four portions.

In a flat nonreactive dish, whisk together the marinade ingredients. Add turkey tenderloins, and turn to coat all sides. Cover and marinate for several hours or overnight, turning occasionally.

Grill tenderloins over a hot grill 6 to 8 minutes per side, depending on thickness. Turkey is done when the meat thermometer reaches 170°F in the thickest part of the tenderloin, and the meat is no longer pink.

Serve immediately on a hot dog bun with BBQ sauce, relish, mustard, or other favourite toppings. ✳

Recipe provided by Ms. Gretta Irwin, Executive Director of the Iowa Turkey Federation. This long-time favourite is served each year at the Iowa State Fair.

LEMON-OREGANO GRILLED TURKEY

1 12-to-14-pound
whole turkey

⅓ cup olive oil

4 medium lemons

1 tablespoon chopped red
onion

1 bunch fresh oregano
leaves

4 cloves garlic

½ teaspoon coarsely ground
black pepper

Cooking spray for grill

In a blender or food processor, combine oil, the juice of two of the lemons, onions, one tablespoon chopped oregano, two cloves of the garlic, and pepper; process until smooth. Prepare grill for medium indirect heat.

Remove neck and giblets from turkey. Use paper towels to dry turkey inside and outside. Tuck in wings and untuck the legs. Loosen skin over breast and legs. Cut one of the remaining lemons and the two remaining garlic cloves into thin slices. Arrange under turkey skin with half of the oregano bunch. Return legs to tucked position.

Cut the remaining lemon into quarters; place in body cavity, along with remaining garlic and oregano. Spoon or brush some of the lemon juice mixture evenly over turkey.

Grill turkey, breast up, above drip pan over indirect heat. Cover grill. Cook 2¼ to 2¾ hours, or until meat thermometer inserted deep in thigh reaches 180°F. Baste with lemon-juice mixture after each hour. Let turkey stand 15 minutes before carving. ✳

POULTRY

6

Honey-Grilled Cauliflower,
page 258

THAI MARINADE TURKEY WINGS

4 turkey wings

THAI MARINADE
½ cup smooth peanut butter
½ cup water
3 tablespoons light soy sauce
3 tablespoons fresh lemon juice
2 tablespoons brown sugar
2 green onions, chopped
3 drops Tabasco sauce

Discard wing tips, and divide wings into 2 pieces. In a large saucepan, cover turkey wings with water, and bring to a boil. Reduce heat to simmer for 20 minutes.

Meanwhile, combine remaining ingredients to make the Thai Marinade, stirring well to dissolve the sugar. Remove the turkey from the water, and marinate in the refrigerator for 2 to 12 hours.

Remove turkey wings from the marinade; grill over medium heat for 20 to 30 minutes, turning often. ✳

RED-HOT BARBECUED TURKEY TENDERLOINS

1 pound turkey tenderloins

BARBECUE SAUCE

¼ cup chili sauce

2 tablespoons ketchup

2 tablespoons Dijon-style mustard

1 tablespoon honey

1 tablespoon Worcestershire sauce

1 tablespoon red wine vinegar

1 teaspoon ground ginger

¾ teaspoon black pepper

¼ teaspoon garlic salt

¼ to ½ teaspoon cayenne pepper

In small microwave-safe container, combine barbecue-sauce ingredients. Microwave on high (100% power) 1 to 2 minutes.

Butterfly tenderloins by slicing each one almost, but not all the way, through lengthwise. Place the butterflied tenderloins individually between two sheets of wax paper, and gently flatten using the smooth side of a meat tenderizer.

Preheat grill for direct-heat cooking. Place turkey on well-oiled grill rack, and brush with barbecue sauce.

Grill 5 to 6 minutes per side or until meat thermometer registers 170°F in thickest part of tenderloin. Turn over halfway through grilling process, and brush each tenderloin with additional barbecue sauce. ❋

Pan Pacific Rice,
* page 256*

FLORENTINE TURKEY BURGERS

1 pound ground turkey

¼ cup light mayonnaise

1 cup fresh spinach, washed, drained, and chopped

1 medium onion, finely chopped

1 clove garlic, minced

¼ teaspoon freshly ground black pepper

2 tablespoons Worcestershire sauce

½ cup bread crumbs

½ cup mozzarella cheese, grated

½ medium red bell pepper, sliced and ribs removed

4 medium kaiser buns, sliced in half

In a bowl, mix turkey, mayonnaise, spinach, onion, garlic, pepper, Worcestershire sauce, and bread crumbs. Form four patties.

Grill over medium-high heat about 6 inches from direct heat source for 6 to 8 minutes per side or until the internal temperature reaches 155°F.

Top burgers with mozzarella cheese and red pepper slices, and continue to cook about 2 more minutes or until the internal temperature reaches 165°F. Toast kaiser buns, and sandwich with turkey burgers. ❋

JALAPEÑO-JELLY-GLAZED TURKEY THIGHS

2 pounds turkey thighs

⅓ cup jalapeño jelly

2 tablespoons butter or margarine

1 tablespoon fresh lime juice

Preheat gas grill to medium high.

Place thighs in a 2-quart, microwave-safe dish; cover with wax paper; and microwave on high for 10 minutes, turning thighs over halfway through cooking.

In a microwave-safe measuring cup, combine jelly and butter. Microwave on high for 45 seconds; stir in lime juice. Set aside 3 tablespoons of the glaze.

Place turkey thighs on grill rack. Cook thighs, brushing with glaze, 10 to 20 minutes or until meat thermometer registers 180°F.

To serve, cut turkey from bones, and serve with reserved glaze. ✽

6

POULTRY

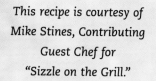

This recipe is courtesy of
Mike Stines, Contributing
Guest Chef for
"Sizzle on the Grill."

1 (12-to-14-pound) fresh turkey
Onions, fresh herbs for stuffing

BRINE

16 cups fresh apple cider, divided
1½ cups coarse kosher salt
¼ cup whole allspice
8 bay leaves
16 cups cold water

THE BIG EASY CIDER-BRINED TURKEY

This recipe requires advance preparation, as the turkey must be brined and then air-dried in the refrigerator before cooking. If you don't have room in the refrigerator to brine the turkey, put the turkey in a large oven bag in a large cooler. Pour the brine into the bag, and seal tightly. Place ice or reusable ice packs around the turkey; close the lid; and let the turkey brine, adding more ice packs as needed to keep the temperature at 40°F or below.

To brine: Simmer 4 cups of apple cider, salt, allspice, and bay leaves in a large stockpot for 5 minutes. Cool, and add remaining cider and the cold water. Leave brine in the pot, or pour into a large food-safe container. After removing the giblets, neck, and pop-up thermometer, add the turkey to the brine; refrigerate overnight or up to 24 hours.

Day of cooking: One hour before cooking, remove turkey from the brine; rinse well with cold water; and pat dry with paper towels. Place the turkey in a large roasting pan. If desired, cut the skin between the leg and the rib cage to improve heat penetration. Loosely stuff any aromatics—onions, herbs—into the cavity of the turkey. Truss legs to keep aromatics inside the cavity during cooking.

Place the prepared turkey in The Big Easy's basket, legs down, and centred as much as possible. Place the basket into the cooker, and turn on the unit according to instructions. Plan your cooking to approximately 10 minutes per pound of turkey.

Turkey is done when an instant-read thermometer inserted in the thickest part of the thigh registers 180°F and 165°F in the breast. Carefully remove turkey basket from the cooking chamber. Place the turkey on a serving platter; tent with foil; and allow the bird to rest for 20 to 30 minutes before carving. ✳

Cranberry-Pecan Rice Pilaf, page 242

6

POULTRY

7 Seafood

188 CB's Grilled Salmon with Shallot & Lemon Glaze

189 CB's Grilled Salmon with Bacon & Tomato Salsa

190 CB's Snapper Grilled on a Bed of Limes

192 Cajun Grilled Mahi-Mahi with Avocado Salad

193 Mary's "Cape" Cod with Bacon & Leeks

194 CB's Rainbow Trout Stuffed with Lemon, Shallots & Herbs

196 Grilled Salmon Salad Vinaigrette

197 Grilled Halibut with Lemon-Caper Butter

198 Fast & Spicy Halibut

199 Halibut Skewers with Mango-Mojito Salsa

200 Smoky Seared Tuna Loin

202 CB's Thai-Glazed Swordfish

203 Grilled Tuna with Roasted Cipollini Onions

204 CB's Grilled Grouper with Garlic Butter

205 Polynesian-Style Marlin with Poke Sauce

206 CB's Grilled Fish Tacos

208 CB's Baja-Style Grilled Sea Bass

209 CB's Grilled Pacific Sardines

210 Grilled Bluefish with Fresh Corn Salsa

211 Grilled Atlantic Croaker

212 Brined, Smoked Bluefish

214 Jim Hatcher's Creole Shrimp & Sausage

215 Cilantro-Pesto Snapper with Red Pepper Sauce

216 Grilled Shrimp & Vegetable Kebabs

218 Grilled Shrimp & Blue Cheese Grits

219 Margarita Grilled Shrimp

220 CB's Grilled Honey & Lime Prawns

221 CB's Grilled Scallops with Asparagus & Toasted Walnuts

222 CB's Grilled Lobster Tail with Bourbon-Herb Sauce

224 CB's Grilled Soft-Shell Crabs

225 Smoky Grilled King Crab

226 Grilled Alaska Crab with Trinidad Salad

227 CB's Stuffed Squid with Chicken-Apple Sausage

(Right) Mary's "Cape" Cod with Bacon & Leeks, page 193

CB'S GRILLED SALMON WITH SHALLOT & LEMON GLAZE

12-to-16-ounce salmon

SAUCE

4 ounces anchovy fillets or paste

2 tablespoons shallots, finely chopped

3 tablespoons extra-virgin olive oil

3 garlic cloves, finely chopped

½ teaspoon Worcestershire sauce

Juice from ½ lemon

3 tablespoons parsley, chopped

1 tablespoon red wine vinegar

Canola oil spray

Rinse the fish under cool water, and pat dry with paper towels. Place portions in freezer to chill, but do not freeze.

Rinse and drain anchovies. Mash them in a bowl with shallot, olive oil, minced garlic, and Worcestershire sauce. Stir in lemon juice; cover; and let stand for at least 1 hour. (If you prefer to make this ahead, chill the fish.)

Preheat grill to high. Remove fish from freezer, and spray both sides with canola oil. Place fish on grates, and sear, skin side down, about 3 to 5 minutes. Use a lightly oiled spatula to turn, and then sear the other side, about 3 to 5 minutes. Move seared fish to unheated section of grill. Brush sauce onto fish, and allow it to finish cooking. Gently insert knife into centre of fillet. Fish is done when the interior is translucent and firm but not dry. Arrange fish on platter, and add more sauce if desired. ❈

Ask me what I want for dinner and I'll nearly always say, "grilled fish." Salmon is a favourite, but this recipe will work with any firm fish.—CB

CB'S GRILLED SALMON WITH BACON & TOMATO SALSA

4 salmon steaks or fillets, approximately 6 ounces each

10 to 12 sprigs fresh thyme

2 slices thick bacon

½ cup red onions, diced

1 tablespoon garlic, minced

Freshly ground coarse salt and black pepper to taste

Canola, safflower, or other neutral, high-temperature oil

10 ounces (about 1 can) mild diced tomatoes with green chiles, well drained

Preheat grill to medium high. Finely chop thyme, and discard stems.

Cut bacon into ¼-inch pieces; lightly brown in a pan; and remove. Add onions to the bacon drippings, and cook until onions are sweated. Combine onions, bacon, and garlic; heat gently.

Season the salmon with salt, pepper, and thyme. Spray salmon with canola oil. Sear on both sides.

Place salmon in a foil pan on an unheated section of the grill. Close hood, and allow salmon to finish cooking until the fish is opaque in the centre; the thickest part of the fish should register 145°F.

Add tomatoes to bacon mixture; simmer 4 to 5 minutes until thick. Spoon salsa over the salmon. ❉

CB'S SNAPPER GRILLED ON A BED OF LIMES

2 snapper fillets or other delicate fish
3 large limes, very thinly sliced
2 teaspoons melted butter per fillet
Smoked paprika for seasoning and colour
Canola oil spray

Preheat the grill to medium high. Carefully rinse the fish, and pat dry with paper towels. Spray one side of the lime slices with canola oil, and arrange them in the centre of the grill to form a "bed" for each fillet.

Lay the fish atop the lime slices, and baste with melted butter and a generous pinch of smoked paprika. Lightly tent the fish fillets with heavy-duty aluminum foil, or cover each with a small foil pan. Reduce the heat to medium, and allow the limes to char and release their juices to flavour the fish.

Check the fish after about 10 to 15 minutes. When fish is opaque and firm to the touch, slip a lightly oiled spatula beneath the limes and lift the fish off the grill. Serve fish on individual plates, and garnish with parsley if desired. ✵

This is an easy, flavourful method for grilling snapper, sole, or any thin fish fillets, which tend to fall apart on a hot grill.—CB

🕒 **Quick Meal** • **4 Servings** • **Prep: 20 min.** • **Grill: 8–10 min.**

CAJUN GRILLED MAHI-MAHI WITH AVOCADO SALAD

4 fillets of mahi-mahi, 4 ounces each

1 tablespoon canola oil

1 tablespoon Cajun seasoning

2 large, ripe avocados, peeled and diced

1 cup corn kernels, cooked

1 16-ounce can black beans, drained and rinsed

¼ cup red onion, diced

1 medium tomato, diced

1 medium green bell pepper, diced

2 tablespoons fresh cilantro, chopped

1 tablespoon jalapeño, minced (optional)

2 tablespoons lime juice

¼ cup olive oil

½ teaspoon cumin

Salt and pepper to taste

Preheat grill to medium high. Brush the fillets with the oil, and sprinkle both sides with Cajun seasoning. Grill for about 4 to 5 minutes on each side, until the fish is cooked to your desired doneness and nicely browned.

Meanwhile, combine in a bowl the avocado, corn, black beans, red onion, tomato, bell pepper, cilantro, and jalapeño. Stir together olive oil, lime juice, and cumin, and add to salad. Season to taste with salt and pepper, and toss.

Top each fillet with some of the avocado salad, and serve immediately. ❋

MARY'S "CAPE" COD WITH BACON & LEEKS

16 ounces cod in 4 equal
portions, skin removed

6 strips thin-cut bacon, cut into
thirds

2 leeks, trimmed and sliced
lengthwise

2 tablespoons fresh ginger, minced

2 tablespoons fresh garlic, minced

¼ cup parsley, chopped

Coarse salt and ground black
pepper to taste

Canola oil spray

Rinse fish under cool water, and pat dry with paper towels. Place fish in freezer to chill, but do not freeze.

In a heavy skillet, slow-fry the bacon until almost crisp; remove to drain on paper towel. When cooled, chop into large bits.

Add leeks to the pan, and sauté in the bacon fat until browned. Remove the leeks; place in bowl with ground ginger, garlic, bacon, and parsley; and toss to combine.

Preheat one side of grill to high. Remove fish from freezer, and spray each side with canola oil. Place fish over hot part of grill to sear, about 3 to 5 minutes on each side. Remove fish to a holding pan on unheated side of the grill to finish cooking. Fish is cooked when the interior is flaky but not dry. Place fish on platter, and top each portion with the leek-and-bacon mixture. ✳

7

SEAFOOD

CB'S RAINBOW TROUT STUFFED WITH LEMON, SHALLOTS & HERBS

2 12-to-14-inch rainbow trout, cleaned (head and tail removed if desired)
Salt and freshly ground pepper
2 tablespoons shallots, minced

2 small lemons, sliced very thin
1 bunch dill, divided
1 bunch tarragon, divided
Canola oil spray
Seasoned wood chips if desired

Preheat grill to high. Season the cavity of each fish with salt and pepper; add 1 tablespoon of shallots to each; and rub all ingredients into the fish. Add lemon slices, dill, and tarragon. Secure stuffing by wrapping fish with kitchen twine or sealing with toothpicks if necessary.

Spray skin of each fish with canola oil. Place fish in grill basket and close.

Reduce heat of grill to medium. Place fish basket on the grill, and cover with a piece of aluminum foil to retain heat and moisture. Close hood, and cook for approximately 5 to 7 minutes. Lift basket off grill to check for grill marks; turn basket; and grill on other side, about 5 to 7 minutes.

Remove basket, and place it in a pan to allow the fish to rest for a few minutes. Using two spatulas to support the fish on each end, remove from the basket, and place on a plate.

To debone fish, insert the tip of a sharp boning knife into the top of the fish and "feel" your way to the spine. Run the knife gently along the spine toward the tail. Use two forks to lift off this half of the fish; then pinch the top end of the spine with two fingers, and peel it away from the bottom half of the fish. Replace the top half.

For a quick sauce, briefly sauté thin lemon slices with pinches of the tarragon and dill in a touch of butter and olive oil until the lemon releases its aroma. Drizzle over each fish serving, and place a lemon slice on top. ❋

Trout is available nearly year-round in just about every market. This recipe is easy because I use a fish basket to hold the stuffed fillets—it makes turning a breeze.—CB

4 Servings • Prep: 30 min. • Grill: 10–15 min.

GRILLED SALMON SALAD VINAIGRETTE

SALAD DRESSING

⅓ cup extra-virgin olive oil

¼ cup tarragon vinegar

1 tablespoon Dijon mustard

1 clove garlic, pressed

Rinse any ice from frozen fish under cold water; pat dry with paper towel. Preheat the grill to medium high. Brush both sides of salmon with oil. Place salmon on grill, and cook about 3 to 4 minutes until good sear marks appear. Turn salmon, and season with salt and pepper. Reduce heat to medium, and close grill lid. Cook an additional 6 to 8 minutes for frozen salmon or 3 to 4 minutes for fresh or thawed fish. Cook just until fish is opaque throughout.

Divide salad among four plates; place salmon portion on top. Drizzle with vinaigrette dressing, and serve. ❊

SALAD

4 salmon steaks or fillets (4 to 6 ounces each), fresh, thawed, or frozen

1 large apple, cored and chopped

1 ripe avocado, peeled and chopped

1 tablespoon lemon juice

1 package (10 ounces) prepared salad greens

1 navel orange, peeled and chopped

¼ medium red onion, sliced very thin

⅓ cup slivered almonds

⅓ cup raisins

2 teaspoons olive, canola, peanut, or grapeseed oil

Salt and pepper

Mix dressing ingredients in a small bowl; set aside. Place chopped apple and avocado in a large salad bowl. Drizzle with lemon juice. Add salad greens, orange, onion, almonds, and raisins; mix.

GRILLED HALIBUT WITH LEMON-CAPER BUTTER

2 halibut fillets (about ¾ pound total)
Olive oil
Salt and pepper
3 tablespoons butter
2 tablespoons capers
2 tablespoons lemon juice, freshly squeezed

Here's a quick sauce for grilled fish that delivers a huge citrus punch. It's less like a lemon-caper butter than caper- and butter-flavoured lemon juice.

Preheat grill to medium high. Pat the fish dry. Brush with olive oil, and season with salt and pepper on both sides. Grill halibut 5 minutes on the first side and 2 to 5 minutes on the other side, depending on the thickness of the fish.

Meanwhile, melt the butter over low heat in a small saucepan. When melted, stir in the capers and lemon juice, and season with salt and pepper. Spoon the sauce over the fish right after it comes off the grill. ✳

Courtesy of Jess Thomson at jessthomson.wordpress.com

FAST & SPICY HALIBUT

4 halibut steaks or fillets (4 to 6 ounces each), fresh, thawed, or frozen

1 tablespoon paprika

1½ teaspoons each dried oregano and dried thyme

1 teaspoon each onion powder and garlic powder

1 teaspoon each black pepper and salt

½ teaspoon cayenne pepper, or to taste

1½ tablespoons butter, melted

Preheat grill to medium high. Mix together all dry-seasoning ingredients until well combined. Rinse any ice glaze from frozen halibut under cold water; pat dry with paper towel. Place fish on a spray-coated or foil-lined baking sheet. Brush butter onto top surfaces of halibut, and sprinkle with ½ teaspoon seasoning mixture.

Grill halibut 5 to 7 inches from heat for 13 to 15 minutes for frozen halibut or 8 minutes for fresh fish. (Note: for best results with frozen fish, cook halibut 4 minutes before adding butter and spices.) Cook just until fish is opaque throughout. ❋

HALIBUT SKEWERS WITH MANGO-MOJITO SALSA

1½ pounds halibut steaks or fillets, cut into 2-inch pieces

8 wooden skewers

¾ cup fresh orange juice

⅓ cup fresh lime or lemon juice

¼ cup dry white wine

¾ cup extra-virgin olive oil, divided

2 tablespoons garlic, crushed

1½ tablespoons ground cumin

Coarse salt and pepper, to taste

2 firm, ripe mangoes, peeled, pitted, and cut into ½-inch pieces

1 small bunch cilantro, trimmed and chopped (about ¾ cup)

2 tablespoons fresh mint, chopped

2 tablespoons red bell pepper, diced

2 tablespoons red onion, diced

2 teaspoons sugar

1 teaspoon red curry paste

¼ teaspoon cinnamon

4 limes, sliced

Prior to grilling, soak wooden skewers in water for at least 30 minutes.

For marinade, combine juices, wine, ½ cup olive oil, garlic, cumin, salt, and pepper. Place fish in a large resealable plastic bag. Pour in marinade; seal bag; and turn several times to coat. Refrigerate for 15 to 30 minutes.

Place mango, cilantro, mint, bell pepper, and onion in a large bowl. In a small bowl, blend sugar, curry paste, and cinnamon until smooth; whisk in ¼ cup olive oil. Gently stir dressing into mango mixture. Cover, and set aside.

Preheat grill to medium high. Thread halibut and lime slices onto skewers, and brush with oil. Place skewers onto grill, and cook, 5 to 6 inches from heat, 4 to 5 minutes per side. Turn once during cooking. Cook just until halibut is opaque throughout. Serve halibut skewers with salsa. ❋

6 Servings • Prep: 6 hr. • Marinate: 2–6 hr. • Grill: 6–10 min.

SMOKY SEARED TUNA LOIN

1 fresh sashimi-grade tuna loin, about 3 pounds

¼ cup soy sauce

2 tablespoons honey

Juice and zest of one lime

1 teaspoon sesame oil

1 teaspoon hot sauce

½ teaspoon ground ginger

½ teaspoon garlic powder

2 tablespoons fresh cilantro, stems and leaves, chopped

2 limes, quartered

Wood chips

Mix all of the ingredients, except the tuna, in a bowl; pour ¾ of it into a sealable plastic bag. Reserve remaining portion for sauce. Place tuna loin in bag; seal; and allow to rest in the refrigerator between 2 and 6 hours.

About 30 minutes before grilling, remove tuna from bag; wipe off excess marinade using paper towels; and discard marinade. Return tuna to the refrigerator to air-dry, and keep chilled. (You can also place in the freezer for up to 10 minutes.)

Preheat the grill to medium high, at least 450°F, and prepare smoker box or scatter wood chips. Remove tuna from the refrigerator, and spray all sides with canola oil.

Put the tuna on the grill, and don't touch until good sear marks appear. (You can actually watch the tuna cooking by checking the sides: the meat will turn opaque and brown-beige as it cooks.) You only want to cook about ¼ inch in for rare; ½ inch in for medium. Use tongs to turn the tuna, and sear the other side.

Remove tuna to a platter, and squeeze lime juice over it. Let it rest for a couple of minutes before slicing and dressing with sauce. ❋

Our smoky seared tuna loin is a terrific summer entrée for an intimate dinner party. We start with the freshest and best tuna "tenderloin" we can buy, and then we do our best to leave it alone. Just add a simple marinade, some heat, some smoke, and WOW!—"Girls on a Grill"
girlsonagrill.com

CB'S THAI-GLAZED SWORDFISH

2 swordfish steaks, about 6 to 8 ounces each (or other firm, white fish, such as halibut or mahi-mahi)
Canola oil spray

THAI GLAZE
½ cup honey
2 tablespoons soy sauce
1 tablespoon fresh ginger, grated
1 teaspoon lime peel, grated
1 teaspoon garlic, minced
Red pepper flakes (optional)
2 tablespoons basil leaves, chopped
Juice from 1 lime

This recipe is inspired by the delightful flavours of Thai cooking.

Mix first six glaze ingredients in a nonreactive bowl.

Preheat one side of grill to medium high. Lightly spray fish steaks with canola oil, and place on hot grates. Sear for about 2 to 3 minutes or until sear marks appear. Lightly spray a flat, thin spatula with canola oil. Quickly slip the spatula under the fish, and turn over to a clean section of the grates to sear the other side, about 2 to 3 minutes.

When both sides are seared but fish is not quite cooked through, remove it to a holding tray away from direct heat, and brush on the glaze. Turn, and repeat on other side of fish. Fish is done when centre is opaque and approximately 145°F. Place fish steaks on platter, and sprinkle with lime juice and chopped basil. ✳

GRILLED TUNA WITH ROASTED CIPOLLINI ONIONS

6 (6-ounce) tuna steaks, about 1-inch thick

2 pounds cipollini onions

⅔ cup balsamic vinegar

1 tablespoon plus ⅓ cup extra-virgin olive oil

1 teaspoon salt, plus more for seasoning

¼ teaspoon freshly ground black pepper, plus more for seasoning

3 tablespoons fresh lemon juice

2 teaspoons fresh thyme leaves, chopped

[*Courtesy of*
christopherranch.com]

7

SEAFOOD

If you can't find cipollini (pronounced chip-oh-LEE-nee) onions in the supermarket, you can substitute pearl onions.

Bring a large pot of water to boil. Add the onions, and cook for 2 minutes. Drain and cool. Peel the onions, and cut off the root ends.

Preheat one side of the grill to high. Toss the onions, vinegar, 1 tablespoon oil, ½ teaspoon of salt, and ¼ teaspoon of pepper in a baking dish. Close cover, and roast over indirect heat until the onions are tender and golden, about 1 hour.

Marinate tuna in the oil, lemon juice, thyme, rest of salt, and dash of pepper, 5 minutes on each side.

Grill the steaks over direct heat to desired doneness, about 3 minutes per side for medium. Spoon the onion mixture around the tuna and serve. ✳

CB'S GRILLED GROUPER WITH GARLIC BUTTER

2 pounds grouper (or black sea bass, monkfish)
   6- to 8-ounce portions, about 1 inch thick
3 tablespoons butter
1½ tablespoons extra-virgin olive oil
1 tablespoon fresh cilantro, finely chopped
2 cloves garlic, minced
¼ teaspoon smoked paprika
¼ teaspoon ground ginger
Juice from ½ lemon
1 tablespoon lemon zest

Rinse fish in cold water; pat dry. Place fish in freezer until chilled but not frozen, about 10 to 15 minutes.

Preheat grill to high. Remove fish from freezer, and spray both sides with canola oil. Sear on both sides, about 4 to 5 minutes each. Use a lightly oiled spatula to turn.

Place seared fish in a holding pan away from direct heat to finish. Fish is done when flaky and opaque.

Combine butter, garlic, paprika, ginger, and lemon zest in saucepan over medium heat until the aromas are released; do not brown the garlic. Reduce heat, and add cilantro, lemon juice, and olive oil; then remove from heat. Spoon the garlic butter sauce over the fish.

An alternative method is to baste the fish while cooking to add a tasty glaze. However, if you are not experienced with grilling fish, the original method works well. ✳

POLYNESIAN-STYLE MARLIN WITH POKE SAUCE

16 ounces fresh marlin cut into 4 portions,
  about 1 inch thick
2 teaspoons fresh ginger, finely minced
1½ cups soy sauce
1 tablespoon brown sugar
½ teaspoon sesame oil
2 tablespoons chili oil
Shredded Napa cabbage (garnish)
Cooked white rice

POKE SAUCE

¼ cup fresh ginger, minced   3 cloves garlic, minced
½ cup cilantro   ½ cup peanut oil
¼ cup scallions, minced   ½ teaspoon Tabasco sauce

Combine ginger, soy sauce, brown sugar, sesame oil, and chili oil in a small bowl. Place the fish in a resealable plastic bag; pour in the marinade; seal bag; and let rest in refrigerator for up to 1 hour.

Mix poke sauce ingredients in a blender or by hand until emulsified. Refrigerate until ready to use. Preheat grill to high. Remove fish from bag, and discard the marinade. Place fish on the grill, and sear one side, about 2 to 3 minutes. Use a lightly oiled spatula to turn and sear the other side, about 2 to 3 minutes. Remove, and plate.

The marlin will be seared on the surface and very rare in the middle. Serve garnished with chopped Napa cabbage, white rice, and ramekin of poke sauce. ❈

CB'S EZ FISH TACO SAUCE

¼ cup sour cream

1 lime, juiced, and grated rind (about 1 tablespoon)

2 tablespoons canned chipotle in adobo, minced

2 tablespoons fresh cilantro leaves, chopped

1 teaspoon capers, rinsed

Mix all ingredients in a nonreactive bowl; cover; and keep cold.

CB'S GRILLED FISH TACOS

3 pounds white flaky fish, such as cod,
   halibut, or mahi-mahi, about 1 inch thick
8 flour tortillas
Shredded cabbage

Hot sauce
Thinly sliced red onion
Thinly sliced green onion
CB's EZ Fish Taco Sauce (See opposite page.)

I prefer to grill fish that is almost frozen, dry on the surface, and about 4 to 6 ounces each—just the right size to fit on a standard spatula.—CB

Rinse fish; cut into 8 portions, about 6 ounces each. Dry the fish, and place on wax paper in the freezer for about 15 minutes to chill—not freeze.

   Preheat one part of grill to high. Remove chilled fish portions from freezer, and spray with canola oil. Place fish on grill over direct heat. Sear one side; then use a lightly oiled spatula to slip under, and turn over the fish to sear the other side.

   When both sides are seared, remove to a tray or part of the grill where the portions can continue to cook over indirect heat.

   Warm the tortillas on the hot grates; top each with one piece of fish, the shredded cabbage, hot sauce, onions, and taco sauce. ❋

CB'S BAJA-STYLE GRILLED SEA BASS

1 whole sea bass (or other firm-flesh fish, such as snapper or trout) about 2 pounds, head and fins removed

½ cup achiote paste (usually found in the Mexican food section of the supermarket)

½ cup orange juice

3 tablespoons lemon juice

3 tablespoons lime juice

Salsa to garnish

Ask your fishmonger to dress and butterfly the fish. Rinse the fish, and pat it dry. Use a sharp knife to score the skin lightly. Spread a mixture of achiote paste and citrus juices over the inside of the fish, avoiding the skin. Refrigerate for at least 2 hours.

Preheat the grill to medium. Spritz the skin of the fish with canola oil; place it, skin side down, on the grill. Tent the fish with heavy-duty aluminum foil, shiny side facing the fish, taking care not to let the foil touch the fish, or cover with a disposable aluminum tray.

Cook the fish until the fish juices and seasonings begin to steam and the flesh of the fish is firming up to your desired taste. Serve with a lightly sweet salsa. ❋

Creamy Zucchini & Garlic,
page 244

CB'S GRILLED PACIFIC SARDINES

2 pounds fresh sardines,
　cleaned and scaled

SAUCE
½ cup olive oil

4 tablespoons unsalted
　butter, melted or clarified

2 tablespoons fresh oregano,
　chopped, or ½ tablespoon
　dried oregano

½ teaspoon mustard, ground

2 garlic cloves, minced

4 tablespoons parsley or
　cilantro, chopped

2 teaspoons coarse salt

2 teaspoons black pepper

Juice from ½ lemon

Whole sardines are one of the most flavourful fish to grill and are an abundant, as well as a renewable, resource. If you have only been exposed to sardines in a can, and you like the taste of grilled fish, you have to try some fresh sardines grilled. These wild-caught Northern Pacific Ocean Sardines are not little tiny things, but about the size of a freshwater trout.

Preheat your grill to medium high. Score the sides of the fish lightly. Spritz the fish with canola oil; grill for about 2 to 3 minutes per side.

For the sauce: Heat oil and the butter in a pan over medium heat; add the oregano and mustard to release their flavours.

Add the garlic, and cook until translucent; reduce heat, and add two tablespoons of the chopped parsley and the salt and pepper. When fish are cooked, arrange on a platter. Squeeze the lemon over the top; then dress the fish with the heated sauce; garnish with the reserved chopped parsley; and serve. ✳

7

SEAFOOD

GRILLED BLUEFISH WITH FRESH CORN SALSA

4 bluefish fillets (6 to 8 ounces each)

Salt and black pepper, to taste

3 ears fresh or frozen corn, kernels removed

6 sprigs fresh cilantro, roughly chopped

2 teaspoons red onion, finely diced

1 jalapeño, seeded and finely chopped

Juice of 2 limes

1 pinch cumin

1 teaspoon canola oil

To make salsa: mix all vegetables and spices together in a nonreactive bowl. Toss; cover for at least one hour.

Preheat grill to medium high. Brush fillets with oil. Cook fish for 2 to 3 minutes on each side. Remove from grill, and place in 225°F oven for 3 to 5 minutes. While fillets are in the oven, heat skillet until it is hot; add salsa; and cook approximately 2 minutes or until all ingredients are warm. Remove from heat. Arrange fish on plates, and garnish with salsa. ❈

GRILLED ATLANTIC CROAKER

4 whole croaker or other lean, white fish, dressed

¼ cup soy sauce

2 tablespoons brown sugar

1 clove garlic, minced

1 tablespoon fresh ginger, minced

2 tablespoons orange peel, finely julienned

2 tablespoons orange juice

¼ teaspoon red pepper flakes, crushed

2 tablespoons butter, melted

4 scallions, sliced

Atlantic croakers are usually caught in the Chesapeake Bay between June and August. Also known as "hardhead," croakers contain delicate white meat with a sweet flavour that ranges from mild to moderately pronounced. You can substitute croaker for any recipe that calls for catfish, perch, sea trout, spot, or striped bass.

Place fish in a bowl. Combine remaining ingredients, and pour over fish. Marinate for one hour in the refrigerator. Preheat grill to medium. Place fish on grill, about 5 inches from heat, and cook about 10 minutes per inch of thickness, turning once halfway through cooking time and basting often with the marinade. When fish is tender and flakes easily, remove from grill, and serve hot over fresh corn salsa. (See recipe on opposite page.) ✳

7

SEAFOOD

BRINED, SMOKED BLUEFISH

2 pounds bluefish fillets or 3
  pounds bluefish steaks
1 cup salt
16 cups water
1 pound hardwood chips
  (whichever type you prefer)
¼ cup neutral-flavoured vegetable
  oil or clarified butter

Dissolve salt in 16 cups of water to make brine. Marinate fish in brine for 30 minutes.

Preheat grill to low, and set up for indirect heat. Place smoker box filled with dry wood chips (alder, apple, or pear work well) directly over heat source.

Remove fish from brine; rinse in cool water; and pat dry with paper towels. If possible, allow fish to dry in the refrigerator for up to 1 hour.

Brush grate where fish will cook with oil. Place fish, skin side down, on unheated side of grill. If your grill doesn't have a thermometer, centre an oven thermometer at the back of grill. Maintain temperature of 200–250°F.

Brush top of fish with oil. Close grill cover, and smoke fillets or steaks about 30 to 45 minutes (for whole fish, about 45 minutes). If the surface of the fish dries out a bit, baste with clarified butter or vegetable oil during the final 10 minutes of cooking.

The fish is done when its flesh is opaque and firm. Serve with chopped hard-boiled egg, chopped onion, capers, and toast triangles. ❈

JIM HATCHER'S CREOLE SHRIMP & SAUSAGE

1 pound jumbo prawns (about 23 per pound), cleaned
1 pound Andouille sausage
Canola oil

CREOLE SAUCE

⅓ cup Creole or stone-ground mustard
1 tablespoon orange marmalade or preserves
2 teaspoons Tabasco sauce

Combine sauce ingredients, and set on grill away from direct heat to warm.

Preheat one section of grill to high and one section to low. Sear the sausages on the hot side of the grill, and move to a pan on the low side to finish.

When the sausages are just about done (160°F internal temperature), spray the prawns with canola oil, and place over direct heat to sear. When grill marks appear, remove them to the pan with the sausages. Add the Creole sauce to coat the prawns and sausages; serve with mac & cheese (page 246) or over white rice. ❈

CILANTRO-PESTO SNAPPER WITH RED PEPPER SAUCE

4 snapper (or mahi-mahi or swordfish)
   fillets (1½ pounds)

2 tablespoons shredded Parmesan cheese

2 fresh garlic cloves

⅓ cup walnuts, chopped

1 tablespoon extra-virgin olive oil

¼ cup fresh cilantro

¾ teaspoon pepper, divided

1 medium shallot

½ cup white wine

1 (12-ounce) jar roasted red peppers
   (drained)

¾ teaspoon salt, divided

1 tablespoon butter

Preheat grill to medium high. Make pesto: place cheese, garlic, and walnuts in food processor; process 15 to 20 seconds or until finely chopped. Add olive oil, cilantro, and ⅛ teaspoon of the pepper. Process until smooth; remove from food processor, and set aside.

Mince shallot finely; combine with wine in saucepan. Bring to boil; reduce heat to medium, and cook about 4 minutes, stirring occasionally, or until liquid has reduced by about one-half.

Put red peppers in food processor; add wine reduction; and process 20 seconds or until smooth. Pour mixture back into same pan, and bring to boil; reduce and simmer 3 to 4 minutes, stirring often, or until sauce thickens.

Season fish with ½ teaspoon of the salt and ¼ teaspoon of the pepper. Grill fish with the lid closed about 4 to 6 minutes on each side or until fish is golden and separates with a fork.

Add butter to sauce, along with remaining salt and pepper; whisk until smooth. Spoon sauce onto serving plates containing yellow rice and peas; place fish on sauce; and top with pesto. ✳

7

SEAFOOD

GRILLED SHRIMP & VEGETABLE KEBABS

2 pounds shrimp, peeled and deveined
2 medium zucchini, cut into ½-inch half-rounds
2 medium yellow squash, cut into ½-inch half-rounds
1 medium onion, cut into ½-inch pieces
4 to 6 wooden skewers

These shrimp kebabs are a tasty main dish when paired with rice or other grain. At a casual gathering, guests can even assemble and grill their own kebabs.

Soak the skewers in water for 20 minutes. For the marinade, whisk together the garlic, oregano, lemon juice, zest, and oil.

Thread each skewer with alternating shrimp and vegetables. Put the skewers in a large baking dish, and pour the marinade over them. Turn the skewers to coat with the marinade, and refrigerate up to 1 hour.

Preheat one side of the grill to high. Lightly spray the hot side of grill with vegetable oil.

Shake any excess marinade off the skewers, and place them on the hot side of the grill. Leave them alone to brown on the one side, a minute or so. Turn skewers, and brown the vegetables on all sides until the shrimp is cooked, about 4 to 6 minutes. ❋

MARINADE
2 garlic cloves, minced
1 tablespoon fresh
   oregano, chopped
2 teaspoons lemon juice
1 teaspoon lemon zest
¼ cup olive oil

[*Courtesy of*
cookthink.com]

GRILLED SHRIMP & BLUE CHEESE GRITS

5 pounds shrimp, peeled and deveined with tail on

¼ cup olive oil

¼ cup soy sauce

¼ cup white wine

2 teaspoons Cajun seasoning or seasoned salt

5 pounds assorted vegetables (peppers, zucchini, onions, mushrooms)

½ cup olive oil

¼ cup fresh basil, sliced

Salt and pepper, to taste

4 cups stone-ground grits

1 cup blue cheese, crumbled

10 skewers

Combine oil, soy sauce, wine, and Cajun seasoning. Add shrimp. Refrigerate and marinate for 1 hour. While the shrimp marinate, dice or julienne the vegetables. Heat a pan over high heat; add oil; and sauté vegetables until softened, about 5 minutes. Add basil, and remove from heat. Season vegetables with salt and pepper.

Cook grits following package directions, about 20 minutes. Add blue cheese, and simmer until thick. Cover to keep warm.

Preheat grill to high. Skewer shrimp, and place on grates. Cook until just opaque, turning once, about 5 minutes. To serve, place grits in centre of platter. Top with vegetables. Surround with shrimp. ❈

4–6 Servings • Prep: 20 min. • Marinate: 30 min. • Grill: 6–8 min.

219

MARGARITA GRILLED SHRIMP

1½ pounds shrimp, peeled and
deveined

¼ cup vegetable oil

3 tablespoons fresh lime juice

3 tablespoons tequila

2 tablespoons triple sec

1 large jalapeño chili, seeded
and minced

1½ teaspoons grated lime zest

1 teaspoon chili powder

½ teaspoon coarse salt

1 teaspoon sugar

This recipe also works well with chicken legs, thighs, or wings.

Whisk all ingredients together, except shrimp, in a medium-size bowl. Allow the mixture to rest for at least 20 minutes. This marinade can be prepared 1 day in advance. Simply cover, and refrigerate for up to 24 hours.

Pour about ¼ cup of the marinade mixture into a container, and reserve. Place shrimp in a large baking dish or sealable plastic bag, and cover with remaining marinade. Cover dish with plastic wrap, or seal bag and refrigerate shrimp for 30 minutes.

Remove shrimp from container, and discard marinade. Grill shrimp on indirect heat for 3 to 4 minutes per side, basting with the reserved marinade. Serve over rice. ✲

7

SEAFOOD

CB'S GRILLED HONEY & LIME PRAWNS

1 pound jumbo prawns (about 21 per pound) cleaned, tails on

MARINADE

2 tablespoons Italian salad dressing

2 tablespoons dry white vermouth

⅓ cup Worcestershire sauce

1 garlic clove, finely minced

2 tablespoons cilantro, finely chopped

1 teaspoon ground ginger

BASTING SAUCE

2 tablespoons Worcestershire sauce

¼ cup olive oil

¼ cup honey

Combine marinade ingredients in a sealable plastic bag, and add prawns. Refrigerate for up to 1 hour. Combine basting-sauce ingredients in a nonreactive bowl, and set aside.

Preheat grill to medium high. Place marinated prawns on hot grates. Use tongs to turn, and sear all sides. When seared, remove the prawns to a holding pan away from direct heat. Brush with basting sauce, and allow to finish cooking, about 3 to 5 minutes. Prawns may be served as a main course over rice or pasta, or with a salad, such as "You Won't Know It's Not Potato Salad," page 257. ✳

CB'S GRILLED SCALLOPS WITH ASPARAGUS & TOASTED WALNUTS

1 dozen sea scallops, cleaned and dried with a paper towel

3 large walnut halves or 6 large hazelnuts, chopped

1 pound asparagus, woody ends removed

Salt and pepper to taste

Juice from ½ lemon

Soy sauce

To toast nuts, place them in a dry skillet over medium-low heat, shaking pan to prevent burning, for about 2 to 3 minutes until aroma is released. When cool, chop nuts, and set aside.

Preheat the grill to medium. Spray the scallops and asparagus with canola oil, and season with salt and pepper to taste. Place asparagus on the grill, and use tongs to turn until all sides are charred and spears are tender, about 4 to 5 minutes. Remove to serving plate, and lightly cover with foil. Use tongs to place the scallops on a clean section of the grill. Leave in one place until seared; use tongs to turn the scallops; and sear the other sides. Remove, and place atop seared asparagus. Serve with a mixture of equal parts fresh lemon juice and soy sauce. Garnish with lemon zest and chopped nuts. ✳

CB'S GRILLED LOBSTER TAIL WITH BOURBON-HERB SAUCE

7

SEAFOOD

2 lobster tails removed from shell,
   about 6 ounces each
Canola oil

SAUCE
5 tablespoons butter, melted
1 tablespoon olive oil
¼ cup shallots, finely diced
1 garlic clove, finely minced
Coarse salt and freshly ground black
   pepper to taste
¼ cup Kentucky bourbon
1 tablespoon chives, finely chopped
1 tablespoon tarragon, finely chopped
2 tablespoons dry white vermouth

Melt butter in a heavy saucepan over medium heat. Add olive oil and shallots, and cook until translucent; stir in garlic, and heat until aroma is released. Add salt and pepper to taste. Add bourbon; allow alcohol to vaporize; remove from heat; and set aside, covered.

Preheat grill to medium high. Dry lobster with paper towel, and then lightly spray with canola oil. Place lobster tails on hot grill to sear, using tongs to turn. When seared, remove to aluminum pan away from direct heat, and continue to cook until lobster is firm but not rubbery, about 15 minutes.

Prior to serving, add the chives, tarragon, and vermouth to the sauce; re-warm to release the flavours. Serve on plates with sauce drizzled over the lobster or as a dipping sauce. ❋

CB'S GRILLED SOFT-SHELL CRABS

8 soft-shell crabs,
  cleaned

Coarse salt and pepper
  to taste

Canola oil spray

1 lime cut into quarters

SAUCE

2 cloves minced garlic

1 tablespoon ginger, minced

1 chipotle pepper, finely diced

3 tablespoon canola oil

1 teaspoon anchovy paste

1 cup fresh cilantro, finely
  chopped

1 cup Thai basil, finely
  chopped

Combine all sauce ingredients, and set aside.

Preheat the grill to high. Season the crabs with salt and pepper to taste; spritz with canola oil; place on clean grates; and sear on both sides—about 3 minutes per side—using tongs to turn.

Remove crabs, and place them on a platter where the sauce is spread as a base. Squeeze limes over grilled crabs; then spoon sauce over the crabs, and serve. ✳

SMOKY GRILLED KING CRAB

2 to 3 pounds Alaska King
　Crab legs, frozen
Wood chips (alder, cedar,
　apple, etc.)
2 to 3 tablespoons olive oil
2 to 3 teaspoons favourite
　seafood spice blend
1 large-size foil cooking bag
　or 2 sheets (15-inch) heavy-
　duty aluminum foil

Soak wood chips in water for 30 minutes; drain. Preheat grill to medium high. Add chips to grill or smoker box.

Rinse crab legs under cold water to remove any ice glaze; pat dry with paper towels. For each pound of crab, use 1 tablespoon olive oil and 1 teaspoon of seafood spice. Blend olive oil and seasoning. Place foil bag in a 1-inch-deep baking pan. Place crab legs in bag. Pour or brush oil blend onto legs; seal the bag tightly. If using foil sheets, place crab legs on the foil, and pour or brush oil blend onto legs. Lay second foil sheet over crab, and tightly crimp edges to seal foil, leaving room for heat circulation inside.

To cook, slide bag onto grill, and cook for 8 to 10 minutes, until the internal temperature of the crab reaches 145°F. (Use an instant-read thermometer, and test crab in shoulder section.) ✽

7

SEAFOOD

⏲ Quick Meal • 4–6 Servings • Prep: 15 min. • Grill: 4–5 min.

GRILLED ALASKA CRAB WITH TRINIDAD SALAD

3 to 4 pounds Alaska Crab legs (King, Snow, or Dungeness), split open to expose meat
⅓ cup butter, melted
¼ to ½ teaspoon chili oil
⅛ teaspoon cayenne pepper

TRINIDAD SALAD
½ cup extra-virgin olive oil
1 lime, juiced and divided
¼ cup dry white wine
2 tablespoons whole-grain mustard
1 can (14 to 15 ounces) palm hearts, drained and sliced crosswise

1 large, firm ripe papaya, skinned and chunked
1 cup celery, thinly sliced
½ fresh small red chili pepper, sliced and minced
¼ small sweet onion, thinly sliced then quartered
2 large, firm ripe avocados, pitted and diced in large chunks

Whisk together olive oil, one-half of the lime juice, wine, and mustard for salad dressing. In large bowl, add salad ingredients, topping with avocado. Pour dressing over avocado; cover; and refrigerate.

Preheat grill to medium high. Blend butter, chili oil, cayenne, and remaining lime juice. Brush butter mixture onto exposed crabmeat; place crab legs on grill; and cook 4 to 5 minutes, until heated. Save the unused sauce so that you can drizzle some over the crab legs at the table. Gently stir salad mixture to coat evenly; serve the dressed salad with the crab legs. ❈

CB'S STUFFED SQUID WITH CHICKEN-APPLE SAUSAGE

6 to 9 small-medium squid, cleaned, gutted, skinned, and fins removed

6 to 9 toothpicks

SERVE WITH

Green-Chile Pesto, Madras Curry Dip, or Moroccan Sauce (See Chapter 10 for recipes.)

STUFFING

1 cup precooked chicken apple or other sausage, removed from casings

3 scallions, finely chopped

2 garlic cloves, crushed

1 teaspoon chili powder

1 tablespoon tarragon leaves, minced

⅛ teaspoon Chinese five-spice powder

Pinch of salt and pepper

Remove tentacles from squid, and finely chop. Add them to a large bowl with other stuffing ingredients, and mix well. Using a small spoon, stuff the squid. Do not overfill. Secure the opening of each squid with a sturdy toothpick or small skewer. Dry the outside of the stuffed squid with a paper towel, and spray with canola oil.

Preheat one side of grill to high. Place the stuffed squid on clean hot grates and sear; use tongs to turn; and sear all sides. Then remove squid to a holding pan on unheated side of the grill, and close hood. Squid is done when the internal temperature of the stuffing registers about 145°F. ❋

8 Sides

230 Aunt Sylvia's Buttermilk Cole Slaw

231 Peg's Magic Beans

232 Greek Potato Salad with Sun-Dried Tomatoes

233 Savoury Corn Pudding

234 Black-Eyed-Pea Salad

235 Carrots & Raisins Revisited

236 CB's Cucumber Salad

237 Marinated Portobello Mushrooms with Roasted-Pepper Vinaigrette

238 CB's Grilled Pear & Gorgonzola Salad

239 CB's Smoky, Cheesy Cornbread

240 CB's Grilled Fennel

241 CB's Grilled Potatoes with Bacon, Cheese & Roasted Jalapeño

242 Cranberry-Pecan Rice Pilaf

243 Livefire's Holiday Potato Torte

244 Creamy Zucchini & Garlic

245 Garlic-Roasted Sweet Potatoes with Arugula

246 Better-than-Mom's Mac & Cheese

247 Potato Casserole

248 Grilled Eggplant with Cheese

249 Harvest Slaw with Sweet Potatoes

250 Grilled Potato Planks

251 Grilled Stuffed Tomatoes Caprese

252 CB's Grilled Broccoli & Cauliflower with Toasted Walnuts

253 Salt-Grilled Potatoes

254 Roasted Asparagus with Cherry Tomatoes, Garlic & Olive Oil

255 Miss Allison's One-Beer Skillet Bread

256 Pan Pacific Rice

257 You Won't Know It's Not Potato Salad

258 Honey-Grilled Cauliflower

259 Devilled Potato Bites

(Right) Creamy Zucchini & Garlic, page 244

AUNT SYLVIA'S BUTTERMILK COLE SLAW

This version of slaw was something my Aunt Sylvia would make for summer backyard barbecues. It's great as a side to grilled meat and a tasty topping over a pulled-pork sandwich!—CB

5 to 6 cups Savoy or other cabbage, tightly packed

1 large carrot, julienned or grated

1 cup jicama or Granny Smith apple, julienned

1 cup sweet onion, diced or thinly sliced

Coarse salt

2 garlic cloves, mashed

⅓ cup buttermilk

¼ cup extra-virgin olive oil

2 tablespoons fresh lemon juice

¼ teaspoon celery seeds

Black pepper, freshly ground

Combine the cabbage, carrot, jicama, and onion in a colander, and lightly season with salt. Put the colander in a large bowl; set a plate on top of the vegetables; and place a can of soup or beans on top of the plate for extra weight. Allow the vegetables to drain for 1 to 2 hours in the refrigerator. Then turn the mixture onto a sheet pan lined with paper towels; pat dry; and transfer to a dry bowl.

In a small bowl, mix the mashed garlic, buttermilk, olive oil, lemon juice, celery seeds, and pepper. Toss the slaw with the dressing, and season with salt, pepper, and lemon juice to taste. May be kept in the refrigerator for up to a day before serving. ❧

PEG'S MAGIC BEANS

[*From "Sizzle on the Grill." I can testify to the great taste of these beans!—CB*]

1 pound maple-cured bacon

1 large white onion, finely chopped

1 pound 80 percent-lean ground beef

1 can (15½ ounces) dark-red kidney beans

1 can (15½ ounces) white cannellini beans or reat northern beans

1 can (15½ ounces) black-eyed peas or navy beans

1 can (8 ounces) baked beans

1 can (15½ ounces) medium to hot chili beans

1 bottle (12 ounces) chili sauce

1 cup brown sugar

6 ounces apple cider vinegar

1 tablespoon garlic powder

1 tablespoon chili powder

½ tablespoon paprika

Hot sauce to taste

The night before cooking beans, fry one pound of maple-cured bacon in a large skillet or frying pan until crisp. Remove the bacon; crumble when cool. Drain fat from skillet, reserving about 1 teaspoon. Cook onion and ground beef in the skillet with the reserved bacon fat until meat is browned. Drain off the fat, and transfer the onions, cooked ground beef, and bacon to the cooking sleeve of a 5-quart slow cooker.

Drain and rinse all of the beans except the chili and baked beans. Then add all of the beans, chili sauce, brown sugar, vinegar, and spices to the rest of the ingredients. Stir well. Cover with plastic wrap, and store in the refrigerator overnight.

The next day, transfer the cooking sleeve with the beans and meat to the slow cooker set on low for a minimum of 4 cooking hours. Serve warm.

GREEK POTATO SALAD WITH SUN-DRIED TOMATOES

1 pound (3 medium) potatoes, cut into
   ¼-inch slices

1 cup (1½ ounces) sun-dried tomatoes,
   halved lengthwise

1 cup seedless cucumber, sliced

½ cup red onion, sliced

1 cup feta cheese, crumbled

½ cup Greek olives or pitted black olives

LEMON DRESSING

¼ cup olive oil

¼ cup water

2½ tablespoons lemon juice

1 large garlic clove, pressed

1 tablespoon oregano, freshly chopped,
   or 1 teaspoon dried oregano leaves

1 teaspoon salt

½ teaspoon pepper

In 2-quart saucepan over medium heat, cover potatoes with 2 inches of water. Bring to a boil; reduce heat; and cook until tender, about 12 minutes. Drain, and set aside. Meanwhile, put the sliced sundried tomatoes in a small bowl, and pour boiling water over them; set aside 10 minutes.

Whisk together all of the dressing ingredients in a large bowl. Thoroughly drain tomatoes, and pat dry with paper towels. Add potatoes, tomatoes, and cucumbers to the bowl, and toss with the dressing. Transfer the potato salad to a serving plate. Garnish with onion, cheese, and olives. 🖐

SAVOURY CORN PUDDING

2 tablespoons butter, melted

4 medium shallots, finely chopped

1 small cubano or jalapeño pepper, seeded and finely chopped

1 ripe tomato, chopped

8 ears fresh corn

¾ cup whole milk

½ cup heavy cream or milk

Salt and pepper to taste

1 to 2 teaspoons red pepper flakes (optional)

2 tablespoons fine yellow cornmeal (optional)

2 to 3 tablespoons fresh lime juice

1 cup fresh basil, slivered

1 tablespoon olive oil

1 tablespoon fresh chives (optional)

1 to 2 teaspoons fresh oregano, finely chopped (optional)

[*Courtesy of cookbook author and food blogger Cathy Erway*]

In 3-quart saucepan over medium-low heat, sauté shallots in butter 6 minutes or until translucent. Add pepper and tomato; cook another 2 to 3 minutes.

Using a sharp paring knife, scrape kernels from the corncobs over a bowl; transfer corn and juices to the saucepan, and stir another 2 to 3 minutes. Add milk, ¼ cup at a time, stirring until absorbed; then pour in the cream, and season with salt, pepper, and pepper flakes if desired. If necessary, thicken mixture with cornmeal, 1 tablespoon at a time, until it is puddinglike. Add the lime juice, basil, olive oil, and optional herbs. 🍎

BLACK-EYED-PEA SALAD

BEANS

1 tablespoon extra-virgin olive oil

1 medium onion, chopped

3 or 4 garlic cloves, minced

1 pound black-eyed peas, rinsed and drained

6 cups water

1 bay leaf

Salt to taste

DRESSING AND SALAD

¼ cup red wine vinegar or sherry vinegar

1 garlic clove, minced

Salt and pepper, freshly ground, to taste

1 to 2 teaspoons cumin, lightly toasted and ground

1 teaspoon Dijon mustard

½ cup broth from the beans

⅓ cup extra-virgin olive oil

1 large red bell pepper, diced

½ cup cilantro, chopped

Heat 1 tablespoon olive oil in a large, heavy soup pot over medium heat; add onion; and cook until tender, about 5 minutes. Add half the garlic. Once it is fragrant, about 30 seconds to 1 minute, add the black-eyed peas and the water. Simmer, skimming off any foam from the surface. Add the bay leaf and salt, to taste (1 to 2 teaspoons). Reduce the heat; cover; and simmer 30 minutes. Taste and adjust salt, if needed. Add the remaining garlic; cover; and simmer until the beans are tender but intact. Remove from the heat; drain over a bowl. Transfer the beans to a large salad bowl.

In a small bowl, whisk together vinegar, garlic, salt, pepper, cumin, and mustard; add ½ cup of the bean broth and the olive oil; blend with the whisk. Taste and adjust seasonings. Toss dressing with the warm beans. Stir in the red pepper and cilantro. Serve warm or at room temperature. 🌶

6 Servings • Prep: 10 min. (1½ hr. to drain yogurt) • Chill: 20–30 min.

235

CARROTS & RAISINS REVISITED

2 cups plain non- or low-fat yogurt

1 tablespoon packed brown sugar

¼ teaspoon orange peel, grated

2 tablespoons orange juice

¼ teaspoon nutmeg or cardamom, ground

¼ teaspoon Tabasco sauce

6 to 7 medium carrots, peeled and shredded coarsely

3 cups dark raisins

3 tablespoons cashews, almonds, or pecans, chopped

Line a medium-size strainer with a double layer of rinsed cheesecloth or a triple layer of white paper towels. Place the strainer over a large bowl, and spoon yogurt into it. Let yogurt drain for 1½ hours; then scrape it into a medium-size bowl. Discard strained liquid.

Stir brown sugar, orange peel and juice, nutmeg, and Tabasco sauce into the yogurt until smooth. Mix in carrots and raisins, and toss to coat. Cover, and chill 20 to 30 minutes. Just before serving, sprinkle with chopped nuts. 🌰

8

SIDES

CB'S CUCUMBER SALAD

2 to 4 medium-size cucumbers (7 to 10 inches each), thoroughly washed and dried

Salt

GINGER DRESSING

3 tablespoons Japanese rice vinegar or apple cider vinegar

1 tablespoon coarse salt

1 tablespoon lemon juice, freshly squeezed

1 tablespoon sugar

1 tablespoon ginger, peeled and finely grated

¼ teaspoon lemon rind, grated

Score the skin of the cucumbers with a fork, or peel off skin in strips. Slice cucumbers into very thin rounds; place sliced cucumbers in a colander; sprinkle with salt; and toss to mix thoroughly. Let cucumbers rest for 15 to 20 minutes. Meanwhile, make the dressing by mixing together the vinegar, salt, lemon juice, sugar, ginger, and lemon rind in a nonmetallic bowl. Set aside.

Once the salted cucumbers have drained, remove them from the colander, and place them into a large, clean dishtowel or cheesecloth; gently blot excess moisture. Then add cucumbers to the bowl, and toss with the dressing. Chill before serving. 🌱

6 Servings
Prep: 10 min.
Marinate: 1 hr.
Grill: 4–6 min.

MARINATED PORTOBELLO MUSHROOMS WITH ROASTED-PEPPER VINAIGRETTE

1 pound fresh portobello
   mushrooms, stems trimmed
Olive oil for skillet

MARINADE

4 tablespoons balsamic
   vinegar
6 garlic cloves, minced
2 tablespoons fresh thyme
   leaves, chopped
⅓ cup olive oil

VINAIGRETTE

1 red pepper, roasted, peeled,
   seeded, and chopped coarsely
1 poblano chile, roasted, peeled,
   seeded, and chopped coarsely
4 garlic cloves, peeled
2 tablespoons red wine vinegar
1 lemon, squeezed for juice
¼ cup olive oil
Coarse salt
Black pepper, freshly ground

In a small bowl, whisk together marinade ingredients. Arrange mushroom caps in a single layer in a nonreactive shallow pan. Pour marinade over mushrooms; cover; and marinate for 1 hour, turning mushrooms several times. In a blender, combine vinaigrette ingredients until smooth. Taste for seasoning.

Heat an oiled grill skillet. Remove mushrooms from marinade; place in pan; and use a food press or a heavy can to press down on them. Sear them about 2 to 3 minutes on each side or until tender. Transfer mushrooms to a cutting board; slice thin; and drizzle with red-pepper vinaigrette. 🌶

CB'S GRILLED PEAR & GORGONZOLA SALAD

2 ripe pears, cored and cut in eighths

3 to 4 leaves of Bibb or other tender lettuce, washed and dried

2 tablespoons extra-virgin olive oil

1 wedge Gorgonzola or blue cheese

4 tablespoons salted roasted almonds, chopped

Preheat grill to medium high. Spray pear slices with canola oil, and sear over direct heat, turning to ensure both sides become fairly dark brown but not blackened.

Arrange the seared pear slices on the lettuce leaves. Drizzle with olive oil; crumble cheese over them; and sprinkle with the roasted almonds. 🌿

CB'S SMOKY, CHEESY CORNBREAD

Preheat grill to medium. Lightly grease a small cast-iron skillet or a 9 x 5 baking pan.

Whisk together first five ingredients; then add oil, eggs, and buttermilk; use spatula to mix until just combined. Ladle batter evenly into pan. Crumble cheese on top, and let rest for 15 minutes; then bake in grill over indirect heat for 30 to 35 minutes. (Check doneness by inserting a toothpick in the centre; it should come out clean.) Remove, and cool for a few minutes. Run a butter knife around the edge; place cooling rack on top of skillet or pan; and flip. Cool for 30 minutes before slicing. ✣

8

SIDES

1½ cups cornmeal

1 cup all-purpose flour

1 teaspooon baking soda

½ teaspooon salt

3 tablespoons sugar

¼ cup vegetable oil

2 large eggs

1 cup buttermilk

4 ounces smoked cheese, such as smoked Gouda or smoked blue cheese

CB'S GRILLED FENNEL

2 large fennel bulbs
2 tablespoons brown sugar
1 teaspoon Worcestershire
   sauce
2 tablespoons peanut oil or
   clarified butter
Coarse salt

Remove the green top and fronds from the fennel, and reserve. Quarter each bulb, leaving the root bottoms in place to hold the leaves together during roasting. Whisk together the brown sugar, Worcestershire sauce, and oil. Marinate the pieces in the mixture for 15 to 20 minutes.

Preheat the grill to medium. Using tongs, arrange fennel slices on grates; turn to sear and caramelize all sides, about 3 to 5 minutes. As the edges begin to crisp and char just a bit, remove to a holding pan to finish over indirect heat with the hood closed. The fennel bulbs are cooked when they are fork-tender but not too soft. Serve on a platter with freshly ground salt and a teaspoon or two of finely minced fennel tops. 🍅

This recipe will drive you crazy-go-nuts because it pairs deliciously with just about any grilled meat or fish.—CB

CB'S GRILLED POTATOES WITH BACON, CHEESE & ROASTED JALAPEÑO

2 large russet potatoes, scrubbed and dried
Olive oil
3 strips cooked centre-cut bacon, crumbled
4 jalapeño peppers, roasted and diced
¼ cup smoked Gouda cheese, shredded
¼ cup Parmesan cheese, shredded
¼ cup sour cream
2 tablespoons green onions, minced
Coarse salt and black pepper, freshly ground
½ cup prepared adobo sauce (See page 290.)

The potatoes can be roasted a day in advance.

Preheat grill to high. Rub potatoes with the oil. Poke small holes in each end to allow steam to escape; then grill over high heat for about 1 hour, turning every 15 minutes. (Or roast on warming rack without turning.)

Slice cooked potatoes in half lengthwise. Scoop all but ¼ inch of the potato into a bowl. Leave the rest inside the skin.

Add the remaining ingredients to the bowl; mix; then spoon into the skins. Top with additional Gouda, and melt over indirect heat with the hood closed. Drizzle with the adobo sauce when you serve. 🐞

8

SIDES

CRANBERRY-PECAN RICE PILAF

2 tablespoons butter or margarine

1 cup uncooked rice

1 can (14½ ounces) chicken broth

1 cup Parmesan cheese, grated

½ cup dried cranberries

½ cup pecans,
   chopped and toasted*

¼ cup green onions, sliced

Salt and black pepper, ground,
   to taste

To toast pecans, spread nuts on small baking sheet. Bake 5 to 8 minutes at 350°F., or until golden brown, stirring frequently.

Melt butter in 2-quart saucepan over medium heat. Add rice; cook, stirring, 2 to 3 minutes. Add broth, and heat to boiling, stirring once or twice. Reduce heat; cover; and simmer 15 minutes or until liquid is absorbed.

Remove from heat. Stir in cheese, cranberries, pecans, and onions. Season to taste with salt and pepper. ❧

LIVEFIRE'S HOLIDAY POTATO TORTE

3 to 4 russet potatoes, scrubbed
  but not skinned
Olive oil
Salt and black pepper to taste
2 tablespoons fresh rosemary,
  chopped
V-slicer or mandolin

Preheat grill to medium high. Generously butter a well-seasoned 10-inch cast-iron or other heavy skillet. Using a V-slicer or mandolin, thinly slice each potato, placing slices in the skillet as you go to prevent oxidation.

Because you will invert the torte after it is cooked, the bottom layer of potatoes will be the top of the torte, so make sure to arrange the slices in an attractive pattern. As you add each layer, brush it with olive oil, and sprinkle with salt and pepper and about ½ teaspoon of rosemary. When you're finished, you should have about 7 layers of potatoes.

Place skillet on the grill, and cook until the potatoes are sizzling nicely, about 12 to 15 minutes. Using heat-resistant gloves or potholders, remove skillet from the grill, and drain off excess oil. Carefully invert the torte onto a clean plate, and then slide the potatoes, bottom side up, back into the skillet. Return to the grill, and cook, with lid closed, for about 20 to 25 minutes or until potatoes are browned and crispy and inner layers are tender. 🌶

CREAMY ZUCCHINI & GARLIC

2½ tablespoons butter

6 garlic cloves, minced

6 medium zucchini, grated

2½ tablespoons garlic powder

1 teaspoon thyme, chopped

2½ tablespoons sour cream

Fresh pepper

Melt the butter in a heavy-bottom skillet over medium heat. Lower the heat; add the minced garlic; and sauté for about 1 to 2 minutes. (Do not let the garlic burn.) Add the grated zucchini, garlic powder, and thyme.

Cook, stirring frequently until the zucchini is tender. Remove from the heat, and stir in the sour cream. Season with fresh pepper. Serve immediately. 🍏

GARLIC-ROASTED SWEET POTATOES WITH ARUGULA

8

SIDES

2 pounds sweet potatoes, peeled and cut into 2-inch pieces

4 garlic cloves, peeled and sliced

2 tablespoons extra-virgin olive oil

½ teaspoon salt

½ teaspoon black pepper, ground

2 Bartlett pears, cored and cut into 2-inch pieces

1 5-ounce package arugula

½ teaspoon lemon peel, grated

Preheat grill or oven to medium high. In large roasting pan, combine potatoes, garlic, oil, salt, and pepper, and toss to coat well. Roast for 30 minutes, tossing occasionally, until tender and browned. Add pears, and roast another 10 minutes.

Place the arugula in a large bowl. Add the cooked potatoes and pears, and toss until the arugula wilts. Sprinkle with the lemon peel. 🌿

Courtesy of christopherranch.com

BETTER-THAN-MOM'S MAC & CHEESE

1 box (16 ounces) corkscrew or
mini penne pasta

¼ cup butter or margarine

¼ cup all-purpose flour

4 cups milk

¾ teaspoon salt

1½ teaspoons Tabasco sauce

1 cup Gruyère cheese, shredded

1 cup sharp cheddar cheese, shredded

BREAD-CRUMB TOPPING

⅓ cup butter or margarine

½ cup dried seasoned bread crumbs

½ teaspoon Tabasco sauce

Prepare pasta as directed on box. Drain; set aside.

Meanwhile, melt butter in 3-quart saucepan over medium heat. Stir in flour until blended and smooth. Gradually whisk in milk, salt, and Tabasco sauce. Cook until thickened and smooth, stirring often. Add cheese to sauce, and stir until melted. In large bowl, toss sauce with cooked pasta. Spoon mixture into an ungreased 2-quart baking dish.

Preheat oven to 375°F. To prepare bread-crumb topping, melt butter or magarine in a small skillet over medium heat. Stir in bread crumbs and Tabasco sauce; blend well. Top pasta mixture with prepared bread crumbs and cheese. Bake 20 minutes until crumbs are toasted and casserole is completely heated. 🐜

POTATO CASSEROLE

Nonstick cooking spray

1 medium onion, halved and thinly sliced

1½ pounds Yukon Gold potatoes, very
   thinly sliced

1⅓ cups low-fat sharp cheddar cheese,
   shredded

⅓ cup real bacon bits

⅓ cup bell pepper, chopped

½ teaspoon garlic salt

Spray a 9 x 9 x 2-inch foil pan liberally with nonstick cooking spray. Layer half the onions, potatoes, cheese, bacon bits, bell pepper, and garlic salt in pan; then layer the other half over the first. Cover the top tightly with foil, and grill over medium heat for 1 hour, rotating pan occasionally to avoid hot spots.

GRILLED EGGPLANT WITH CHEESE

4 small eggplants

Olive oil

Salt and pepper

½ pound soft goat cheese or feta, crumbled

2 teaspoons garlic, minced

1 teaspoon red pepper flakes

1 tablespoon fresh basil, finely chopped

Cut eggplants in half lengthwise. Brush cut edges with olive oil, and season with salt and pepper. In a small bowl, combine cheese, garlic, red pepper flakes, and basil with a pinch of salt, and then refrigerate until ready to use. Preheat the grill to medium. Place eggplant halves on grill over direct heat, skinless side down. Roast until almost soft (2 to 3 minutes). Remove from grill, and cool slightly. Then spread or sprinkle the cheese mixture on the warm eggplant, and serve immediately. 🌿

8 Servings • Prep: 10 min. • Cook: 3½ min. • Chill: up to 8 hr.

249

HARVEST SLAW WITH SWEET POTATOES

12 ounces sweet potatoes, cubed
12 ounces packaged broccoli slaw
½ cup dried cranberries or raisins
1 green apple, diced
½ cup almonds, sliced
1 teaspoon cinnamon, ground
¼ teaspoon garlic salt
¼ teaspoon black pepper
½ cup ranch dressing

Place sweet potatoes in a microwave-safe dish or plastic food bag. Microwave for 3½ minutes; let cool for 5 minutes. In a large bowl, combine the potatoes with the rest of the ingredients. Toss with ranch dressing. Chill up to 8 hours before serving. 🐢

GRILLED POTATO PLANKS

1½ pounds (about 3 large) unpeeled baking
  potatoes, cut into ½-inch-thick slices
3 tablespoons olive oil
2 teaspoons fresh rosemary, finely chopped
1 garlic clove, minced
½ teaspoon salt

Preheat grill to medium high. Combine oil, rosemary, garlic, and salt in dish. Add potato slices, and turn until well-coated. Grill potatoes for about 8 minutes. Turn, and continue grilling 10 minutes longer or until cooked. Remove from grill, and serve. ❧

GRILLED STUFFED TOMATOES CAPRESE

6 plum tomatoes, stemmed,
    tops cut off, and insides
    scooped out
Small bocconcini or other
    fresh mozzarella, cut into 6
    1-inch cubes

DRY INGREDIENTS

½ cup Italian bread crumbs
⅓ cup Parmesan or Romano
    cheese, freshly grated,
    plus extra for topping
8 fresh basil leaves, chopped, with
    6 additional leaves for garnish

WET INGREDIENTS

1 tablespoon balsamic vinegar
2 tablespoons extra-virgin
    olive oil
1 teaspoon sugar
Dash hot sauce

8

SIDES

Clean and scoop out the plum tomatoes; then insert 1 bocconcini or piece of mozzarella into each.

Separately combine the dry and wet ingredients, and then mix them together well. Stuff the tomatoes with the mixture, mounding it slightly. Top each tomato with extra grated Parmesan, and place them into a greased muffin pan.

Preheat your grill for indirect cooking, with one side hot and one side warm. Grill the tomatoes over the hot side for about 4 minutes, turning them often. Then move them to the warm side; close the grill lid; and let them cook an additional 5 minutes, turning pan occasionally, until all the cheese is melted.

Top each tomato with a small basil stem and leaf, and serve hot as a side dish or appetizer. 🌷

Thanks to girlsonagrill.com for their contribution as guest chefs and writers.

CB'S GRILLED BROCCOLI & CAULIFLOWER WITH TOASTED WALNUTS

2 large broccoli heads

1 large cauliflower head

Canola oil spray

¼ cup fruit vinegar (such as pear, raspberry, apple, or blueberry)

¼ cup walnuts, chopped and toasted

Preheat grill to medium. Trim broccoli and cauliflower into florets about the size of a golf ball. Put them on a large sheet pan, and spray with oil.

Using tongs, move florets to the grill. Turn each one as it sears and chars just a bit. Remove as they finish cooking, 7 to 12 minutes.

Arrange in a mound on a serving platter; drizzle with vinegar; and garnish with walnuts. ❧

SALT-GRILLED POTATOES

2 medium russet, white, or yellow-flesh
  potatoes, or 3 or 4 small red potatoes
Coarse salt

Preheat grill to medium high. Poke several holes in each potato to vent steam. Cover bottom of an aluminum loaf pan with salt. Place potatoes in pan, and cover completely with salt. Grill over direct heat with grill lid closed for 40 minutes or until potatoes are done. Use oven mitts to remove pan from grill. Remove potatoes from pan, and brush off excess salt. 🍎

ROASTED ASPARAGUS WITH CHERRY TOMATOES, GARLIC & OLIVE OIL

2 pounds pencil asparagus, woody ends trimmed

2 cups cherry tomatoes, washed and stemmed

12 garlic cloves, peeled and smashed

¼ cup extra-virgin olive oil

1 teaspoon coarse salt

½ teaspoon black pepper, freshly ground

¼ cup fresh lemon juice, reserve lemon halves

Preheat the grill to medium high. In a large bowl, combine the asparagus, tomatoes, and garlic. Drizzle with the olive oil, and season with the coarse salt and pepper. Toss to coat; then transfer to a large aluminum baking sheet. Drizzle the lemon juice over the asparagus; add the lemon halves to the pan; and place on the grill. Roast until the asparagus stalks are tender and the tomatoes begin to caramelize, about 20 to 25 minutes. Remove from the grill, and serve hot or at room temperature. ❦

MISS ALLISON'S ONE-BEER SKILLET BREAD

3 cups self-rising flour

¼ cup sugar

Pinch salt

1 can beer

1 egg, beaten

OPTIONAL ADDITIONS

Chopped onions, corn, bacon
  bits, bell pepper, jalapeño,
  or chopped herbs

Preheat grill to medium low. Mix flour, sugar, salt, and beer, and lightly knead into a dough. Pour dough into a well-seasoned cast-iron skillet, or add a bit of bacon grease to the bottom and sides of a pan. Brush the top of the dough with the beaten egg; then top with the onions, corn, or other additions.

Place skillet on grill over indirect heat. Close lid. After about 50 minutes, move the skillet over direct heat, and continue cooking for 10 minutes.

Skillet bread is done when toothpick inserted in the centre comes out clean. Flip bread over onto a cooling rack. Serve in wedges. 🌶

8

SIDES

PAN PACIFIC RICE

1 cup long grain rice
1 cup green onions, sliced
¾ cup salted cashews
¼ cup seasoned rice vinegar
1 tablespoon sesame seeds, toasted*

*To toast sesame seeds, spread them on a small baking sheet. Bake at 350°F for 5 to 8 minutes, stirring occasionally, or until golden brown.

Cook rice according to package directions; there should be about 3 cups of cooked rice. While it's still hot, combine the rice with the onions, cashews, vinegar, and sesame seeds. Toss well. ✿

YOU WON'T KNOW IT'S NOT POTATO SALAD

2 1-pound bags frozen cauliflower florets

1 10-ounce bag frozen peas and carrots

1¾ cups reduced-fat mayonnaise or salad dressing

1 teaspoon granulated sugar

1 teaspoon salt

¼ teaspoon pepper

¼ teaspoon paprika

1 tablespoon cider vinegar

1 teaspoon yellow mustard

1 cup celery, chopped (2½ stalks)

⅔ cup onion, chopped (about 1 medium)

4 hard-boiled eggs, peeled, chopped, and cooled

Place cauliflower, peas, and carrots in a large microwavable bowl; cover with microwavable waxed paper. Cook on high 20 to 25 minutes, pausing halfway to stir; then continue to cook. Drain in colander, and rinse with cold water to stop cooking process. Place colander with vegetables over same bowl; refrigerate at least 30 minutes.

In a small bowl, make the dressing by combining the next seven ingredients; set aside.

Remove vegetables from refrigerator, and pat dry with paper towels; discard any liquid in bowl. Chop large florets into ¾-inch chunks. Return to bowl with the other vegetables, and add the celery, onion, and chopped eggs.

Coat with the dressing. If desired, cover and refrigerate at least 1 hour or until well-chilled before serving. 🐞

8

SIDES

HONEY-GRILLED CAULIFLOWER

1 cauliflower head, rinsed
  and cut into florets

1 cup honey

Salt and pepper

Nonstick cooking spray

6 wooden skewers (soaked in
  water)

Preheat grill to medium. In a microwavable bowl filled with 1 inch of water, microwave cauliflower on high for 5 minutes or until the florets are crisp on the outside and tender on the inside.

Arrange four florets on each wooden skewer, and spritz with cooking spray. Place skewers over direct heat; turn until there is an even, light charring on each floret.

Brush honey onto the cauliflower; then salt and pepper to taste. Put back on the grill for another minute or until the honey melts into cauliflower. Remove, and serve immediately. 🐛

Quick Meal • 6–12 Servings • Prep: 10 min. • Cook 10–20 min.

259

DEVILLED POTATO BITES

12 to 15 small potatoes
Water
Pinch of coarse salt
2 teaspoons mustard
2 tablespoons mayonnaise
½ cup fresh dill, chopped

Wash each potato, and cut the top off. Cut larger potatoes in half. (See photo.) Bring a large pot of water to a boil, and add salt. Carefully drop potatoes into the pot, and boil for 10 to 20 minutes, depending on size, until easily pierced with a fork.

Scoop the centre of each cooked potato into a bowl. Add mustard and mayonnaise; mix well; and spoon into the potato halves. Top with dill.

"As I looked at these pretty little red and blue-purple potatoes, I decided to do something kind of like a devilled egg that showed off their colours. I separated the blue and red potato fillings and used a couple of whole red potatoes (no skin) to make a little more. These are perfect appetizers for a party, or a great snack or side dish. They're also a great substitute for potato salad at a BBQ."—Diana Johnson, dianasaurdishes.com

9 Desserts

262   Bacon Chocolate Chip Cookies

263   CB's Cranberry-Apple Skillet Crisp

264   CB's Pie-Iron Peach Pie

266   CB's Grilled Pears
      with Honey & Thyme

267   CB's Nutella & Marshmallow
      Quesadillas

268   Chocolate-Chip Cookie-Dough Dip

270   Grilled Brownie Sundae
      with Blueberry Sauce

271   Frozen Strawberry Pie

272   Nectarine Pizza
      with Goat Cheese & Thyme

274   Grilled Pineapple
      with Rum & Coconut

275   Peanut Butter & Marshmallow
      Finger Sandwiches

276   Dulce de Leche Grilled Cheese

(Right) Grilled Brownie Sundae with
Blueberry Sauce, page 270

BACON CHOCOLATE CHIP COOKIES

1 cup all-purpose flour
1 cup bread flour
½ teaspoon salt
½ teaspoon baking soda
1½ cup turbinado sugar or light brown sugar
¾ cup unsalted butter, melted

1 egg
1 egg yolk
⅛ teaspoon cinnamon
1 tablespoon vanilla extract
2 cups semi-sweet chocolate chips or chunks
¼ pound bacon, fried crisp and crumbled

Preheat the grill to 325°F, and set up for indirect cooking. Grease cookie sheets, or line them with parchment paper or baking mats. Sift the flour, salt, and baking soda; set aside.

Using a mixer, combine the sugar and butter; add eggs, cinnamon, and vanilla; and mix until creamy. Blend in the sifted ingredients; then fold in the chocolate chips and crumbled bacon, using a spatula or a wooden spoon.

Drop ¼-cup-size dough balls onto a cookie sheet, spaced about 3 inches apart, and bake for 9 minutes; then turn and bake for an additional 7 to 9 minutes. Let the cookies cool slightly on the sheet for a few minutes before moving them to a rack to finish cooling.

Courtesy of Curt McAdams of the Livefire grilling blog.

8–10 Servings • Prep: 30 min. • Chill: 1 hr. • Grill: 30 min.

263

CB'S CRANBERRY-APPLE SKILLET CRISP

FILLING

1 pound cranberries, fresh or frozen

1¼ cups granulated sugar

3 tablespoons orange peel, grated

¼ cup water

5 pounds apples (combination of Granny Smith, Honey Crisp, or other firm baking apple), peeled, cored, and cut into ½-inch pieces

1 cup raisins

3 tablespoons instant tapioca

1 teaspoon vanilla extract

1 teaspoon nutmeg

1 teaspoon pumpkin pie spice

TOPPING

¾ cup all-purpose flour

½ cup packed light brown sugar

½ cup granulated sugar

1 teaspoon cinnamon, ground

12 tablespoons (1½ sticks) unsalted butter, cut into ½-inch pieces and chilled

¾ cup old-fashioned oats

9

DESSERTS

Simmer the cranberries, ¾ cup of the sugar, grated orange peel, and water in an ovenproof pot over medium-high heat. When the mixture has a jamlike consistency, remove to a bowl.

Add the apple slices, remaining sugar, and raisins to the pot to cook. When the apples have softened, about 5 to 10 minutes, combine them in the bowl with the cranberries. Blend in the remaining filling ingredients.

For the topping: In a food processor, blend the flour, sugars, cinnamon, and butter. Remove to a medium-size bowl. Pour oats into the food processor, and

pulse until they are the texture of coarse crumbs. Combine with the flour mixture, and using your fingers, pinch the topping to make peanut-size clumps. Chill for 1 hour.

Preheat grill to medium high. Pour filling into a greased cast-iron skillet; scatter topping over it.

Bake over indirect heat, hood closed, for about 30 minutes. (Rotate the pan after 15 minutes for even baking.) The crisp is done when the juices are bubbling and the topping is brown. Serve hot with whipped cream or vanilla ice cream. ✤

⏱ **Quick Snack • 2 Servings • Prep: 5 min. • Grill: 5 min.**

CB'S PIE-IRON PEACH PIE

Canola oil spray

1 can (8 ounces) sliced peaches, drained

2 teaspoons brown sugar, plus extra for topping

2 teaspoons butter

Lemon zest to taste

4 slices sandwich bread

Cinnamon

1 pie iron

A pie iron is an old-fashioned cooking device with a long, wooden handle that is used to make grilled sandwiches or pies over an open fire. They're pretty easy to find on-line or at a camping supply store.

Preheat the grill to medium. Get the pie iron hot by placing it, closed, over the heat for 5 minutes on each side. Then open it, and lightly grease the inside with canola oil spray.

Mix together the peaches, brown sugar, butter, and lemon zest. For each pie, place a slice of bread on one side of the iron. Add about 2 to 3 table-spoons of the peach mixture to the centre of the slice. Top with a second slice of bread. Close the pie iron, and return to the grill. Heat for about 5 minutes or until the bread toasts.

Remove, and sprinkle with brown sugar and cinnamon before serving. 🍃

CB'S GRILLED PEARS WITH HONEY & THYME

Canola oil spray

**1 ripe pear, cored and
   sliced into eighths**

1 tablespoon honey

**1 teaspoon fresh
   thyme, chopped**

This easy dessert will cook quickly, especially if the grill is already hot.

Preheat the grill to medium. Spray the pear slices with canola oil, and grill, turning as needed, until they are slightly soft and grill marks appear. Arrange four slices in a fan shape on each plate. Drizzle with honey, and sprinkle with thyme. Serve with a dollop of ice cream or whipped cream if desired. 🥄

CB'S NUTELLA & MARSHMALLOW QUESADILLAS

4 soft flour tortillas

8 tablespoons Nutella or thick chocolate sauce

8 tablespoons marshmallow creme

2 tablespoons butter, melted (½ tablespoon per tortilla)

2 teaspoons cinnamon

2 teaspoons sugar

Preheat grill to low. Warm, but do not brown, the tortillas; then lay them flat on a work surface. Spread 2 tablespoons of Nutella and 2 tablespoons of marshmallow creme on top of each one; fold them in half; and return them to the grill. Cover with an inverted aluminum pan for quick heating.

When the Nutella and marshmallow are sufficiently heated and oozing slightly out of the tortillas, remove the quesadillas from the grill, and quickly brush them with melted butter. Finish with a sprinkling of cinnamon and sugar. Serve warm.

CHOCOLATE-CHIP COOKIE-DOUGH DIP

½ cup (1 stick) butter
⅓ cup brown sugar
1 teaspoon vanilla extract
1 package (8 ounces) cream cheese
½ cup confectioner's sugar
¾ cup semi-sweet mini
   chocolate chips

Fresh fruit for dipping
   (such as strawberries,
   pineapple, peaches,
   melon, grapes, or
   bananas)
1 package vanilla wafers
   or graham crackers

9

DESSERTS

Melt the butter with the brown sugar in a small saucepan over medium heat. Stir continuously until the brown sugar dissolves. Remove from heat; whisk in vanilla extract; and set aside to cool.

Using a hand mixer, beat the cream cheese and confectioner's sugar for 1 minute. Slowly add the cooled butter mixture, and beat 1 more minute. Stir in the chocolate chips, using a spatula or a wooden spoon. Transfer the dip to a serving bowl, and refrigerate at least 1 hour and as long as 24 hours. (Remove the dip from the refrigerator about 15 to 30 minutes before serving to allow it to soften.)

Garnish with additional chocolate chips if desired. Serve with fresh fruit and vanilla wafers or graham crackers. ❧

GRILLED BROWNIE SUNDAE WITH BLUEBERRY SAUCE

BLUEBERRY SAUCE

¼ cup sugar

2 tablespoons lemon juice

2 cups blueberries, fresh or frozen

SUNDAE & TOPPINGS

Vanilla ice cream or frozen yogurt

Whipped cream (optional)

Chopped nuts (optional)

BROWNIES

½ cup sugar

2 tablespoons butter

2 tablespoons water

1½ cups semi-sweet chocolate chips

2 eggs, slightly beaten

½ teaspoon vanilla

⅔ cup flour

¼ teaspoon baking soda

½ teaspoon salt

In a small saucepan, bring the blueberry sauce ingredients to a boil. Stir for 1 minute, and remove from heat. Set aside. Bring sugar, butter, and water to a boil in a medium saucepan over low heat; remove from heat, and add chocolate chips, stirring until melted. Blend in eggs and vanilla. In a separate bowl, combine flour, baking soda, and salt; then add to the chocolate mixture.

Preheat grill to medium. Spoon batter into an oiled 9 x 9-inch metal pan. Bake over indirect heat with the lid down for 30 minutes or until a toothpick inserted into the centre of the brownies comes out clean. Cool before slicing.

Scoop ice cream onto each brownie; sprinkle with nuts if desired; and drizzle sauce over the top.

FROZEN STRAWBERRY PIE

CRUST

4 tablespoons sugar

14 chocolate graham crackers, crushed

1 tablespoon butter, melted

FILLING

12 ounces white chocolate chips

6 egg whites

2 cups heavy cream, sweetened

1 teaspoon vanilla

1 pound fresh strawberries

1 cup strawberry glaze or jelly

Combine sugar with chocolate graham crackers; add butter; press into a springform pan; and bake at 375°F for 6 to 7 minutes. Set aside to cool.

Melt white chocolate chips in a double boiler, and let cool slightly. Beat egg whites until stiff, and then set aside. Whip cream with vanilla; set aside.

Wash the strawberries; pat dry with paper towels; and chop, reserving a few for garnish. Place into a bowl with the strawberry jelly. Fold the egg whites into the whipped cream; then fold in the strawberry mixture, followed by the white chocolate. Pour the filling into the pie crust, and freeze.

Remove the pie from the freezer about 15 minutes before serving to soften slightly. Garnish with the reserved strawberries. ❧

NECTARINE PIZZA WITH GOAT CHEESE & THYME

¼ cup water

3 tablespoons honey

Few sprigs thyme

2 teaspoons balsamic vinegar

Prepared pizza dough (one-fourth package per pie)

Olive oil, for brushing

¾ cup goat cheese, crumbled

2 to 3 nectarines, thinly sliced

Coarse salt, to taste

Preheat grill to high. Heat water until boiling; then add honey and thyme. When the liquid is reduced by half, stir in the balsamic vinegar; set aside.

Divide the dough into four equal parts. On a well-floured surface, roll out one-quarter of the dough into an 8-inch round "pie." Refrigerate until ready to grill. (If you will only be making one pie, refrigerate the rest of the dough for up to two days.)

Brush one side of the pie lightly with olive oil, and place it, oiled side down, directly on the grill. After about 1 minute, rotate the pie 180 degrees to cook it evenly. Dough will begin to puff or bubble and brown in about 2 to 3 minutes.

Slide the pie off the grill and onto a flat surface, such as a cutting board, and flip it over. Reduce the heat to low. Lightly brush the pie with olive oil. Sprinkle with the goat cheese; then top with the nectarines. Return it to the grill, and close grill lid. Let the dough become crisp and the cheese soften, about 3 minutes.

Remove from grill, and drizzle immediately with the honey-balsamic reduction and a pinch of coarse salt. You can garnish with more crumbled cheese if desired. Slice into 4 wedges and serve warm. 🌱

Courtesy of Liz Vidyarthi at zested.wordpress.com

8 servings shown

GRILLED PINEAPPLE WITH RUM & COCONUT

1 ripe pineapple, peeled and cut
  crosswise into 6 slices

2 to 3 tablespoons dark rum

1 teaspoon granulated sugar

1 cup whipped cream

¼ cup shredded coconut, toasted

With or without a scoop of ice cream, this grilled dessert will be a huge hit at your next outdoor party.

Pour the rum and sugar in a bowl with the pineapple. Mix to coat the slices evenly; cover with plastic wrap; and let it rest for 3 to 5 minutes. Preheat the grill to medium high.

Lightly sear the pineapple directly over the heat for about 10 minutes, using tongs to turn once. Make sure the fruit does not become overly charred.

Remove pineapple from grill, and top with whipped cream and coconut. You can also add a heaping scoop of your favourite ice cream if desired. ☙

PEANUT BUTTER & MARSHMALLOW FINGER SANDWICHES

½ cup heavy cream

2 ounces semi-sweet chocolate, chopped

1 pound cake

½ cup peanut butter

⅓ cup marshmallow creme

2 tablespoons unsalted butter, melted

In a microwave-safe bowl heat cream and chocolate on high for 30 seconds; stir; heat for about another 30 seconds, making sure that cream does not boil over. Let the mixture stand until the chocolate is melted, about 5 minutes, stirring occasionally.

Preheat the grill to medium high. Using a knife, trim off the top of the cake so that it is even on all sides. Cut the cake in half horizontally. Spread the peanut butter on one half and the marshmallow on the other. Put the two halves together, and brush the top and bottom with butter.

Grill, turning once, until both sides are warm and golden, about 3 to 5 minutes. Transfer to a platter, and cut the cake into thin finger sandwiches. Serve with the chocolate dipping sauce. ☙

🕐 **Quick Snack** • **4 Servings** • **Prep: 15 min.** • **Grill: 3 min.**

DULCE DE LECHE GRILLED CHEESE

1 teaspoon vanilla extract
8 ounces mascarpone cheese, room temperature
8 slices cinnamon-raisin bread
6 tablespoons butter, softened
4 tablespoons raspberry preserves
1 jar (14 to 16 ounces) of dulce de leche*
Fresh red raspberries for garnish, optional
Whipped cream for garnish, optional

*Dulce de leche is a thick, creamy spread made from caramelized milk and sugar. It is much-loved in Latin American countries.

In a bowl, stir vanilla into the mascarpone. Stirring will make the cheese lighter and easier to spread. Butter one side of each bread slice.

Preheat grill to medium. Place the bread slices, buttered side down, in a cast-iron or other heavy skillet over direct heat. Grill until golden brown and crisp, about 3 minutes. Place the bread, toasted side down, on a clean work surface. Spread 1 tablespoon of raspberry preserves, 2 tablespoons of mascarpone cheese, and 1 tablespoon dulce de leche over each slice. Top with another piece of bread, toasted side up, and drizzle with more dulce de leche. Garnish with fresh raspberries or whipped cream if desired. 🌿

10 Marinades, Sauces & Rubs

280   Plum Marinade

281   Captain Jessie's
      Jamaican Jerk Marinade

281   Three-Way Marinade

282   Korean Kalbi Marinade

282   Garlic-Yogurt Marinade

283   Savannah Smoker's
      Special Pork Brine

284   Spicy Grilled-Veggie
      Marinade

285   CB's Herbed Poultry Rub

285   CB's Lavender Rub
      for Lamb

285   CB's Pacific Northwest
      Seasoning for Game

286   CB's Wet Salt Rub for Fish

286   Jan's Dry Rub

287   Chili-Cinnamon Rub
      for Chicken

287   Savannah Smoker's
      Mohunken Rub

288   CB's Chimichurri Sauce

288   CB's Curry, Garlic &
      Black-Pepper Sauce

288   CB's Hot Thai-Style
      Dipping Sauce

289   CB's Filipino Adobo Sauce

290   Provençal Citrus-Tarragon
      Sauce

290   Chipotle BBQ Sauce

290   Jalapeños in Adobo Sauce

291   Madras Curry Dip

291   Dried-Cherry Chutney

291   Green-Chile Pesto

292   Moroccan Sauce

292   Creamy Gorgonzola Sauce

293   Maître d' Butter

(Right) Jan's Dry Rub, page 286

PLUM MARINADE

Yield: approx. ¾ cup
Prep: 5 min.
Marinate: 4–6 hr.
Use with: steak, chicken

½ cup plum preserves
3 tablespoons green onion, minced
2 tablespoons white vinegar
2 tablespoons hoisin sauce
2 teaspoons fresh ginger, minced
1 teaspoon dry mustard
½ teaspoon ground red pepper
Green onion, minced (optional)

In a bowl, whisk together all ingredients until completely emulsified. Marinate meat in a sealable plastic bag or covered container in the refrigerator.

CAPTAIN JESSIE'S JAMAICAN JERK MARINADE

Yield: 1 cup
Prep: 10 min.
Marinate: 4 hr.–overnight
Use with: meat
　　and poultry

1 white onion, chopped
½ cup scallions, chopped
2 teaspoons fresh thyme
　　or
1 teaspoon dried thyme

Spices from the Caribbean give this marinade a kick to heat up your mouth!

1 whole Scotch Bonnet or
　　habanero pepper, seeded
　　and chopped
1 teaspoon coarse salt
2 teaspoons light brown
　　sugar
1 teaspoon allspice
½ teaspoon ground
　　nutmeg
½ teaspoon ground
　　cinnamon
1 teaspoon black pepper
1 tablespoon soy sauce
1 tablespoon
　　Worcestershire sauce
1 tablespoon vegetable oil
1 tablespoon apple cider
　　vinegar

In a food processor or blender, add the onions, scallions, thyme, and peppers. Stir in the other spices, and pulse until mixture becomes a light slurry. Marinate meat in a sealable plastic bag or covered container in the refrigerator.

Note: when working with fresh peppers, use food-safe gloves; do not touch your eyes, mouth, or nose until you have washed your hands with soap and water.

10

MARINADES, SAUCES & RUBS

THREE-WAY MARINADE

Yield: 1 cup
Prep: 5 min.
Marinate: 4–12 hr.
Use with: flank
　　steak, London broil

CLASSIC MARINADE

1 cup prepared Italian-
　　style vinaigrette
1 teaspoon garlic, minced
¼ teaspoon black pepper,
　　coarsely ground

MEXICAN VARIATION

To classic marinade, add
1 tablespoon fresh lime
　　juice
1 teaspoon cumin, ground
1 teaspoon chipotle chili
　　powder
½ teaspoon salt

ASIAN VARIATION

To classic marinade, add
2 tablespoons reduced-sodium
　　soy sauce
2 tablespoons fresh ginger,
　　minced
1 tablespoon packed brown
　　sugar
1 tablespoon sesame seeds,
　　toasted
1½ teaspoons dark sesame oil

In a bowl, whisk together all ingredients until completely emulsified. Marinate meat in a sealable plastic bag or covered container in the refrigerator.

KOREAN KALBI MARINADE

Yield: approx. 1 cup
Prep: 5 min.
Marinate: overnight
Use with: short ribs

1 tablespoon soy sauce
¼ cup sugar
2 tablespoons honey
¼ cup Chinese rice wine
2 teaspoons Korean toasted-sesame oil
2 green onions, minced
4 teaspoons (1 to 2 cloves) garlic, chopped
2 tablespoons roasted sesame seeds
2 tablespoons water
1 teaspoon ginger root, grated

The recipe is a classic one used for most Korean kalbi (grilled short ribs).

Mix ingredients in nonreactive bowl. Use some as an overnight marinade for meat—placed in a sealable plastic bag or covered container in the refrigerator—and reserve some for glazing during the final 5 to 7 minutes of cooking.

GARLIC-YOGURT MARINADE

Yield: 1 cup
Prep: 5 min.
Marinate: 2–4 hr.
Use with: steak

1 cup plain yogurt
¼ cup chopped fresh parsley
2 tablespoons lemon juice
1 tablespoon sweet paprika
1 tablespoon minced garlic
1 teaspoon salt

In a bowl, whisk together all ingredients until completely emulsified. Marinate meat in a sealable plastic bag or covered container in the refrigerator.

SAVANNAH SMOKER'S SPECIAL PORK BRINE

Yield: 32+ cups

Prep: 5 min.

Use with: pork

32 cups water

2 cups dark brown sugar

2 cups coarse salt

¼ cup ground ginger

¼ cup garlic powder

½ cup apple cider vinegar

¼ cup ground cumin

4 large sprigs fresh rosemary

¼ cup black pepper, coarsely ground

2 tablespoons Worcestershire sauce

2 tablespoons Tabasco sauce

2 medium-size lemons chopped, squeezed, and smashed

Fill a large pot with the water. Then add the remainder of the ingredients, and stir. Brine meat overnght or for 24 hours.

Submitted by Sizzle on the Grill contributor "Savannah Smoker."

10

SPICY GRILLED-VEGGIE MARINADE

Yield: 1½ cups
Prep: 5 min.
Marinate: 1 hr.
Use with: vegetables

⅔ cup white wine vinegar
½ cup soy sauce
2 tablespoons fresh ginger, minced
2 tablespoons olive oil
2 tablespoons sesame oil
2 large cloves garlic, minced
2 teaspoons Tabasco sauce

In a bowl, whisk together all ingredients until completely emulsified. Marinate in a sealable plastic bag or covered container in the refrigerator.

CB'S HERBED POULTRY RUB

Prep: 5 min.
Use with: chicken, turkey

Equal parts fresh parsley, sage, rosemary, and thyme, finely chopped
½ part coarse salt

Blend ingredients in a spice mill or with a mortar and pestle until the mixture becomes a coarse paste.

CB'S LAVENDER RUB FOR LAMB

Prep: 5 min.
Use with: lamb

3 parts lavender flowers
1 part fresh lemon sage, finely chopped
1 part fresh rosemary, chopped
½ part coarse salt
½ part cumin, ground

Blend ingredients in a spice mill or with a mortar and pestle until the mixture becomes a coarse paste.

CB'S PACIFIC NORTHWEST SEASONING FOR GAME

Prep: 5 min.
Use with: duck, pheasant, chukar, quail

2 parts dried cherries or cranberries
1 part rosemary
1 part orange zest
½ part coarse salt

Blend ingredients in a spice mill or with a mortar and pestle until the mixture becomes a coarse paste.

CB'S WET SALT RUB FOR FISH

Prep: 5 min.
Use with: fish

1 part coarse salt
1 part fresh lemon thyme,
    finely minced
½ part anchovy paste
2½ parts dry white vermouth

Whisk together all ingredients
until blended.

JAN'S DRY RUB

Yield: approx. 3 cups
Prep: 5 min.
Use with: pork ribs,
    chicken

*Seasoned salt:
2 tablespoons salt
2 teaspoons sugar
½ teaspoon paprika
¼ teaspoon tumeric
¼ teaspoon onion
    powder
¼ teaspoon garlic
    powder
¼ teaspoon cornstarch

1¼ cups sugar
¼ cup seasoned salt*
¼ cup garlic salt
¼ cup + 1½ teaspoon celery
    salt
¼ cup onion salt
½ cup paprika
3 tablespoons chili powder
2 tablespoons black pepper
1 tablespoon lemon pepper
2 teaspoons celery seed
2 teaspoons dry sage, ground
1 teaspoon dry mustard
½ teaspoon dry thyme, ground
½ teaspoon cayenne pepper

Blend all ingredients in a
large bowl.

*"Sizzle on the Grill" contributor KyNola
says his wife, Jan, came up with this
recipe to match a secret version at a
local BBQ restaurant.*

CHILI-CINNAMON RUB FOR CHICKEN

Yield: approx. ¼ cup
Prep: 5 min.
Use with: chicken

2 teaspoons ancho chili powder
2 teaspoons cinnamon, ground
2 teaspoons cumin, ground
4 teaspoons fresh thyme
2 teaspoons salt
2 teaspoons brown sugar

Blend the spices, salt, and sugar
in a small bowl.

Ancho chili powder works well in this recipe, but you can use chipotle or other, milder chili powders.

SAVANNAH SMOKER'S MOHUNKEN RUB

Yield: 3+ cups
Prep: 5 min.
Use with: pork

½ cup brown sugar
1 cup white sugar
1 cup paprika
¼ cup garlic powder
¼ cup coarse salt
2 tablespoons chili powder
2 teaspoons cayenne pepper
4 teaspoons black pepper
2 teaspoons dried oregano
 or Italian seasoning
2 teaspoons cumin
1 tablespoon mustard power
Yellow mustard to taste

Blend all ingredients in a
small bowl.

CB'S CHIMICHURRI SAUCE

Yield: 1½ to 2 cups
Prep: 10 min.
Use with: steak, seafood,
    chicken

2 garlic cloves
3 tablespoons fresh thyme
½ cup fresh parsley or cilantro

2 tablespoons fresh mint
1 tablespoon fresh oregano
2 tablespoons fresh chervil
Juice of 1 lime
¼ cup red pepper flakes or
    jalapeño peppers, minced
1 cup extra-virgin olive oil

Mince herbs. Combine with lime juice and pepper flakes or jalapeños in a food processor, and pulse to blend thoroughly; then drizzle in the olive oil, and pulse to form a light, semi-thick sauce. Refrigerate for at least 1 hour to allow flavours to meld.

CB'S CURRY, GARLIC & BLACK-PEPPER SAUCE

Yield: ¾ cup
Prep: 15 min.
Cook: 15–20 min.
Use with: chicken wings,
    pork chops

½ cup tamari or soy sauce
¼ cup clarified butter*
1 teaspoon curry spice
2 tablespoons garlic, finely minced
½ teaspoon black pepper, ground
½ teaspoon ginger powder
2 tablespoons dark brown sugar

Combine ingredients, in order, in a small nonreactive sauce pan. Simmer, stirring, until mixture reduces to a gravy-like consistency.

*To clarify butter, simmer it until it forms a white foamy residue on top. Skim off the foam, using a ladle. What's left should be a clear golden liquid.

CB'S HOT THAI-STYLE DIPPING SAUCE

Yield: 3+ cups
Prep: 10 min.
Cook: 2–5 min.
Use with: chicken wings

2 cups chunky peanut butter
½ cup coconut milk or
    coconut slurry
3 tablespoons water
1 tablespoon lime rind,
    grated
¼ cup fresh lime juice

3 tablespoons tamari or soy sauce
1 tablespoon anchovy paste
Anchovy fillets, finely minced
2 tablespoons Worcestershire
    sauce
2 tablespoons Tabasco sauce
1 tablespoon fresh ginger, minced,
    or 1 teaspoon ginger powder
¼ teaspoon white or black pepper
4 medium garlic cloves, finely
    minced, or 2 tablespoons garlic
    powder

¼ cup fresh mint, finely chopped
¼ cup fresh cilantro, finely chopped

Heat peanut butter in the microwave on low until it is a bit runny—but not too warm. Stir in the coconut milk or coconut slurry. Add the remaining ingredients, in order, slowly folding everything together using a spatula. Add extra mint and cilantro to taste.

CB'S FILIPINO ADOBO SAUCE

Yield: 3+ cups
Prep: 5 min.
Cook: 30–40 min. (until sauce thickens)
Use with: chicken, pork

1 cup soy sauce
½ cup rice wine vinegar (may substitute apple cider vinegar)
1 tablespoon garlic, minced
1 tablespoon fresh ginger, minced
2 cups coconut milk

1 teaspoon smoked paprika
1 small jalapeño, diced
1 cup water
Whole chicken, cut into eighths, or 2-pound pork loin, cubed
1 tablespoon lime juice, freshly squeezed

Combine the soy sauce, vinegar, garlic, ginger, ½ cup of the coconut milk, paprika, jalapeño, and water in a deep pot, and slowly simmer on low for about 5 to 10 minutes until ingredients are blended and sauce is heated evenly.

Add meat; cook for about 15 to 20 minutes. When it starts to get firm, remove meat from pot; pat dry with a paper towel; and reserve to finish on the grill.

Turn up the heat a bit, and add the remaining coconut milk. Reduce until the sauce has the consistency of runny cake batter. Add lime juice, and strain before serving.

My friend, Chris, an avid griller who lives in Hawaii, prepares some of the tastiest Filipino food. Adobo is a traditional Filipino dish in which meat or poultry is dipped in a rich, sour-spicy sauce.—CB

PROVENÇAL CITRUS-TARRAGON SAUCE

Yield: 1½ cups
Prep: 5 min.
Use with: halibut, salmon
   crab, scallops

¼ cup apple cider vinegar
2 tablespoons Dijon mustard
⅓ cup olive oil

2 tablespoons honey
⅓ cup fresh tarragon leaves
1 can (11 ounces) mandarin orange
   slices, drained, or 2 fresh
   mandarin oranges,
   peeled, sectioned, and seeded
½ teaspoon coarse salt

Combine the vinegar and mustard in a blender or food processor, and pulse until smooth; slowly add olive oil until fully incorporated. Add the honey, tarragon, and oranges; blend or pulse again until almost smooth. Salt to taste.

CHIPOTLE BBQ SAUCE

Yield: 2½ cups
Prep: 5 min.
Cook: 25 min.
Use with: meat or poultry

2 tablespoons vegetable oil
1 cup chopped red onion
1 small shallot, minced
1½ tablespoons tomato paste

5 garlic cloves, minced
¾ cup dry red wine
½ can (7 ounces) of chipotle chilies
   in adobo
1 cup ketchup
¼ cup apple cider vinegar
2 tablespoons dark brown sugar
2 teaspoons Worcestershire sauce
¼ teaspoon cumin, ground

Heat oil in saucepan over medium heat. Add onion and shallot, and sauté for about 4 minutes or until soft. Blend in tomato paste, stirring for 2 minutes. Add garlic, stir for another 2 minutes; add wine and chipotle chilies; simmer for 2 minutes. Add remaining ingredients; simmer for 15 minutes, stirring often. Season with salt and pepper. Remove from heat, and cool slightly.

JALAPEÑOS IN ADOBO SAUCE

Yield: 3 cups
Prep: 10–15 min.
Use with: poultry or pork

10 jalapeño peppers, smoked
   or grilled, split, and seeded
1 can (18 ounces) tomatoes,
   diced
10 large garlic cloves, crushed
   and minced

2 tablespoons fresh cilantro,
chopped
2 tablespoons apple cider vinegar
1 tablespoon red pepper flakes
1 teaspoon cumin
1 teaspoon oregano
1 teaspoon coarse salt
Juice from ½ large lime
Juice from ½ large lemon
6 tablespoons olive oil
Pinch of brown sugar, if necessary

After preparing the jalapeño peppers, mix all ingredients, and seal in nonreactive container. Sauce can be kept in the refrigerator for several weeks.

MADRAS CURRY DIP

Yield: 1½ cups
Prep: 5 min.
Use with: fish fillets, crab, scallops

1 cup plain Greek-style yogurt
3 tablespoons fresh lime juice
1 tablespoon curry powder

2 to 3 tablespoons mango chutney
1 teaspoon garlic, minced
2 to 3 tablespoons fresh cilantro, chopped
1 green onion, sliced
½ teaspoon hot pepper sauce, or to taste

In a small bowl, whisk together the yogurt, lime juice, and curry powder. Stir in the chutney, garlic, cilantro, green onion, and hot sauce until all ingredients are blended. Cover, and refrigerate until ready to serve.

DRIED-CHERRY CHUTNEY

Yield: 3 cups
Prep: 10 min.
Cook: 23–25 min.
Use with: pork

1½ cups port or sherry
1½ cups dried cherries
1 large shallot, minced
2 cloves garlic, minced
1 teaspoon peppercorns, crushed

4 whole cloves, crushed, or ¼ teaspoon ground cloves
4 to 5 allspice berries, crushed, or ¼ teaspoon ground allspice
1 teaspoon whole cumin seeds, crushed
1 teaspoon coriander seeds, crushed
2 tablespoons to ¼ cup fruit preserves

Heat wine in a microwave on high for 30 seconds; make sure wine is not boiling; then pour it into a bowl over cherries. Let it sit for 1 hour.

Over medium-high heat, sauté shallots and garlic until transparent. Add the wine, cherries, and spices. Reduce heat to medium; simmer for 3 or 4 minutes; add preserves; and cook until thickened, about 20 minutes.

GREEN-CHILE PESTO

Yield: approx. 2 cups
Prep: 15 min.
Use with: meat, poultry, fish

6 large, long green chilies or 4 medium poblano chilies, roasted, peeled, and seeded
¾ cup pine nuts
2 cups lightly packed fresh basil, leaves and stems

6 garlic cloves, peeled and chopped
1 cup extra-virgin olive oil
¾ cup Parmesan cheese, grated
½ cup Romano cheese, grated
½ teaspoon salt
½ teaspoon black pepper, ground

Chop the chilies, and set aside.

In a skillet over medium heat, toast the pine nuts; then let them cool to room temperature.

In a food processor, combine chilies, pine nuts, basil, and garlic. Process, scraping down sides of the bowl once or twice, until smooth. Drizzle in olive oil. Transfer the mixture to a bowl, and blend in the cheese, salt, and pepper. Use immediately, or cover and refrigerate for up to 3 days; freeze (without cheese) for up to 3 months.

MOROCCAN SAUCE

Yield: approx. 1 cup
Prep: 5 min.
Cook: 12–13 min.
Use with: cod, halibut, salmon, crab, scallops

1½ tablespoons garlic, minced
½ cup olive oil
½ cup unsalted butter
2 tablespoons harissa
1½ tablespoons fresh lemon juice or 1 to 2 tablespoons sherry

Coarse salt, to taste
Black pepper, cracked, to taste
2 tablespoons Italian (flat-leaf) parsley, chopped
2 tablespoons salted almonds, chopped (optional)

Place the garlic, olive oil, and butter in a small saucepan over low heat. Cook until the garlic begins to soften, about 10 minutes. Add the harissa and lemon juice, blending with a whisk; continue cooking 2 to 3 minutes more. Season to taste with salt and pepper. Garnish with parsley and, if desired, almonds.

Discover the flavours of North Africa in this zesty sauce made using fiery-hot harissa, a traditional seasoning for couscous. If harissa is not available, substitute 1 tablespoon of pimenton (smoked Spanish paprika).

CREAMY GORGONZOLA SAUCE

Yield: 2+ cups
Prep: 5 min.
Chill: 30 min. to 1 hr.
Use with: steaks, vegetables

1 cup reduced-fat cream cheese, softened
1 cup plain non-fat yogurt
½ cup Gorgonzola cheese, crumbled
¼ cup onion, minced
1 teaspoon pepper

Combine all ingredients in a small bowl; mix well. Chill for 30 minutes to 1 hour before serving.

MAÎTRE D' BUTTER

Yield: 2 cups
Prep: 10 min.
Refrigerate: 1 hr. or overnight
Use with: steak, chicken, fish, vegetables

1 pound (4 sticks) unsalted butter, softened
3 tablespoons lemon juice (about 1 lemon)
¼ cup Italian (flat-leaf) parsley, chopped, or other herbs or spices as desired

In a large bowl, mash the butter. Add lemon juice and parsley and, using a wooden spoon, blend.

Spread a 1-foot-square piece of plastic wrap across a work surface, and scoop the butter mixture on top. Gently wrap the plastic film around the butter, forming a cylinder. Tie off the ends of the wrap with string or a twist tie. Chill or freeze until needed.

Maître d' Butter is simply softened butter, with seasonings, that is rolled and chilled. You can serve it in slices on top of grilled steaks, fish, or vegetables. Experiment by combining your favourite herbs and spices.

10

MARINADES, SAUCES & RUBS

RESOURCES

This list of manufacturers and associations is meant to be a general guide to additional industry and product-related sources. It is not intended as a listing of products and manufacturers represented by the photographs in this book.

Companies and Associations

Butterball

www.butterball.com

The company provides recipes, tips, and ideas, and product information on its Web site.

Canadian Beef

www.beefinfo.org

Recipes, information, preparation tips, cooking lessons, and more from the Canadian Cattleman's Association

Char-Broil

www.charbroil.com

Official Web site for the Char-Broil company.

Chicken Farmers of Canada

www.chicken.ca

The Chicken Farmers of Canada offer nutritional and food-safety tips, recipes, and information on its Web site.

Christopher Ranch

www.christopherranch.com

Christopher Ranch provides product information and recipes on its Web site.

Food Safety

www.foodsafety.gc.ca

The Government of Canada's official food safety website provides information on safe preparation and storage, recalls, food allergies, and public health.

Lean on Lamb

www.leanonlamb.com

The Tri-Lamb group offers nutritional information, preparation and cooking tips, and recipes on its Web site.

Litehouse Foods

www.litehousefoods.com

The company's Web site features recipes and product information.

Manitoba Chicken Producers

www.chicken.mb.ca

The Manitoba Chicken Producers provide culinary inspiration and information on its Web site.

Mann's Fresh Vegetables

www.broccoli.com

The company's Web site features product information and recipes.

Marie's

www.maries.com

The company's Web site features product information and recipes.

Ocean Mist Farms

www.oceanmist.com

Ocean Mist Farms provides recipes, videos, and nutrition information on its Web site.

Perdue

www.perdue.com

Perdue provides recipes, information, and tips on its Web site.

Pillsbury

www.pillsbury.com

The company's Web site features recipes, holiday cooking guides, and product information.

Potatoes Goodness Unearthed

www.healthypotato.com

Recipes and information about healthy eating.

Put Pork on Your Fork

www.putporkonyourfork.com

Pork Marketing Canada's guide to everything you need to know about cooking and enjoying pork, including nutritional information, safety tips, recipes, and more.

SeaChoice

www.seachoice.org

Canada's most comprehensive sustainable seafood program provides resources for consumers, including recipes.

Sizzle on the Grill

www.sizzleonthegrill.com

Char-Broil-sponsored newsletter and Web site featuring grilling tips and recipes.

Tabasco

www.tabasco.com

The company's Web site features product information, recipes, and merchandise.

The Turkey Farmers of Canada

www.turkeyfarmersofcanada.ca

Consumers are welcome to enjoy recipes, look up nutritional facts and information, and explore preparation and serving tips.

The Turkey Farmers of Ontario

www.turkeyfarmers.on.ca

The organization-sponsored Web site provides recipes, history, and general information.

Tyson Foods

www.tyson.com

Provides recipes and product information.

Food Blogs and Recipe Databases

Amanda's Cookin'

www.amandascookin.com

Amanda Formaro shares her home cooking and craft ideas.

Appoggiatura

http://haleysuzanne.wordpress.com

Haley Johnson is a home cook with a keen appreciation for regional cooking.

Canadian Living

www.canadianliving.com/food

An index of recipes for every season and occasion, from one of Canada's leading magazines.

Closet Cooking

http://closetcooking.blogspot.com

Kevin Lynch searches for and creates his own new recipes in his closet-size kitchen in Toronto.

Couture au Chocolat

http://coutureauchocolat.com

Bay area residents Vicky Chen and Liza Mock share an endless curiosity and love of new foods on their food and fashion blog.

Cookthink

www.cookthink.com

Features a recipe database and kitchen tips.

Dana McCauley's Food Blog

www.homemakers.com/blog/danasblog

A collection of blogs and recipes from the former food editor of *Homemaker's* magazine and a frequent guest on *Canada AM, Breakfast Television, The Today Show, and CNN.*

Danica's Daily

http://danicasdaily.com

This blog focuses on recipes for a healthy lifestyle.

Dianasaur Dishes

www.dianasaurdishes.com

Diana Johnson shares recipes for healthy meals that are affordable and easy to make.

Easy and Tasty Food

http://easyandtastyfood.com

Judy Cheske enjoys classic dishes, as well as exploring undiscovered meals from all over the world to create recipes that are both easy and tasty.

Food & Drink

www.lcbo.ca/fooddrink

Entertain in style with this tremendous database of recipes from the magazine of Ontario's Liquor Control Board.

FoodBuzz

www.foodbuzz.com

A community that publishes food blogs, recipes, restaurant reviews, and photos.

Food Network

www.foodnetwork.ca/recipes

Recipes, menus, and food information.

Marcia's Kitchen

www.happyinthekitchen.com

Marcia Franknberg's main inspiration for cooking is hearing her daughter say, "Feed me Mama!"

Mochachocolata Rita

http://mochachocolatarita.blogspot.com

Rita Suttarno, living in Hong Kong, shares her eating, cooking, and baking experiences.

Not Eating Out in New York

www.noteatingoutinny.com

Cathy Erway is the author of *The Art of Eating In: How I Learned to Stop Spending and Love the Stove,* which is based on her two-year mission to forego restaurant food, and her blog, which is filled with original recipes for the busy-but-thrifty.

Poblano Pepper Recipes

http://poblanorecipes.blogspot.com

A collection of recipes featuring poblano peppers.

The Purple Foodie

www.purplefoodie.com

Shaheen Peerbhai of Bombay chronicles her cooking and baking experiences.

SippitySup

www.sippitysup.com

Greg Henry shares his interest in recipes that feature familiar ingredients handled in a fresh way.

Ted's World Famous BBQ

www.tedreader.com

Everything you need to know about grilling from an award-winning chef, food entertainer, and author.

The Spice House

www.thespicehouse.com

The spice merchant's Web site offers merchandise, spice history, and a recipe collection.

Zested

http://zested.wordpress.com

Liz Vidyarthi, a freelance food photographer, chronicles her experiences eating in New York and traveling in East Africa.

"Sizzle on the Grill" Contributors

The BBQ Grail

http://thebbqgrail.com

Larry Gaian, food author, posts recipes and barbecue information on his site.

Cape Cod Barbecue

www.capecodbbq.com

Mike Stines, contributing guest chef for "Sizzle on the Grill," is the executive chef at a Cape Cod restaurant specializing in barbecue and grilled foods.

Cooking Outdoors

www.cooking-outdoors.com

Gary House, "The Outdoor Cook," shares his adventures while cooking over an open fire.

Dr. BBQ

www.drbbq.com

The Web site of food personality Ray Lampe, where he posts information, recipes, and answers to questions.

FireCooker

www.firecooker.com

A site built by and for barbecue fans, with recipes, grilling techniques, and forums.

Girls on a Grill

www.girlsonagrill.com

These guest chefs are sisters who share their recipes featuring fresh ingredients cooked over an open fire.

LiveFire

http://livefireonline.com

Curt McAdams explores barbecuing and grilling, in addition to local foods and markets, breads, and other baking.

Patio Daddio BBQ

www.patiodaddiobbq.com

Member of the Kansas City Barbeque Society and regular contributor to "Sizzle on the Grill" John Dawson shares his barbecue thoughts and recipes.

INDEX

A

Adobo Sauce
    CB's Filipino, 289
    Jalapeños in, 290
Almonds
    in Carrots & Raisins Revisited, 235
    in CB's Grilled Pear & Gorgonzola Salad, 238
    CB's Nut-Crusted Ribs with Bourbon Mop Sauce, 132–33
    in Harvest Slaw with Sweet Potatoes, 249
Appetizers, 28–67
    Avocado Chimichurri Bruschetta, 45
    The Big Easy Yardbird Wings, 65
    CB's Avocado, Crab & Jalapeño Roll-Ups, 38–39
    CB's Caramelized Onion "Lollipops," 60
    CB's Feta-Stuffed Portobellos, 61
    CB's Fire-Charred Green Beans with Vinaigrette, 41
    CB's Grilled Melon Salad, 66
    CB's Grilled Scallops with Prosciutto, 64
    CB's Prosciutto-Wrapped Dates, 57
    CB's Smoked Eggs, 52
    Dr. BBQ's Bacon-Brie, 62
    Frittata on the Grill, 47
    Grilled Oysters with Bacon, Tomato & Tarragon, 35
    Grilled Oysters with Blood Orange & Ginger, 36
    Grilled Portobello Mushrooms with Pepperoni & Cheese, 32
    Grilled Romaine Salad, 54
    Hot Corn Dip, 33
    Hot Sweet-Onion Dip, 31
    Moink Balls, 49
    Patio Daddio BBQ's Pulled-Pork Pasties, 44
    Pirate Mike's Peg Leg Chicken Drums, 51
    Reuben Dip, 48
    'Shroom Bombs, 53
    Smoked Chicken "Pâté", 56
    Smokin' Soon's Hobo Potato Skins, 37
    Smoky Baby Blue Artichokes, 30
    Spiced Cranberry Wings, 43
    Tall Paul's Scotch Eggs on the Grill, 40
    Thai Grilled Salt-and-Pepper Squid, 59
Apples
    CB's Cranberry-Apple Skillet Crisp, 263
    CB's Stuffed Squid with Chicken-Apple Sausage, 227
    in Grilled Salmon Salad Vinaigrette, 196
    in Harvest Slaw with Sweet Potatoes, 249
Artichokes
    Grilled Stuffed Chicken Breasts with Artichokes & Italian Cheeses, 158
    Smoky Baby Blue, 30
Arugula, Garlic-Roasted Sweet Potatoes with, 245
Asian Marinade, 281
Asparagus
    CB's Grilled Scallops with Asparagus & Toasted Walnuts, 221
    Roasted Asparagus with Cherry Tomatoes, Garlic & Olive Oil, 254
Aunt Sylvia's Buttermilk Cole Slaw, 230
Avocado
    Cajun Grilled Mahi-Mahi with Avocado Salad, 192
    CB's Avocado, Crab & Jalapeño Roll-Ups, 38–39

Chimichurri Bruschetta, 45
Grilled Beef Tacos with Avocado Salsa, 77
in Grilled Salmon Salad Vinaigrette, 196
in Trinidad Salad, 226

B

Bacon
    Bacon Chocolate Chip Cookies, 262
    CB's Bacon-Wrapped Pork Loin, 111
    CB's Grilled Potatoes with Bacon, Cheese & Roasted Jalapeño, 241
    CB's Grilled Salmon with Bacon & Tomato Salsa, 189
    Dr. BBQ's Bacon-Brie Appetizer, 62
    Grilled Oysters with Bacon, Tomato & Tarragon, 35
    Grilled Stuffed Pork Chops, 115
    Mary's "Cape" Cod with Bacon & Leeks, 193
    Moink Balls, 49
    in Panzanella Salad, 175
    in Pirate Mike's Peg Leg Chicken Drums, 51
    in Potato Casserole, 247
    in 'Shroom Bombs, 53
    in Smoky Grilled Meat Loaf, 83
    in Tall Paul's Scotch Eggs on the Grill, 40
Balsamic Garlic Sauce, 152
Barbecued Chicken Thighs au Vin, 159
Barbecue Mop, 121
Barbecuing, 13
Basil, with CB's Grilled Soft-Shell Crabs, 224
Basting Sauce, for CB's Grilled Honey & Lime Prawns, 220
BBQ Sauces. See also Sauces
    Bourbon, 166–67
    CB's White, 154–55
    Chipotle, 290
Beans
    Black-Eyed-Pea Salad, 234
    in Cajun Grilled Mahi-Mahi with Avocado Salad, 192
    CB's Fire-Charred Green Beans with Vinaigrette, 41
    Peg's Magic Beans, 231
Beef, 68–99
    The Big Easy Coffee-Brined Beef Roast, 98
    Cajun Meat-Loaf Muffins, 75
    "California Roll" Salad, 84
    CB's Beef Skewers "On Fire," 95
    CB's Burgers with Caramelized Onion Spread, 70
    CB's Cowboy-Style Beef Ribs, 99
    CB's Grilled Hanger Steak "Moutarde," 92
    CB's Polynesian-Style Tri-Tip, 87
    CB's Rib Eyes with Balsamic-Mushroom Sauce, 78–79
    CB's Salted Margarita Flank Steak, 88
    CB's Sliders, 72–73
    CB's Slow-Grilled Rib Eyes, 82
    Flank-Steak Tournedos with Goat Cheese, 89
    Ginger-Maple Steak with Napa Cabbage & Grilled Onions, 81
    Grilled Beef Tacos with Avocado Salsa, 77
    Grilled Flank Steak with Lemon & Rosemary Marinade, 94
    Grilled Flat-Iron Steaks with Mustard-Bourbon Sauce, 80
    Jamaican Jerk Burgers, 74
    Livefire's Grilled Beef Wellington, 91
    Moink Balls, 49
    Pomsey's Tailgate Tips, 86
    Reuben Dip, 48
    Smoky Grilled Meat Loaf, 83
    Szechuan Steak Wraps with Spicy Peanut

Mayonnaise, 93
Thai-Style Burgers, 76
Tomato-Mozzarella-Polenta Burgers, 71
Turkish-Style Sirloin with Roasted Garlic-Fig Sauce, 97
Beef temperature chart, 24
Beer
    CB's Beer-Brined Chicken Quarters, 170
    Miss Allison's One-Beer Skillet Bread, 255
Better-Than-Mom's Mac & Cheese, 246
The Big Easy, 14, 18
The Big Easy Coffee-Brined Beef Roast, 98
The Big Easy Yardbird Wings, 65
Black-Eyed-Pea Salad, 234
Blueberries
    Blueberry Sauce, 270
    Grilled Brownie Sundae with Blueberry Sauce, 270
Blue cheese
    Grilled Shrimp & Blue Cheese Grits, 218
    Smoky Baby Blue Artichokes, 30
Bluefish
    Grilled Bluefish with Fresh Corn Salsa, 210
    Maryland Smoked Bluefish, 212
Boar, CB's Grilled Wild Boar Tenderloin, 146
Bok choy, in Szechuan Steak Wraps with Spicy Peanut Mayonnaise, 93
Bommarito, Tommy, 98
Bourbon
    -BBQ Cornish Hens, 166–67
    -BBQ sauce, 166–67
    Grilled Flat-Iron Steaks with Mustard-Bourbon Sauce, 80
    -Herb Sauce, 223
    Mop Sauce, 132–33
Bread
    Avocado Chimichurri Bruschetta, 45
    CB's Smoky, Cheesy Cornbread, 239
    Miss Allison's One-Beer Skillet Bread, 255
    in Panzanella Salad, 175
Breadcrumb Topping, for Better Than Mom's Mac & Cheese, 246
Brie cheese, Dr. BBQ's Bacon-Brie Appetizer, 62
Brine
    for Brined Pork Chops with Mustard & Herbs, 102
    for Brined, Smoked Bluefish, 212
    CB's Beer-Brined Chicken Quarters, 170
    for CB's Caribbean-Spice Pork Roast, 107
    for CB's Chicken with Rosemary Butter & White BBQ Sauce, 154–55
    for CB's Mojito-Mopped Pulled Pork, 126–27
    Coffee Brine, 98
    for Grilled Stuffed Pork Chops, 115
    Savannah Smoker's Special Pork Brine, 283
    The Big Easy Cider-Brined Turkey, 184–85
Brined Pork Chops with Mustard & Herbs, 102
Brined, Smoked Bluefish, 212
Brining, 18, 98, 170, 185
Broccoli
    CB's Grilled Broccoli & Cauliflower with Toasted Walnuts, 252
    in Harvest Slaw with Sweet Potatoes, 249
Brownie Sundae, Grilled, with Blueberry Sauce, 270
Bruschetta, Avocado Chimichurri, 45
Bulgur, for Turkish-Style Sirloin with Roasted Garlic-Fig Sauce, 97
Burgers
    CB's Burgers with Caramelized Onion Spread, 70
    CB's Grilled Pork Burgers with Chorizo,

120
CB's Sliders, 72–73
Florentine Turkey, 182
Jamaican Jerk, 74
Lamb Burgers with Feta Spread, 141
Pacific Rim Chicken Burgers with Ginger
      Mayo, 160–61
Thai-Style, 76
Tomato-Mozzarella-Polenta, 71
Uncle Dane's Grilled Pork Patties, 129
Butter, Maître d,' 293
Butterflied Leg of Lamb with Chinese
      Seasonings, 140

C

Cabbage
      Aunt Sylvia's Buttermilk Cole Slaw, 230
      in CB's Grilled Fish Tacos, 206–7
      Ginger-Maple Steak with Napa Cabbage &
            Grilled Onions, 81
Cajun Grilled Mahi-Mahi with Avocado Salad,
      192
Cajun Meat-Loaf Muffins, 75
Calamari
      Stuffed Squid with Chicken-Apple
            Sausage, 227
      Thai Grilled Salt-and-Pepper Squid, 59
Capers, Grilled Halibut with Lemon-Caper
      Butter, 197
Captain Jessie's Jamaican Jerk Marinade, 281
Caramelized Onion Spread, 70
Caribbean Spice Sauce, 107
Carrots
      & Raisins Revisited, 235
      in You Won't Know It's Not Potato Salad,
            257
Cashews
      in Carrots & Raisins Revisited, 235
      in Pan Pacific Rice, 256
Casserole, CB's "Get Creative" Pork Chop, 119
Cauliflower
      CB's Grilled Broccoli & Cauliflower with
            Toasted Walnuts, 252
      Honey-Grilled, 258
      in You Won't Know It's Not Potato Salad,
            257
CB's Avocado, Crab & Jalapeño Roll-Ups,
      38–39
CB's Bacon-Wrapped Pork Loin, 111
CB's Baja-Style Grilled Sea Bass, 208
CB's Beef Skewers "On Fire," 95
CB's Beer-Brined Chicken Quarters, 170
CB's Burgers with Caramelized Onion Spread,
      70
CB's Caramelized Onion "Lollipops," 60
CB's Caribbean-Spice Pork Roast, 107
CB's Char Siu Pork Tenderloin, 121
CB's Chicken with Rosemary Butter & White
      BBQ Sauce, 154–55
CB's Chili-Rubbed Ribs, 109
CB's Chimichurri Sauce, 288
CB's "Cincinnati-Chili" Pork Chops, 114
CB's Cowboy-Style Beef Ribs, 99
CB's Cranberry-Apple Skillet Crisp, 263
CB's Cucumber Salad, 236
CB's Curry, Garlic & Black-Pepper Sauce, 288
CB's EZ Fish Taco Sauce, 206–7
CB's Fennel & Vermouth Pork Tenderloin, 108
CB's Feta-Stuffed Portobellos, 60
CB's Filipino Adobo Sauce, 289
CB's Fire-Charred Green Beans with
      Vinaigrette, 41
CB's Five-Spice Pork Chops, 103
CB's "Get Creative" Pork Chop Casserole, 119
CB's Grilled Broccoli & Cauliflower with
      Toasted Walnuts, 252

CB's Grilled Chicken Cacciatore, 156
CB's Grilled Chicken Meatballs, 173
CB's Grilled Chicken with Balsamic Garlic
      Sauce, 152
CB's Grilled Fennel, 240
CB's Grilled Fish Tacos, 206–7
CB's Grilled Flat-Iron Steaks with Mustard-
      Bourbon Sauce, 80
CB's Grilled Ginger Chicken Tenderloins with
      Spicy Peanut Sauce, 164
CB's Grilled Grouper with Garlic Butter, 204
CB's Grilled Hanger Steak "Moutarde," 92
CB's Grilled Honey & Lime Prawns, 220
CB's Grilled Lobster Tail with Bourbon-Herb
      Sauce, 223
CB's Grilled Loin of Venison, 148
CB's Grilled Melon Salad, 66
CB's Grilled Pacific Sardines, 209
CB's Grilled Pear & Gorgonzola Salad, 238
CB's Grilled Pears with Honey & Thyme, 266
CB's Grilled Pork Burgers with Chorizo, 120
CB's Grilled Pork Chops Marsala, 106
CB's Grilled Pork Chops with Garlic &
      Cilantro, 104–5
CB's Grilled Pork Paillards with Two-Mustard
      Sauce, 112
CB's Grilled Potatoes with Bacon, Cheese &
      Roasted Jalapeño, 241
CB's Grilled Salmon with Bacon & Tomato
      Salsa, 189
CB's Grilled Salmon with Shallot & Lemon
      Glaze, 188
CB's Grilled Scallops with Asparagus &
      Toasted Walnuts, 221
CB's Grilled Scallops with Prosciutto, 64
CB's Grilled Soft-Shell Crabs, 224
CB's Grilled Wild Boar Tenderloin, 146
CB's Herb & Honey Glazed Ham, 122–23
CB's Herbed Poultry Rub, 285
CB's Hot Thai-Style Dipping Sauce, 288
CB's Korean-Style Chicken, 153
CB's Lamb Chops with Toasted Cumin &
      Rosemary, 136
CB's Lamb Sirloin with Red-Wine Sauce, 137
CB's Lavender Rub for Lamb, 285
CB's Low & Slow Lamb Roast, 142
CB's Mojito-Mopped Pulled Pork, 126–27
CB's Nut-Crusted Ribs with Bourbon Mop
      Sauce, 132–33
CB's Nutella & Marshmallow Quesadillas, 267
CB's Pacific Northwest Seasoning for Game,
      285
CB's Pie-Iron Peach Pie, 264
CB's Polynesian-Style Tri-Tip, 87
CB's Pork Loin with Chili, Curry & Coffee Rub,
      118
CB's Pork Neck Roast with Cumin-Spice Rub,
      113
CB's Prosciutto-Wrapped Dates, 57
CB's Rainbow Trout Stuffed with Lemon,
      Shallots & Herbs, 194
CB's Rib Eyes with Balsamic-Mushroom
      Sauce, 78
CB's Salted Margarita Flank Steak, 88
CB's Sliders, 72–73
CB's Slow-Grilled Rib Eyes, 82
CB's Smoked Eggs, 52
CB's Smoky, Cheesy Cornbread, 239
CB's Snapper Grilled on a Bed of Limes, 190
CB's Spit-Roasted Rabbit, 147
CB's Stuffed Squid with Chicken-Apple
      Sausage, 227
CB's Tailgate Grilled Baby Back Ribs, 117
CB's Thai-Glazed Swordfish, 202
CB's V8 Chicken, 162
CB's Wet Salt Rub for Fish, 286

CB's White BBQ Sauce, 154–55
Char-Broil, 14
Cheese
      Better Than Mom's Mac & Cheese, 246
      CB's Feta-Stuffed Portobellos, 61
      in CB's "Get Creative" Pork Chop
            Casserole, 119
      in CB's Grilled Chicken Meatballs, 173
      in CB's Grilled Melon Salad, 66
      CB's Grilled Pear & Gorgonzola Salad, 238
      in CB's Grilled Pork Chops Marsala, 106
      CB's Grilled Potatoes with Bacon, Cheese
            & Roasted Jalapeño, 241
      in CB's Prosciutto-Wrapped Dates, 57
      CB's Smoky, Cheesy Cornbread, 239
      in Creamy Gorgonzola Sauce, 292
      Dr. BBQ's Bacon-Brie Appetizer, 62
      Dulce de Leche Grilled Cheese, 276
      Feta Spread, 141
      Flank-Steak Tournedos with Goat Cheese,
            89
      in Frittata on the Grill, 47
      in Greek Potato Salad with Sun-Dried
            Tomatoes, 232
      in Greek Salad Olive-Grilled Chicken, 163
      in Green-Chili Pesto, 291
      Grilled Eggplant with, 248
      Grilled Portobello Mushrooms with
            Pepperoni &, 32
      in Grilled Romaine Salad, 54
      Grilled Shrimp & Blue Cheese Grits, 218
      Grilled Stuffed Chicken Breasts with
            Artichokes & Italian Cheeses, 158
      in Grilled Stuffed Pork Chops, 115
      in Grilled Stuffed Tomatoes Caprese, 251
      in Hot Corn Dip, 33
      in Hot Sweet-Onion Dip, 31
      Nectarine Pizza with Goat Cheese &
            Thyme, 272
      in Panzanella Salad, 175
      in Potato Casserole, 247
      in Reuben Dip, 48
      in Smoked Chicken "Pâté", 56
      in Smokin' Soon's Hobo Potato Skins, 37
      Smoky Baby Blue Artichokes, 30
      in Tall Paul's Scotch Eggs on the Grill, 40
      Tomato-Mozzarella-Polenta Burgers, 71
Chef Erick's Lamb Kebabs with Mint Pesto,
      144–45
Cherries
      in CB's Pacific Northwest Seasoning for
            Game, 285
      Dried-Cherry Chutney, 291
Chicken, 152–73
      Barbecued Chicken Thighs au Vin, 159
      The Big Easy Yardbird Wings, 65
      CB's Beer-Brined Chicken Quarters, 170
      CB's Chicken with Rosemary Butter &
            White BBQ Sauce, 154–55
      in CB's Filipino Adobo Sauce, 289
      CB's Grilled Chicken Cacciatore, 156
      CB's Grilled Chicken Meatballs, 173
      CB's Grilled Chicken with Balsamic Garlic
            Sauce, 152
      CB's Grilled Ginger Chicken Tenderloins
            with Spicy Peanut Sauce, 164
      CB's Korean-Style, 153
      CB's Stuffed Squid with Chicken-Apple
            Sausage, 227
      CB's V8 Chicken, 162
      Chili-Cinnamon Rub for Chicken, 287
      Coffee & Cocoa Grilled Chicken Thighs,
            168
      Greek Salad Olive-Grilled, 163
      Grilled Chicken Marsala, 165
      Grilled Stuffed Chicken Breasts with

Artichokes & Italian Cheeses, 158
Grilled Yogurt-Mint Chicken, 157
Pacific Rim Chicken Burgers with Ginger
Mayo, 160–61
Peach-Barbecued, 171
Pirate Mike's Peg Leg Chicken Drums, 51
Sesame-Crusted Chicken with Wasabi
Cream Sauce, 169
Smoked Chicken "Pâté", 56
Spiced Cranberry Wings, 43
Tequila Lime, 172
Chili-Cinnamon Rub For Chicken, 287
Chili Rub, 109
Chimichurri
Avocado Chimichurri Bruschetta, 45
CB's Chimichurri Sauce, 288
Chipotle
BBQ Sauce, 290
in CB's "Cincinnati-Chili" Pork Chops, 114
in CB's EZ Fish Taco Sauce, 206–7
in CB's Grilled Soft-Shell Crabs, 224
in Grilled Pork & Pineapple Tacos, 125
-Lime Mayonnaise, 74
in Mexican Marinade, 281
Chocolate
Bacon Chocolate Chip Cookies, 262
CB's Nutella & Marshmallow Quesadillas,
267
-Chip Cookie-Dough Dip, 269
Coffee & Cocoa Grilled Chicken Thighs,
168
Grilled Brownie Sundae with Blueberry
Sauce, 270
Peanut Butter & Marshmallow Finger
Sandwiches, 275
Chorizo, CB's Grilled Pork Burgers with, 120
Christopherranch.com, 203
Chutney, Dried-Cherry, 291
Cider-Brined Turkey, The Big Easy, 184–85
Cilantro
with CB's Grilled Soft-Shell Crabs, 224
-Pesto Snapper with Red Pepper Sauce
Cincinnati Rub, 114
Cinnamon, Chili-Cinnamon Rub for Chicken,
287
Classic Marinade, 281
Cocoa & Coffee Grilled Chicken Thighs, 168
Coconut
Grilled Pineapple with Rum &, 274
-Peanut Sauce, 131
Cod, Mary's "Cape" Cod with Bacon & Leeks,
193
Coffee
& Cocoa Grilled Chicken Thighs, 168
The Big Easy Coffee-Brined Beef Roast, 98
CB's Pork Loin with Chili, Curry & Coffee
Rub, 118
Cola Ribs, 128
Cookies
Bacon Chocolate Chip, 262
Chocolate-Chip Cookie-Dough Dip, 269
Cookthink.com, 94, 197, 217
Corn
in Cajun Grilled Mahi-Mahi with Avocado
Salad, 192
with Cola Ribs, 128
Grilled Bluefish with Fresh Corn Salsa,
210
Hot Corn Dip, 33
Savoury Corn Pudding, 233
Cornbread, CB's Smoky, Cheesy, 239
Cornish Hens, Bourbon-BBQ, 166–67
Crab
CB's Avocado, Crab & Jalapeño Roll-Ups,
38–39
CB's Grilled Soft-Shell, 224
Grilled Alaska Crab with Trinidad Salad,

226
Smoky Grilled King, 225
Cranberry
CB's Cranberry-Apple Skillet Crisp, 263
-Pecan Rice Pilaf, 242
Spiced Cranberry Wings, 43
Cream cheese
in Chocolate-Chip Cookie-Dough Dip, 269
in Creamy Gorgonzola Sauce, 292
Creamy Gorgonzola Sauce, 292
Creamy Zucchini & Garlic, 244
Creole Sauce, 214
Crisp, CB's Cranberry-Apple Skillet, 263
Croaker, Grilled Atlantic, 211
Cuban-Spice Rub, 126–27
Cucumber
CB's Cucumber Salad, 236
Wasabi, 84
Cumin & Rosemary Rub, 136
Cumin-Spice Rub, 113
Curry
CB's Curry, Garlic & Black-Pepper Sauce,
288
CB's Pork Loin with Chili, Curry & Coffee
Rub, 118
Madras Curry Dip, 291

D

Danicasdaily.com, 165
Dates, CB's Prosciutto-Wrapped, 57
Dawson, John, 45, 54
Defrosting foods, 22
Desserts, 260–77
Bacon Chocolate Chip Cookies, 262
CB's Cranberry-Apple Skillet Crisp, 263
CB's Grilled Pears with Honey & Thyme,
266
CB's Nutella & Marshmallow Quesadillas,
267
CB's Pie-Iron Peach Pie, 264
Chocolate-Chip Cookie-Dough Dip, 269
Dulce de Leche Grilled Cheese, 276
Frozen Strawberry Pie, 271
Grilled Brownie Sundae with Blueberry
Sauce, 270
Grilled Pineapple with Rum & Coconut,
274
Nectarine Pizza with Goat Cheese &
Thyme, 272
Peanut Butter & Marshmallow Finger
Sandwiches, 275
Devilled Potato Bites, 259
Dips
Chocolate-Chip Cookie-Dough Dip, 269
Creamy Gorgonzola Sauce, 292
Dr. BBQ's Bacon-Brie Appetizer, 62
Hot Corn, 33
Hot Sweet-Onion Dip, 31
Madras Curry Dip, 291
Reuben Dip, 48
Direct heat, 13
Dr. BBQ's Bacon-Brie Appetizer, 62
Dried Cherry Chutney, 291
Dulce de Leche Grilled Cheese, 276

E

Eggplant, Grilled, with Cheese, 248
Eggs
CB's Smoked, 52
Frittata on the Grill, 47
Tall Paul's Scotch Eggs on the Grill, 40
in You Won't Know It's Not Potato Salad,
257

F

Fast & Spicy Halibut, 198
Fennel

CB's Fennel & Vermouth Pork Tenderloin,
108
CB's Grilled, 240
Grapefruit-Fennel Salad, 138
Feta
CB's Feta-Stuffed Portobellos, 61
in CB's Grilled Melon Salad, 66
in Greek Potato Salad with Sun-Dried
Tomatoes, 232
in Greek Salad Olive-Grilled Chicken, 163
in Grilled Eggplant with Cheese, 248
in Grilled Romaine Salad, 54
Lamb Burgers with Feta Spread, 141
Feta Spread, 141
Figs, Roasted Garlic-Fig Sauce, 97
Fish. See Seafood; specific fish
Five-Spice Lamb Chops with Grapefruit-
Fennel Salad, 138–39
Five-Spice Marinade, 138
Flank-Steak Tournedos with Goat Cheese, 89
Florentine Turkey Burgers, 182
Frankenberg, Marcia, 172
Fresh Citrus Salsa, 103
Frittata on the Grill, 47
Frozen Strawberry Pie, 271
Fruit. See specific fruits

G

Gaian, Larry, 56
Game
CB's Grilled Loin of Venison, 148
CB's Grilled Wild Boar Tenderloin, 146
CB's Pacific Northwest Seasoning for
Game, 285
CB's Spit-Roasted Rabbit, 147
Garlic
CB's Curry, Garlic & Black-Pepper Sauce,
288
CB's Grilled Chicken with Balsamic Garlic
Sauce, 152
CB's Grilled Grouper with Garlic Butter,
204
CB's Grilled Pork Chops with Garlic &
Cilantro, 104–5
Creamy Zucchini &, 244
Roasted Asparagus with Cherry
Tomatoes, Garlic & Olive Oil, 254
-Roasted Sweet Potatoes with Arugula,
245
Turkish-Style Sirloin with Roasted Garlic-
Fig Sauce, 97
-Yogurt Marinade, 282
Ginger
Carrots, 84
CB's Grilled Ginger Chicken Tenderloins
with Spicy Peanut Sauce, 164
Dressing, 236
Grilled Oysters with Blood Orange &, 36
in Hawaiian-Style Marlin with Poke
Sauce, 205
-Maple Steak with Napa Cabbage &
Grilled Onions, 81
Mayonnaise, 160–61
Girls on a Grill, 201, 251
Glazes
for CB's Hawaiian-Style Tri-Tip, 87
for CB's Spit-Roasted Rabbit, 147
for Jalapeño-Jelly-Glazed Turkey Thighs,
183
Shallot & Lemon, 188
Thai, 202
Goat cheese
in CB's Grilled Melon Salad, 66
Flank-Steak Tournedos with, 89
in Grilled Eggplant with Cheese, 248
Nectarine Pizza with Thyme &, 272

Gorgonzola
    CB's Grilled Pear & Gorgonzola Salad, 238
    Creamy Gorgonzola Sauce, 292
Grapefruit-Fennel Salad, 138
Greek Potato Salad with Sun-Dried Tomatoes, 232
Greek Salad Olive-Grilled Chicken, 163
Green Beans with Vinaigrette, CB's Fire-Charred, 41
Green-Chili Pesto, 291
Grill care, 21
Grilled Alaska Crab with Trinidad Salad, 226
Grilled Atlantic Croaker, 211
Grilled Beef Tacos with Avocado Salsa, 77
Grilled Bluefish with Fresh Corn Salsa, 210
Grilled Breaded Pork Chops, 124
Grilled Brownie Sundae with Blueberry Sauce, 270
Grilled Chicken Marsala, 165
Grilled Eggplant with Cheese, 248
Grilled Flank Steak with Lemon & Rosemary Marinade, 94
Grilled Halibut with Lemon-Caper Butter, 197
Grilled Lamb & Mango Tostadas, 143
Grilled Oysters with Bacon, Tomato & Tarragon, 35
Grilled Oysters with Blood Orange & Ginger, 36
Grilled Pineapple with Rum & Coconut, 274
Grilled Pork & Pineapple Tacos, 125
Grilled Portobello Mushrooms with Pepperoni & Cheese, 32
Grilled Potato Planks, 250
Grilled Romaine Salad, 54
Grilled Salmon Salad Vinaigrette, 196
Grilled Shrimp & Blue Cheese Grits, 218
Grilled Shrimp & Vegetable Kebabs, 217
Grilled Stuffed Chicken Breasts with Artichokes & Italian Cheeses, 158
Grilled Stuffed Pork Chops, 115
Grilled Stuffed Tomatoes Caprese, 251
Grilled Tuna with Roasted Cipollini Onions, 203
Grilled Yogurt-Mint Chicken, 157
Grilling methods, 13–14
Grilling safety, 20–23
Grills, 14, 21
Grits, Grilled Shrimp & Blue Cheese Grits, 218
Grouper, CB's Grilled, with Garlic Butter, 204

H

Halibut
    Fast & Spicy Halibut, 198
    Grilled Halibut with Lemon-Caper Butter, 197
    Skewers with Mango-Mojito Salsa, 199
Ham
    CB's Grilled Scallops with Prosciutto, 64
    CB's Herb & Honey Glazed Ham, 122–23
    CB's Prosciutto-Wrapped Dates, 57
    in Livefire's Grilled Beef Wellington, 91
Harissa, in Moroccan Sauce, 292
Harvest Slaw with Sweet Potatoes, 249
Heat, 16
Hedrick, Mike, 51, 65
Herb-Marinated Grilled Turkey & Panzanella Salad, 174–75
Honey
    CB's Grilled Honey & Lime Prawns, 220
    CB's Grilled Pears with Honey & Thyme, 266
    CB's Herb & Honey Glazed Ham, 122–23
    -Grilled Cauliflower, 258

Honu, Ka, 53

Hot Corn Dip, 33
Hotdogs, Tangy Turkey Dogs, 178
Hot Sweet-Onion Dip, 31
House, Gary, 47
Hygiene, 20–21

I

Ice cream and frozen desserts
    Frozen Strawberry Pie, 271
    Grilled Brownie Sundae with Blueberry Sauce, 270
Indian Tandoori Ribs, 130
Indirect heat, 13
Infrared cooking, 14, 18

J

Jalapeño
    in Adobo Sauce, 290
    CB's Avocado, Crab & Jalapeño Roll-Ups, 38–39
    CB's Grilled Potatoes with Bacon, Cheese & Roasted, 241
    -Jelly-Glazed Turkey Thighs, 183
Jamaican Jerk Burgers, 74
Jamaican Jerk Marinade, 176
Jamaican Jerk Turkey Thighs, 176
Jan's Dry Rub, 286
Jim Hatcher's Creole Shrimp & Sausage, 214

K

Kebabs
    CB's Beef Skewers "On Fire," 95
    Chef Erick's Lamb Kebabs with Mint Pesto, 144–45
    Grilled Shrimp & Vegetable, 217
    Lemonade Turkey Kebabs, 177
Korean Kalbi Marinade, 282

L

Lamb, 134–45
    Burgers with Feta Spread, 141
    Butterflied Leg of Lamb with Chinese Seasonings, 140
    CB's Lamb Chops with Toasted Cumin & Rosemary, 136
    CB's Lamb Sirloin with Red-Wine Sauce, 137
    CB's Lavender Rub for, 285
    CB's Low & Slow Lamb Roast, 142
    Chef Erick's Lamb Kebabs with Mint Pesto, 144–45
    Five-Spice Lamb Chops with Grapefruit-Fennel Salad, 138–39
    Grilled Lamb & Mango Tostadas, 143
Lamb temperature chart, 24
Lampe, Ray, 62
Lavender Rub for Lamb, CB's, 285
Leeks, Mary's "Cape" Cod with Bacon &, 193
Lemon
    & Rosemary Marinade, 94
    CB's Grilled Salmon with Shallot & Lemon Glaze, 188
    CB's Rainbow Trout Stuffed with Lemon, Shallots & Herbs, 194
    in CB's White BBQ Sauce, 154–55
    Dressing, 232
    Grilled Flank Steak with Lemon & Rosemary Marinade, 94
    Grilled Halibut with Lemon-Caper Butter, 197
    Lemonade Turkey Kebabs, 177
    -Oregano Grilled Turkey, 179
Lemonade Turkey Kebabs, 177
Lime
    CB's Grilled Honey & Lime Prawns, 220
    in CB's Mojito-Mopped Pulled Pork, 126–27

in CB's Salted Margarita Flank Steak, 88
CB's Snapper Grilled on a Bed of Limes, 190
Chipotle-Lime Mayonnaise, 74
in Halibut Skewers with Mango-Mojito Salsa, 199
in Margarita-Grilled Shrimp, 219
Tequila Lime Chicken, 172
Livefire's Grilled Beef Wellington, 91
Livefire's Holiday Potato Torte, 243
Lobster Tail, CB's Grilled, with Bourbon-Herb Sauce, 223
Louisianacookin.com, 218

M

Mac & Cheese, Better Than Mom's, 246
Madras Curry Dip, 291
Mahi-Mahi, Cajun Grilled, with Avocado Salad, 192
Maître d' Butter, 293
Mango
    Grilled Lamb & Mango Tostadas, 143
    Halibut Skewers with Mango-Mojito Salsa, 199
    in Lemonade Turkey Kebabs, 177
Maple syrup
    Ginger-Maple Steak with Napa Cabbage & Grilled Onions, 81
    in Grilled Stuffed Pork Chops, 115
Margarita Grilled Shrimp, 219
Marinades
    Asian, 281
    for Beef "California Roll" Salad, 84
    Captain Jessie's Jamaican Jerk Marinade, 281
    for CB's Beef Skewers "On Fire," 95
    CB's Grilled Honey & Lime Prawns, 220
    Classic, 281
    for Cola Ribs, 128
    Five-Spice, 138
    Garlic-Yogurt Marinade, 282
    Ginger-Maple Marinade and Dressing, 81
    for Grilled Beef Tacos, 77
    for Grilled Shrimp & Vegetable Kebabs, 217
    for Grilled Yogurt-Mint Chicken, 157
    for Hawaiian-Style Marlin, 205
    for Indian Tandoori Ribs, 130
    for Iowa State Fair Turkey Dogs, 178
    Jamaican Jerk, 176
    Korean Kalbi, 282
    Lemon & Rosemary Marinade, 94
    for Margarita Grilled Shrimp, 219
    Marinated Portobello Mushrooms with Roasted-Pepper Vinaigrette, 237
    Mexican, 281
    Plum, 280
    Spicy Grilled-Veggie, 284
    for Szechuan Steak Wraps, 93
    Thai, 180
    Three-Way, 281
Marinated Portobello Mushrooms with Roasted-Pepper Vinaigrette, 237
Marlin, Polynesian-Style, with Poke Sauce, 205
Marsala Sauce, 106
Marshmallow
    CB's Nutella & Marshmallow Quesadillas, 267
    Peanut Butter & Marshmallow Finger Sandwiches, 275
Maryland Smoked Bluefish, 212
Mary's "Cape" Cod with Bacon & Leeks, 193
Mayonnaise
    Chipotle-Lime, 74
    Spicy Peanut, 93
McAdams, Curt, 91, 262

Meatballs
 CB's Grilled Chicken, 173
 Moink Balls, 49
Meat loaf
 Cajun Meat-Loaf Muffins, 75
 Smoky Grilled, 83
Melons
 CB's Grilled Melon Salad, 66
 in Lemonade Turkey Kebabs, 177
Mexican Marinade, 281
Mint Pesto, 145
Miss Allison's One-Beer Skillet Bread, 255
Moink Balls, 49
Mojita Mop, 127
Moroccan Sauce, 292
Mushrooms
 CB's Feta-Stuffed Portobellos, 61
 CB's Rib Eyes with Balsamic-Mushroom
  Sauce, 78–79
 Grilled Portobello Mushrooms with
  Pepperoni & Cheese, 32
 in Livefire's Grilled Beef Wellington, 91
 Marinated Portobello Mushrooms with
  Roasted-Pepper Vinaigrette, 237
 'Shroom Bombs, 53
Mustard
 Brined Pork Chops with Mustard & Herbs,
  102
 CB's Grilled Hanger Steak "Moutarde," 92
 CB's Grilled Pork Paillards with Two-
  Mustard Sauce, 112
 Grilled Flat-Iron Steaks with Mustard-
  Bourbon Sauce, 80

N

Nectarine Pizza with Goat Cheese & Thyme,
 272
Nutella & Marshmallow Quesadillas, CB's,
 267

O

Olives
 in Greek Potato Salad with Sun-Dried
  Tomatoes, 232
 Greek Salad Olive-Grilled Chicken, 163
Onions
 CB's Burgers with Caramelized Onion
  Spread, 70
 CB's Caramelized Onion "Lollipops," 60
 in Chef Erick's Lamb Kebabs with Mint
  Pesto, 144–45
 Ginger-Maple Steak with Napa Cabbage &
  Grilled, 81
 Grilled Tuna with Roasted Cipollini
  Onions, 203
 Hot Sweet-Onion Dip, 31
Oranges
 in CB's Grilled Pork Chops with Garlic &
  Cilantro, 104–5
 Fresh Citrus Salsa, 103
 Grilled Oysters with Blood Orange &
  Ginger, 36
 in Grilled Salmon Salad Vinaigrette, 196
 in Provençal Citrus-Tarragon Sauce, 290
Oysters
 Grilled Oysters with Bacon, Tomato &
  Tarragon, 35
 Grilled Oysters with Blood Orange &
  Ginger, 36

P

Pacific Rim Chicken Burgers with Ginger
 Mayo, 160–61
Palm hearts, in Trinidad Salad, 226
Pan Pacific Rice, 256

Panzanella Salad, 175
Papaya, in Trinidad Salad, 226
Pasta
 Better Than Mom's Mac & Cheese, 246
 CB's "Get Creative" Pork Chop Casserole,
  119
Patio Daddio BBQ's Pulled-Pork Pasties, 44
Peach
 CB's Pie-Iron Peach Pie, 264
 Peach-Barbecued Chicken, 171
Peanuts
 in CB's Hot Thai-Style Dipping Sauce, 288
 Peanut Butter & Marshmallow Finger
  Sandwiches, 275
 Pork Spareribs with Coconut-Peanut
  Sauce, 131
 Spicy Peanut Mayonnaise, 93
 Spicy Peanut Sauce, 164
 in Thai Marinade Turkey Wings, 180
Pears
 CB's Grilled Pear & Gorgonzola Salad, 238
 CB's Grilled Pears with Honey & Thyme,
  266
 in Garlic-Roasted Sweet Potatoes with
  Arugula, 245
Peas
 in You Won't Know It's Not Potato Salad,
  257
Pecans
 in Carrots & Raisins Revisited, 235
 CB's Nut-Crusted Ribs with Bourbon Mop
  Sauce, 132–33
 Cranberry-Pecan Rice Pilaf, 242
Peg's Magic Beans, 231
Pepperoni, Grilled Portobello Mushrooms
 with Cheese &, 32
Peppers
 in Cajun Grilled Mahi-Mahi with Avocado
  Salad, 192
 CB's Avocado, Crab & Jalapeño Roll-Ups,
  38–39
 in CB's Beef Skewers "On Fire," 95
 in CB's Grilled Chicken Cacciatore, 156
 CB's Grilled Potatoes with Bacon, Cheese
  & Roasted Jalapeño, 241
 in Chef Erick's Lamb Kebabs with Mint
  Pesto, 144–45
 Cilantro-Pesto Snapper with Red Pepper
  Sauce, 215
 Green-Chili Pesto, 291
 Jalapeño-Jelly-Glazed Turkey Thighs, 183
 Jalapeños in Adobo Sauce, 290
 Marinated Portobello Mushrooms with
  Roasted-Pepper Vinaigrette, 237
Pesto
 Cilantro-Pesto Snapper with Red Pepper
  Sauce, 215
 Green-Chili, 291
 Mint, 145
Pie
 CB's Pie-Iron Peach, 264
 Frozen Strawberry, 271
Pie Crust, 271
Pie irons, 264
Pineapple
 CB's Hawaiian-Style Tri-Tip, 87
 Grilled Pineapple with Rum & Coconut,
  274
 Grilled Pork & Pineapple Tacos, 125
Pirate Mike's Peg Leg Chicken Drums, 51
Pizza, Nectarine Pizza with Goat Cheese &
 Thyme, 272
Plum Marinade, 280
Poke Sauce, 205
Polenta, Tomato-Mozzarella-Polenta Burgers,

 71
Polynesian-Style Marlin with Poke Sauce, 205
Pomsey's Tailgate Tips, 86
Pork, 100–133
 Brined Pork Chops with Mustard & Herbs,
  102
 CB's Bacon-Wrapped Pork Loin, 111
 CB's Caribbean-Spice Pork Roast, 107
 CB's Char Siu Pork Tenderloin, 121
 CB's Chili-Rubbed Ribs, 109
 CB's "Cincinnati-Chili" Pork Chops, 114
 CB's Fennel & Vermouth Pork Tenderloin,
  108
 CB's Five-Spice Pork Chops, 103
 CB's "Get Creative" Pork Chop Casserole,
  119
 CB's Grilled Pork Burgers with Chorizo,
  120
 CB's Grilled Pork Chops Marsala, 106
 CB's Grilled Pork Chops with Garlic &
  Cilantro, 104–5
 CB's Grilled Pork Paillards with Two-
  Mustard Sauce, 112
 CB's Herb & Honey Glazed Ham, 122–23
 CB's Mojito-Mopped Pulled Pork, 126–27
 CB's Nut-Crusted Ribs with Bourbon Mop
  Sauce, 132–33
 CB's Pork Loin with Chili, Curry & Coffee
  Rub, 118
 CB's Pork Neck Roast with Cumin Spice
  Rub, 113
 CB's Tailgate Grilled Baby Back Ribs, 117
 Cola Ribs, 128
 Grilled Breaded Pork Chops, 124
 Grilled Pork & Pineapple Tacos, 125
 Grilled Stuffed Pork Chops, 115
 Indian Tandoori Ribs, 130
 Patio Daddio BBQ's Pulled-Pork Pasties, 44
 Smoky Grilled Meat Loaf, 83
 Spareribs with Coconut-Peanut Sauce,
  131
 Uncle Dane's Grilled Pork Patties, 129
Pork Brine, Savannah Smoker's Special, 283
Pork temperature chart, 25
Portobello mushrooms
 CB's Feta-Stuffed, 61
 Grilled Portobello Mushrooms with
  Pepperoni & Cheese, 32
 Marinated Portobello Mushrooms with
  Roasted-Pepper Vinaigrette, 237
Potato Casserole, 247
Potatoes
 with CB's "Cincinnati-Chili" Pork Chops,
  114
 CB's Grilled Potatoes with Bacon, Cheese
  & Roasted Jalapeño, 241
 Deviled Potato Bites, 259
 Greek Potato Salad with Sun-Dried
  Tomatoes, 232
 Grilled Potato Planks, 250
 Livefire's Holiday Potato Torte, 243
 Potato Casserole, 247
 Salt Grilled, 253
 Smokin' Soon's Hobo Potato Skins, 37
Poultry Rub, CB's Herbed, 285
Poultry temperature chart, 24
Prawns, CB's Grilled Honey & Lime Prawns,
 220
Prosciutto
 CB's Grilled Scallops with, 64
 CB's Prosciutto-Wrapped Dates, 57
 in Livefire's Grilled Beef Wellington, 91
Provençal Citrus-Tarragon Sauce, 290

Q

Quantam grills, 14
Quesadillas, CB's Nutella & Marshmallow

Quesadillas, 267

R

Rabbit, CB's Spit-Roasted, 147
Raisins
 Carrots & Raisins Revisited, 235
 in CB's Cranberry-Apple Skillet Crisp, 263
RED grills, 14
Red-Hot Barbecued Turkey Tenderloins, 181
Red-Hot Barbecue Sauce, 181
Red-Wine Sauce, 137
Reuben Dip, 48
Rib Eyes
 CB's Rib Eyes with Balsamic-Mushroom Sauce, 78–79
 CB's Slow-Grilled, 82
Ribs
 CB's Chili-Rubbed, 109
 CB's Cowboy-Style Beef, 99
 CB's Nut-Crusted Ribs with Bourbon Mop Sauce, 132–33
 CB's Tailgate Grilled Baby Back, 117
 Cola, 128
 Indian Tandoori, 130
 Pork Spareribs with Coconut-Peanut Sauce, 131
Rice
 Cranberry-Pecan Rice Pilaf, 242
 Pan Pacific, 256
Roasted Asparagus with Cherry Tomatoes, Garlic & Olive Oil, 254
Roasted Garlic-Fig Sauce, 97
Roasted-Pepper Vinaigrette, 237
Roasting temperatures, 27
Rotisserie cooking, 19, 27
Rubs
 for CB's Beer-Brined Chicken Quarters, 170
 for CB's Hawaiian-Style Tri-Tip, 87
 CB's Herbed Poultry Rub, 285
 CB's Lavender Rub for Lamb, 285
 for CB's Nut-Crusted Ribs with Bourbon Mop Sauce, 132–33
 CB's Pacific Northwest Seasoning for Game, 285
 CB's Pork Loin with Chili, Curry & Coffee Rub, 118
 CB's Wet Salt Rub for Fish, 286
 Chili, 109
 Chili-Cinnamon Rub for Chicken, 287
 Cincinnati, 114
 Coffee & Cocoa, 168
 Cuban Spice Rub, 126–27
 Cumin & Rosemary, 136
 Cumin Spice Rub, 113
 for Grilled Chicken Marsala, 165
 Jan's Dry Rub, 286
 Savannah Smoker's Mohunken Rub, 287
Rum, Grilled Pineapple with Coconut &, 274

S

Safety, 20–23
Salad dressings
 for Black-Eyed-Pea Salad, 234
 Ginger, 236
 Grilled Salmon Salad Vinaigrette, 196
 Lemon Dressing, 232
Salads
 Aunt Sylvia's Buttermilk Cole Slaw, 230
 Beef "California Roll," 84
 Black-Eyed-Pea, 234
 Cajun Grilled Mahi-Mahi with Avocado, 192
 Carrots & Raisins Revisited, 235
 CB's Cucumber, 236
 CB's Grilled Melon, 66
 CB's Grilled Pear & Gorgonzola, 238

Grapefruit-Fennel, 138
Greek Potato Salad with Sun-Dried Tomatoes, 232
Greek Salad Olive-Grilled Chicken, 163
Grilled Romaine, 54
Grilled Salmon Salad Vinaigrette, 196
Harvest Slaw with Sweet Potatoes, 249
Panzanella, 175
Trinidad, 226
You Won't Know It's Not Potato Salad, 257
Salmon
 CB's Grilled Salmon with Bacon & Tomato Salsa, 189
 CB's Grilled Salmon with Shallot & Lemon Glaze, 188
 Grilled Salmon Salad Vinaigrette, 196
Salsa
 Avocado, 77
 Fresh Citrus, 103
 Fresh Corn, 210
 Mango-Mojito, 199
 Tomato, 189
Salt curing, 88
Salt-Grilled Potatoes, 253
Sandwiches. *See also* Burgers
 CB's Grilled Chicken Meatballs, 173
 CB's Mojito-Mopped Pulled Pork, 126–27
 CB's Pork Loin with Chili, Curry & Coffee Rub, 118
 Dulce de Leche Grilled Cheese, 276
 Peanut Butter & Marshmallow Finger Sandwiches, 275
 Pomsey's Tailgate Tips, 86
Sardines, CB's Grilled Pacific, 209
Sauces
 Balsamic Garlic, 152
 Balsamic-Mushroom, 79
 Barbecue Mop, 121
 Blueberry Sauce, 270
 Bourbon-BBQ, 166–67
 Bourbon-Herb, 223
 Bourbon Mop, 132–33
 Caribbean Spice, 107
 for CB's Chili-Rubbed Ribs, 109
 CB's Chimichurri, 288
 CB's Curry, Garlic & Black-Pepper, 288
 CB's EZ Fish Taco, 206–7
 CB's Filipino Adobo, 289
 for CB's Grilled Honey & Lime Prawns, 220
 for CB's Grilled Pacific Sardines, 209
 for CB's Grilled Soft-Shell Crabs, 224
 CB's Hot Thai-Style Dipping, 288
 CB's White BBQ, 154–55
 Chipotle BBQ, 290
 Chipotle-Lime Mayonnaise, 74
 Coconut-Peanut, 131
 Creamy Gorgonzola, 292
 Creole, 214
 Dried-Cherry Chutney, 291
 Garlic, Citrus & Cilantro, 105
 Ginger Mayonnaise, 160–61
 Glaze for CB's Hawaiian-Style Tri-Tip, 87
 Green-Chili Pesto, 291
 for Grilled Halibut with Lemon-Caper Butter, 197
 Jalapeños in Adobo Sauce, 290
 Marsala, 106
 Mint Pesto, 145
 Mojita Mop, 127
 Moroccan, 292
 Mustard-Bourbon, 80
 Peanut, 164
 Poke, 205
 for Pomsey's Tailgate Tips, 86
 Provençal Citrus-Tarragon, 290
 Red-Hot Barbecue, 181

Red-Wine, 137
Roasted Garlic-Fig Sauce, 97
Shallot & Lemon Glaze, 188
Spicy Peanut Mayonnaise, 93
Two-Mustard, 112
Sausage
 CB's Grilled Pork Burgers with Chorizo, 120
 CB's Stuffed Squid with Chicken-Apple Sausage, 227
 Jim "Houston" Hatcher's Creole Shrimp & Sausage, 214
 Tall Paul's Scotch Eggs on the Grill, 40
Savannah Smoker's Mohunken Rub, 287
Savannah Smoker's Special Pork Brine, 283
Savoury Corn Pudding, 233
Scallops
 CB's Grilled Scallops with Asparagus & Toasted Walnuts, 221
 with Prosciutto, CB's Grilled, 64
Scotch Eggs on the Grill, Tall Paul's, 40
Sea bass, CB's Baja-Style Grilled, 208
Seafood, 186–227
 Brined, Smoked Bluefish, 212
 Cajun Grilled Mahi-Mahi with Avocado Salad, 192
 CB's Avocado, Crab & Jalapeño Roll-Ups, 38–39
 CB's Baja-Style Grilled Sea Bass, 208
 CB's Grilled Fish Tacos, 206–7
 CB's Grilled Grouper with Garlic Butter, 204
 CB's Grilled Honey & Lime Prawns, 220
 CB's Grilled Lobster Tail with Bourbon-Herb Sauce, 223
 CB's Grilled Pacific Sardines, 209
 CB's Grilled Salmon with Bacon & Tomato Salsa, 189
 CB's Grilled Salmon with Shallot & Lemon Glaze, 188
 CB's Grilled Scallops with Asparagus & Toasted Walnuts, 221
 CB's Grilled Soft-Shell Crabs, 224
 CB's Rainbow Trout Stuffed with Lemon, Shallots & Herbs, 194
 CB's Snapper Grilled on a Bed of Limes, 190
 CB's Stuffed Squid with Chicken-Apple Sausage, 227
 CB's Thai-Glazed Swordfish, 202
 CB's Wet Salt Rub for Fish, 286
 Cilantro-Pesto Snapper with Red Pepper Sauce, 215
 Fast & Spicy Halibut, 198
 Grilled Alaska Crab with Trinidad Salad, 226
 Grilled Atlantic Croaker, 211
 Grilled Bluefish with Fresh Corn Salsa, 210
 Grilled Halibut with Lemon-Caper Butter, 197
 Grilled Salmon Salad Vinaigrette, 196
 Grilled Shrimp & Blue Cheese Grits, 218
 Grilled Shrimp & Vegetable Kebabs, 217
 Grilled Tuna with Roasted Cipollini Onions, 203
 Halibut Skewers with Mango-Mojito Salsa, 199
 Jim Hatcher's Creole Shrimp & Sausage, 214
 Margarita Grilled Shrimp, 219
 Mary's "Cape" Cod with Bacon & Leeks, 193
 Polynesian-Style Marlin with Poke Sauce, 205
 Smoky Grilled Crab, 225

Smoky Seared Tuna Loin, 200–201
Thai Grilled Salt-and-Pepper Squid, 59
Seafood temperature chart, 26
Searing, 13, 14, 16
Sesame-Crusted Chicken with Wasabi Cream
  Sauce, 169
Shallots
  & Lemon Glaze, 188
  CB's Rainbow Trout Stuffed with Lemon,
    Shallots & Herbs, 194
Shellfish
  CB's Avocado, Crab & Jalapeño Roll-Ups,
    38–39
  CB's Grilled Scallops with Prosciutto, 64
  CB's Grilled Soft-Shell Crabs, 224
  Grilled Alaska Crab with Trinidad Salad,
    226
  Grilled Oysters with Bacon, Tomato &
    Tarragon, 35
  Grilled Oysters with Blood Orange &
    Ginger, 36
  Smoky Grilled Crab, 225
Shrimp
  Grilled Shrimp & Blue Cheese Grits, 218
  Grilled Shrimp & Vegetable Kebabs, 217
  Jim Hatcher's Creole Shrimp & Sausage,
    214
  Margarita Grilled, 219
'Shroom Bombs, 53
"Sizzle on the Grill," 86, 231, 283, 286
Smoked Bluefish, Brined, 212
Smoked Chicken "Pâté," 56
Smoked Eggs, CB's, 52
Smoking methods, 17
Smoking temperatures, 27
Smokin' Soon's Hobo Potato Skins, 37
Smoky Baby Blue Artichokes, 30
Smoky Grilled King Crab, 225
Smoky Grilled Meat Loaf, 83
Smoky Seared Tuna Loin, 200–201
Snapper
  CB's Snapper Grilled on a Bed of Limes,
    190
  Cilantro-Pesto Snapper with Red Pepper
    Sauce, 215
Spiced Cranberry Wings, 43
Spicy Grilled-Veggie Marinade, 284
Spicy Peanut Mayonnaise, 93
Spicy Peanut Sauce, 164
Spinach
  in CB's Feta-Stuffed Portobellos, 61
  in Grilled Stuffed Pork Chops, 115
Spread, Feta, 141
Squash, in Grilled Shrimp & Vegetable
  Kebabs, 217
Squid
  CB's Stuffed Squid with Chicken-Apple
    Sausage, 227
  Thai Grilled Salt-and-Pepper, 59
Stephens, Brys, 94
Stines, Mike, 184
Strawberry Pie, Frozen, 271
Stuffing
  CB's Stuffed Squid with Chicken-Apple
    Sausage, 227
  for Grilled Stuffed Pork Chops, 115
Sundae, Grilled Brownie, with Blueberry
  Sauce, 270
Sweet potatoes
  with Cola Ribs, 128
  Garlic-Roasted Sweet Potatoes with
    Arugula, 245
  Harvest Slaw with Sweet Potatoes, 249
Swordfish, CB's Thai-Glazed, 202
Szechuan Steak Wraps with Spicy Peanut
  Mayonnaise, 93

T

Tacos
  CB's Grilled Fish Tacos, 206–7
  Grilled Beef Tacos with Avocado Salsa, 77
  Grilled Pork & Pineapple, 125
Tall Paul's Scotch Eggs on the Grill, 40
Tandoori Ribs, Indian, 130
Tangy Turkey Dogs, 178
Temperatures
  Cooking charts, 24–26
  Food safety, 22
  General grilling, 16
  Guidelines, 26–27
  Terminology, 25
Tequila Lime Chicken, 172
Thai Glaze, 202
Thai Grilled Salt-and-Pepper Squid, 59
Thai Marinade, 180
Thai Marinade Turkey Wings, 180
Thai-Style Burgers, 76
Thawing foods, 22
Three-Way Marinade, 281
Tomatoes
  in Cajun Grilled Mahi-Mahi with Avocado
    Salad, 192
  in CB's Avocado, Crab & Jalapeño Roll-
    Ups, 38–39
  in CB's Grilled Chicken Cacciatore, 156
  CB's Grilled Salmon with Bacon & Tomato
    Salsa, 189
  in Chef Erick's Lamb Kebabs with Mint
    Pesto, 144–45
  Greek Potato Salad with Sun-Dried
    Tomatoes, 232
  Greek Salad Olive-Grilled Chicken, 163
  Grilled Oysters with Bacon, Tomato &
    Tarragon, 35
  Grilled Stuffed Tomatoes Caprese, 251
  -Mozzarella-Polenta Burgers, 71
  in Panzanella Salad, 175
  Roasted Asparagus with Cherry
    Tomatoes, Garlic & Olive Oil, 254
Torte, Livefire's Holiday Potato, 243
Tostadas, Grilled Lamb & Mango, 143
Trinidad Salad, 226
Trout, CB's Rainbow Trout Stuffed with
  Lemon, Shallots & Herbs, 194
Tuna
  Grilled Tuna with Roasted Cipollini
    Onions, 203
  Smoky Seared Tuna Loin, 200–201
Turkey, 174–85
  Florentine Turkey Burgers, 182
  Herb-Marinated Grilled Turkey &
    Panzanella Salad, 174–75
  Jalapeño-Jelly-Glazed Turkey Thighs, 183
  Jamaican Jerk Turkey Thighs, 176
  Lemonade Turkey Kebabs, 177
  Lemon-Oregano Grilled Turkey, 179
  Red-Hot Barbecued Turkey Tenderloins,
    181
  Smoky Grilled Meat Loaf, 83
  Tangy Turkey Dogs, 178
  The Big Easy Cider-Brined Turkey, 184–85
  Thai Marinade Turkey Wings, 180
Turkey & poultry temperature chart, 24
Turkish-Style Sirloin with Roasted Garlic-Fig
  Sauce, 97
Two-Mustard Sauce, 112

U

Uncle Dane's Grilled Pork Patties, 129

V

Vegetables. *See also* salads; *specific vegetables*
  in CB's Beef Skewers "On Fire," 95
  in CB's Grilled Chicken Cacciatore, 156
  in Chef Erick's Lamb Kebabs with Mint
    Pesto, 144–45
  with Grilled Shrimp & Blue Cheese Grits,
    218
  Grilled Shrimp & Vegetable Kebabs, 217
  Spicy Grilled-Veggie Marinade, 284
  You Won't Know It's Not Potato Salad, 257
Venison, CB's Grilled Loin of, 148
Vidyarthi, Liz, 272
Vinaigrette
  CB's Fire-Charred Green Beans with, 41
  Grilled Salmon Salad Vinaigrette, 196
  Roasted-Pepper, 237

W

Walnuts
  CB's Grilled Broccoli & Cauliflower with
    Toasted Walnuts, 252
  CB's Grilled Scallops with Asparagus &
    Toasted Walnuts, 221
  CB's Nut-Crusted Ribs with Bourbon Mop
    Sauce, 132–33
Wasabi
  Cucumbers, 84
  Sesame-Crusted Chicken with Wasabi
    Cream Sauce, 169
Wokthink.com, 102
Wood chips, 17
Wraps, Szechuan Steak Wraps with Spicy
  Peanut Mayonnaise, 93

Y

Yogurt
  in Creamy Gorgonzola Sauce, 292
  Garlic-Yogurt Marinade, 282
  Grilled Yogurt-Mint Chicken, 157
  Madras Curry Dip, 291
You Won't Know It's Not Potato Salad, 257

Z

Zucchini
  Creamy Zucchini & Garlic, 244
  in Grilled Shrimp & Vegetable Kebabs, 217

Have a home gardening, decorating, or improvement project? Look for these and other fine **Creative Homeowner** books wherever books are sold

ULTIMATE GUIDE TO OUTDOOR PROJECTS
Hardscape and landscape projects that add value and enjoyment to your home.

Over 1,200 photos and illustrations.
368 pp.
8½" x 10⅞"
$19.95 (US)
$23.95 (CAN)
BOOK #: CH277873

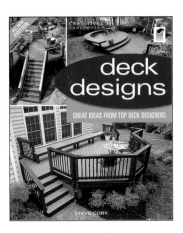

DECK DESIGNS
Features plans and ideas from top deck designers and builders.

Over 480 photographs and illustrations.
240 pp.
8½" x 10⅞"
$19.95 (US)
$21.95 (CAN)
BOOK #: CH277382

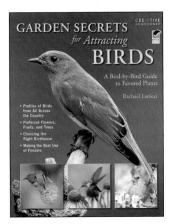

GARDEN SECRETS FOR ATTRACTING BIRDS
Provides information to turn your yard into a mecca for birds.

Over 250 photographs.
160 pp.
8½" x 10⅝"
$ 14.95 (US)
$ 17.95 (CAN)
BOOK #: CH274561

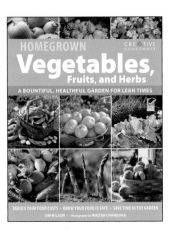

HOMEGROWN VEGETABLES
A complete guide to growing your own vegetables, fruits, and herbs.

Over 275 photographs and illustrations.
192 pp.
8½" x 10⅞"
$16.95 (US)
$20.95 (CAN)
BOOK #: CH274551

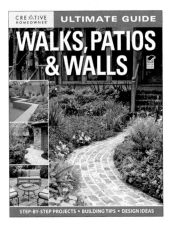

ULTIMATE GUIDE: WALKS, PATIOS & WALLS
Build landscape structures from concrete, brick, and stone.

Over 300 photographs.
240 pp.
8½" x 10⅞"
$16.95 (US)
$20.95 (CAN)
BOOK #: CH277992

CHAR-BROIL'S EVERYBODY GRILLS!
More than 200 recipes for delicious grilled, barbecued, and smoked dishes.

Over 250 photographs.
304 pp.
8½" x 10⅞"
$24.95 (US)
$27.95 (CAN)
BOOK #: CH253001

For more information and to order direct, go to **www.creativehomeowner.com**